CANADIAN CAPITALISM

A STUDY OF POWER IN THE CANADIAN BUSINESS ESTABLISHMENT

JORGE NIOSI

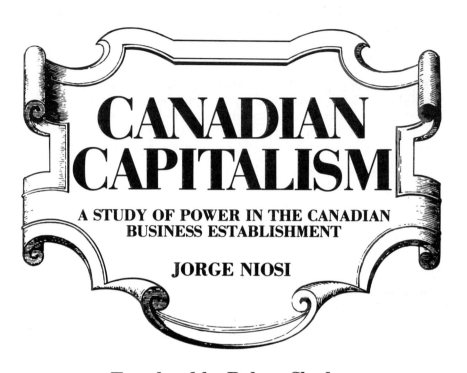

CANADIAN CAPITALISM

A STUDY OF POWER IN THE CANADIAN BUSINESS ESTABLISHMENT

JORGE NIOSI

Translated by Robert Chodos

James Lorimer & Company, Publishers
Toronto, 1981

Originally published as *La bourgeoisie canadienne.*

Copyright © 1980 Les Editions du Boréal Express.

Translation copyright © 1981 by James Lorimer & Company,
Publishers. All rights reserved.

ISBN 0-88862-410-7 paper
      0-88862-411-5 cloth

Cover design: Brant Cowie

Cover photograph: Richard Kim. Limousine and chauffeur courtesy of
        Culliton's Limousine, Toronto.

Canadian Cataloguing in Publication Data

Niosi, Jorge, 1945-
   Canadian capitalism

Translation of: La bourgeoisie canadienne.
Bibliography: p. 203.
ISBN 0-88862-411-5 (bound). — ISBN 0-88862-410-7 (pbk.)

1. Capitalists and financiers — Canada.
2. Corporations — Canada. 3. Corporations,
Government — Canada. 4. Elite (Social sciences) —
Canada. I. Title.

HN105.3.N5513   332'.0971   C81-094326-3

This book has been published with the help of a grant from the
Social Science Federation of Canada, using funds provided by the
Social Sciences and Humanities Research Council of Canada.

James Lorimer & Company, Publishers
Egerton Ryerson Memorial Building
35 Britain Street
Toronto M5A 1R7, Ontario

Printed and bound in Canada

6 5 4 3 2 1   81 82 83 84 85 86

Contents

Tables and Figures

Preface

Data for this study were gathered from a wide variety of public sources. Most important among these are the monthly bulletins issued by the Quebec and Ontario Securities Commissions on insider trading of shares, and the proxies filed by American corporations with the New York Stock Exchange. These three sources give detailed information on stockholdings by all officers and directors of corporations whose stock is traded in those jurisdictions. They also provide data on the owners — institutional as well as individual — of blocks of 10 per cent or more of the capital stock of these enterprises. These sources have been essential in the identification of the focus of control of most corporations on my lists.

The annual surveys of the *Financial Post* service and the manuals published by Moody's in New York complemented the above-mentioned sources and served to identify the largest Canadian-owned and foreign subsidiaries in Canada. I have also relied on the financial press, both Canadian (*Financial Post, Financial Times, Canadian Business*) and American (*Wall Street Journal, Business Week, Fortune, Forbes*), to get more specific information on particular corporations. Reliance on such secondary sources may have led to occasional errors of fact, for which the author takes responsibility.

Government sources have been also very useful in identifying the largest publicly-owned enterprises in Canada and in studying their control. Among these sources are several annual publications by Statistics Canada on federal and provincial enterprise finance, and the proceedings of various parliamentary commissions.

The *Martindale-Hubbell Law Directory* and the *Financial Post Directory of Directors* helped greatly in carrying out a detailed analysis of the boards of directors, i.e., in identifying inside and outside directors of the corporations studied. In this area, I also relied on the annual reports of the companies.

I am grateful to Robert Parent, who helped me collect data in the

library of the New York Stock Exchange. These data helped me in the
preparation of chapter 5. I would also like to thank Philip Ehrensaft,
Philippe Faucher, Paul-André Linteau and Tom Naylor, who read the
manuscript and made very useful suggestions.

Jorge Niosi
Department of Sociology
University of Quebec at Montreal
October 1979

Translator's Note

La bourgeoisie canadienne, of which this is a translation, was written in the fall of 1979. The studies on which the central chapters are based used data that were valid as of the end of 1975. Events between 1975 and 1979 that tended to support the conclusions of these studies were alluded to in the text. Since the fall of 1979, additional events have occurred that have a bearing on these conclusions, and these have been referred to in this edition in footnotes.

Introduction

This book is the second in a series of studies of the ruling class in Canada. *The Economy of Canada: A Study of Ownership and Control*[1] represents the first stage of the project, and my goal in this second stage is to complete the economic sketch of the bourgeoisie begun in that earlier work by exploring its internal composition more thoroughly.

There are two major sections of the capitalist class, based on the kind of ownership each enjoys: there are juridical or legal owners, and economic owners. Juridical owners of large companies are the beneficial owners of shares giving them the right to a periodic dividend, while economic ownership is the result of a kind of control that does not necessarily come from legal ownership. In some companies, stock ownership is so dispersed that control is in the hands of the "inside" directors, the senior officers. But even in firms where an individual, family or partnership has control through juridical ownership, these officers share in economic ownership through a variety of rewards (generous salaries, expense accounts, stock options). Together, wealthy controlling stockholders and senior corporate officers form the core of the Canadian bourgeoisie (or, to use the popular expression, "the establishment"), and they are the main subject of this study.

Outside this core, there is a wide circle of "organic intellectuals" — legal and financial advisers, consulting engineers, actuaries, notaries — that provides the ruling class with valuable assistance in a number of areas, including the control of large corporations, the focus of this study. While they do not run these companies and very rarely own large blocks of shares, they do participate in corporate management as advisers and "outside" directors. This group often facilitates the contact that corporations maintain with governments, political parties and universities, an essentially political function on which little research has been done. Khayyam Z. Paltiel's work on the financing of Canadian political parties and R. Mahon's exploration of hegemony in the government apparatus are pioneering studies, almost unique in their field.[2] However, this function of the stratum of intellectuals is beyond the scope of this book, and only the intellectuals' role in the control of large corporations will be examined.

This study questions the validity of that large body of Canadian nationalist literature that sees foreign capital as the dominant economic and political force. I maintain that, on the contrary, it is the Canadian bourgeoisie that plays a dominant role in Canada, in the private sector where it controls at least 70 per cent of all corporate assets, as well as in the public sector, where most government-owned corporations are run by this Canadian capitalist class and its key advisers. This work is even more firmly opposed to liberal views of Canadian society as a classless society in which equality of opportunity prevails and great fortunes are a thing of the past. We will see that the control of large corporations is in fact often passed from one generation of rich owners and managers to another, with the help of their advisers and experts.

The book begins with a review of the main conclusions of my first book; then, in chapter 2, I examine the main factors which have influenced the formation of the Canadian capitalist class. These factors seem to be: the decline of independent commodity production, the diversification of economic activity, the concentration of capital, the mobility of capital within the Canadian-owned sector and the resistance of this sector to foreign capital, population changes and government intervention.

In chapter 3, I look more closely at an underrepresented minority within the Canadian bourgeoisie: the francophones. This "founding people" constitutes almost 30 per cent of the population, and yet controls only 10 per cent of the entries on a list of major corporations used in this study. To find out more about the francophone bourgeoisie, I studied all public companies under French Canadian control with assets of more than $10 million. From this research, it was possible to conclude that a francophone bourgeoisie does exist, that it has developed rapidly since the Second World War and that its members are newcomers to wealth. The major figures in this group are Desmarais, Bombardier, Campeau, Simard, Parizeau, Allard, Latraverse, etc. A product of post-war economic growth in Canada as a whole and Quebec in particular, this group has been active primarily in low-technology sectors (retailing, finance, real estate, services). The support of the Quebec government has been an important asset to the francophone establishment, and its members in turn have played an active role in encouraging the growing scope and power of that government since the Quiet Revolution. Politically, the francophone bourgeoisie is federalist and Liberal, as its economic interests are Canada-wide and it is trying to carve out a place for itself beside (and in opposition to) the old Conservative Anglo-Saxon establishment.

Chapter 4 is devoted to the question of control of federal and provincial crown corporations, and attempts to answer another question: is
there a state bourgeoisie? According to Fernando H. Cardoso,[3] a state
bourgeoisie consists of the full-time executives of publicly-owned
companies that operate on a commercial or quasi-commercial basis. In
other words, these "public managers" are the senior employees in that
half of the state apparatus made up of enterprises selling goods and
services to the public, such as Canadian National, Air Canada, Sidbec or
the Canada Development Corporation. An analysis of the control of
these enterprises reveals that large crown corporations are run by
members of the private-sector Canadian bourgeoisie — most of the
time in person. As a result, it seems necessary to discard the idea of the
"state bourgeoisie" as an autonomous sector of the Canadian bourgeoisie.

Finally, in chapter 5 the control of foreign-owned companies is examined, using a list of 130 large subsidiaries operating in all sectors of
activity. The companies on the list account for 50 per cent of the assets
of all foreign-owned non-financial companies in Canada and include an
even larger proportion of foreign-controlled financial institutions. The
question addressed is whether a comprador bourgeoisie* exists as an
autonomous sector of the Canadian capitalist class, and if so, what its
relationship is with indigenous capital and the upper-class intelligentsia.
The data led to the conclusion that such a sector does indeed exist, and
its economic boundaries are clearly established by the almost total
absence of companies under joint Canadian-American control. Instead
of surrounding itself with a distinct circle of advisers, the comprador
bourgeoisie maintains ties with the intellectuals (lawyers, financial consultants, consulting engineers, etc.) who serve the indigenous capitalist
class. In the final analysis, foreign-owned companies are controlled in
part by powerful international capitalists (the Fords, Reynolds, Kecks,
Oppenheimers, Tates, Lyles, Mountains, Ruperts, etc.) and in part by
career executives in their head offices.

In the conclusion, I draw some inferences from the principal results of
my research about what should follow this study. These results should
be filled out by research on the control of the mass media and Canadian
multinationals and further study of the intelligentsia that is so closely
linked to the ruling class.

I do not deny that Canada is a dependent country. Philip Ehrensaft
and Warwick Armstrong have shown that Canada is the richest of the
semi-industrial countries and the most prosperous of the peripheral

---

*The *comprador bourgeoisie* comprises those persons who administer foreign-
owned branch plants in Canada — more precisely, the group of Canadian
inside directors of foreign-owned branch plants in Canada.

societies.[4] Tom Naylor and other analysts of Canadian society have adopted essentially the same perspective. It would be absurd to ignore the central role of the commercial, financial and technological dependence that links Canada's economy to that of the United States.

On the other hand, it seems to me that the almost exclusive emphasis that has been placed on Canada's external dependence has diverted attention from the analysis of social classes in Canada and led some observers to neglect their internal conflicts and dynamics. Thus, for example, while there is an extensive literature dealing with foreign investment in Canada, there are comparatively few studies of the control of Canadian-owned companies. For similar reasons, federal-provincial conflicts are often interpreted as an effect of foreign capital on Canadian political life (according to Garth Stevenson and Kari Levitt, this is the source of Canadian "provincialism"). And Hugh G.J. Aitken's interpretation of government intervention in the economy and growth of publicly-owned corporations as "defensive expansionism" in the face of the dynamism of the American economy has been too readily adopted.

As in my first book, I have tried to correct this simplistic view of Canada as an American subsidiary. I have attempted to show that Canada's indigenous bourgeoisie, although troubled by regional and ethnic cleavages and by struggles between large- and small-scale capitalism, is nevertheless healthy and vigorous. I have also reinterpreted the "provincialism" that has been developing in Canada (partly as a result of the growth of provincial crown corporations) as the response of regional bourgeoisies to the growing concentration of economic activity in Ontario. For regional capital, provincial crown corporations are shields against large-scale monopoly and are promoters of local enterprise.

In this study I also put to the test the theory of state monopoly capitalism, the principal Eurocommunist explanation of the growth of publicly-owned corporations in advanced capitalist countries. The data in chapter 4, and indirectly those in chapters 3 and 5 as well, tend to show that this theory is not useful in analysing state-owned enterprises in Canada.

CHAPTER 1

Who Controls
Canadian Capitalism?

Studies of the control of large corporations, in Canada and elsewhere, can be divided into three major schools. The prevalent Marxist school sees banks and other financial institutions as controlling non-financial corporations. According to the theory of internal control, widely taught in management departments and faculties of commerce, professional managers have power in joint-stock companies without actually owning them. The third school consists of radical sociologists, who maintain that large joint-stock companies are under the control of an economic or corporate elite comprising all the members of the boards of directors of these companies. The main aim of this chapter is to look critically at these three interpretations in the light of recent data from official and private sources.

It is also the writer's intention to demonstrate the existence of a Canadian bourgeoisie, to determine its internal composition and to analyse the ways in which it controls large corporations. But before one can answer the question "Who controls Canadian capitalism?", a critical look at existing interpretations is necessary. Control can be defined as the power to choose a majority of the members of the board of directors of a corporation. And since large Canadian corporations are joint-stock companies, the stockholders, who hold the key to control, are of interest.

Do the Banks Control Canadian Industry?

A substantial majority of the world's Marxist economists and sociologists have tried to show, in a variety of contexts, that non-financial companies are controlled by banks. In this endeavour, they are following a school of thought that owes its origins to Rudolf Hilferding and V.I. Lenin, who studied the relationship between banks and industrial corporations in early-twentieth-century central and eastern Europe.[1] They found that the banks tended to gain control of industry by various means: stock issues, industrial and commercial credit, holdings of stocks and bonds in industrial firms, interlocking directorships, etc. The precondition for this kind of bank/industry relationship is a highly centralized financial system based on multipurpose banks; a financial system of this sort existed in continental Europe in the early twentieth century.

In other countries, the thesis has been subtly changed to make it applicable to other financial systems. In the United States, for example, a number of writers have argued that their control of huge pension funds gives the *commercial* banks a dominant position in American industry.[2] Since 1974, however, the total size of the pension funds administered by banks has declined, in absolute terms. This situation has given rise to a third Marxist theory of finance capital, the Pastré thesis.[3] Olivier Pastré maintains that the debt of large industrial corporations leads to their control by commercial banks.

A minority school of American Marxists, of which Paul Baran, Paul Sweezy, Harry Magdoff and Edward Herman are notable representatives, challenges these interpretations, at least in the American context.[4] This school argues that among American financial institutions, only the investment banks have participated in the control of industry, and their power eroded rapidly after the Depression.

In reading the Marxist literature of different countries and different eras on the subject, one is struck by the variety of theses being presented. Writers move from one to another without realizing it. Most important, however, a review of the literature leads to the conclusion that while the classical thesis is an accurate description of bank/industry relations as they existed in continental Europe between 1870 and 1930, banks have never had the same level of power over industry in Britain, the United States or Canada. This is because of the greater diversity of the banking system, the specialization of large banks in commercial credit, and a variety of other factors specific to each country.[5]

In Canada, most Marxists have adopted the most classical version of the theory of finance capital. For example, this interpretation underlies Libbie and Frank Park's very important book, *Anatomy of Big Business*.[6] Newly available sources, however, such as the bulletins of the Quebec and Ontario Securities Commissions and the Statistics Canada publication *Inter-Corporate Ownership*, make it possible to arrive at a more precise determination of the role of financial institutions in the control of industry in Canada.

In fact, the chartered banks hold little stock, and their policy has always been not to undertake long-term investments in corporate securities. Corporate stocks and bonds have never made up more than 5 per cent of total bank assets, and even this figure was reached only between 1900 and 1915, when the banks invested heavily in railway stock. At present, the banks place a maximum of only 1 per cent of their assets in corporate securities, and this percentage is declining. Even these securities are held as liquid assets and not as investments. The only companies controlled by the chartered banks are the real estate companies that manage the banks' own buildings and investment subsidiaries such as RoyNat, Roy Fund and UNAS Investment, all set up in recent years. The testimony, reports and studies yielded by royal commissions and parliamentary banking and commerce committees all lead to the same conclusions. The very close personal relations that link the chartered banks to industrial corporations are in no sense an indication that the relationship between these firms is one of ownership. Rather, they arise out of the fact that the banks provide commercial credit to industrial corporations and also reflect the tendency of the same capitalists to hold stock in both kinds of companies.

Turning to other financial institutions, the investment dealers were too weak to carve out a controlling position in Canadian industry and arrived on the scene too late, when only hydroelectricity and a few branches of industry were available for reorganization. Canadian railways were highly concentrated from the beginning, and were well along the road to development by the time the brokerage houses were founded. While in the United States, firms such as J.P. Morgan & Co. occupied a very important position by 1880, in Canada the major brokerage houses were founded quite a bit later: A.E. Ames & Co. in 1889, Dominion Securities Corporation in 1901, Royal Securities Corporation in 1903, Wood Gundy & Co. in 1905, Nesbitt Thomson in 1912.

Before 1914, the prestige, capital and well-oiled distribution networks of the London and New York firms relegated Montreal and Toronto to entirely secondary positions, and it was only during the First World War that the Canadian houses began to grow appreciably. Between 1904 and 1914, 73 per cent of Canadian bonds were sold in Britain, 9 per cent in the United States and only 18 per cent in Canada; for the period 1915-20, the proportions became 3 per cent, 30 per cent and 67 per cent respectively. This was the real beginning of the Canadian securities industry.

Between 1909 and 1913 and again between 1925 and 1930, these investment dealers participated actively in merger waves and reorganizations in sectors accessible to them, and in some cases they emerged in positions of control. A striking example of this "peripheral finance capitalism" is Nesbitt Thomson's establishment in 1925 of Power Corporation to run a half-dozen hydroelectric companies that it had acquired in the course of its participation in initial securities issues and reorganizations. The Nesbitt and Thomson families kept control of their hydroelectric empire until it was bought out by the Quebec government in the 1960s, and of Power Corporation until Paul Desmarais took over in 1968.

But not all investment dealers achieved a similar stature. Wood Gundy & Co. participated in a number of industrial and commercial reorganizations — of Simpsons Ltd., Abitibi Paper, Canada Cement, Canada Power and Paper, and others — but in almost all cases investment dealers did not maintain a controlling position and had to be satisfied with a substantial minority block of shares. In a few companies, such as Massey-Harris until 1942, this was enough to give them de facto control, although their actual percentage of the voting shares was fairly small.

The same factors that brought about the decline of the American investment dealers also contributed to the weakening of the Canadian dealers. The fall in stock prices and the resulting reduction in the number of mergers between 1930 and 1945, the growing role of the Bank of Canada in the issuing of public securities from the time of its founding in 1935, the ever-increasing participation of government in industrial finance, and the appearance and development of institutional investors relegated Canadian brokerage houses to a more limited role in industrial finance and control. Increasing American control of Canadian resource and manufacturing industries also had the effect of taking away the brokerage firms' stock-in-trade. Today the investment dealers (who lost the right to call themselves bankers in 1934) sit on the boards of large corporations as financial consultants, in much the same way that members of prestigious law firms sit on these boards as legal advisers. Neither group controls the companies it advises.

As has been noted, a more modern version of the theory of finance capital maintains that institutional investors (especially the trust departments of commercial banks but also investment and life insurance companies) accumulate large blocks of shares in companies by buying stock with pension funds of which they are trustees. Instead of being interested purely in a return on their investment, they behave increasingly as controlling stockholders of these companies. Trust companies, legally independent of the banks, administer more than a third of Canadian pension funds; individual trustees administer 55 per cent; retirement savings companies administer 6 per cent, and the rest are under joint management by more than one type of financial intermediary.[7] Pension funds are thus not as concentrated in the hands of one kind of institution in Canada as they are in the United States. However, in the inflationary environment of recent years, trust companies bought stock and tended to dispose of fixed-income securities such as bonds. This gave them a potential source of power in the companies they held stock in. But did they exercise this power? The Royal Commission on Banking and Finance (Porter Commission) arrived at a negative answer to this question in 1964:

> Concern has been expressed at the concentration of equity holdings in the trust companies' own portfolios and in administered accounts. As already indicated, these appear to represent well under 20 per cent of all Canadian common stocks and are spread between a fairly sizable number of companies, many of whose E.T. & A. [estate, trust and agency] clients vote their shares independently. Moreover, the trust companies' normal policy is to support existing management except in very unusual circumstances or unless they have very large stockholdings in one or a number of accounts, in which case they normally have an officer on the board to keep a watching brief in the interests of their clients.[8]

There is no publicly available information that would make it possible to estimate the extent of the major trust companies' influence or control in the companies in which they hold stock. What is evident, however, is that no federal or provincial legislation puts any formal obstacle in the way of a trust company takeover of a corporation through pension funds; there is no legislation preventing a trust company from concentrating the investment of these funds in a few securities. Trust companies' potential for gaining control of the corporations in which they hold stock is enhanced by the high degree of concentration in the trust sector itself. In 1969, four trust companies (Royal Trust, Montreal Trust, National Trust and Canada Permanent Trust) administered 75 per cent of the assets held in estate, trust and agency funds and 50 per cent of the company and guaranteed funds. In 1926, Royal Trust, Montreal Trust, National Trust and Toronto General Trust (which merged with Canada Permanent in 1961) held 95 and 43 per cent respectively of these same funds. The extremely centralized control of these funds has not changed over the years.

One must then ask whether control of industry by the banks, the existence of which in direct form was refuted earlier, nevertheless exists in direct form as a result of control by the banks of the trust companies. A number of writers have stressed the large number of interlocking directorships between the banks and the trust companies, and this has been seen as conclusive evidence that the trust companies were controlled by the banks. But as a result of the recommendations of the Porter Commission, the Bank Act of 1967 forbade interlocking directorships between the chartered banks and the trust companies, and also prohibited the banks from holding more than 10 per cent of the voting stock of a trust company, as of July 1971. The banks and trust companies have complied with the new legislation. Thus, the existence of any form of indirect control of industrial corporations by the banks through the trust companies would now be impossible to prove; control by the trust companies through the pension funds they administer would be legally and economically possible, but improbable.

The "Managerial Revolution"

The theory of internal or managerial control originated in 1932 with the publication of Adolf A. Berle and Gardiner C. Means' book, *The Modern Corporation and Private Property*.[9] Berle and Means studied the control of the 200 largest non-financial corporations in the United States. They came to the conclusion that during the first three decades of the twentieth century, stock in large corporations had become dispersed. In this situation, power had passed to professional managers who owned only a tiny fraction of the stock and perpetuated themselves through the mechanism of voting by proxy. Berle and Means identified three stages in the control of large corporations: first, majority control by the founders of the corporation, which lasted only one generation; second, minority control by an individual or group holding less than half of the corporation's shares; and third, internal control, with the stock totally dispersed.

In 1963, R.J. Larner reproduced Berle and Means' research, and concluded that the tendency towards internal control of large corporations in the United States had continued and even intensified.[10] Many economists and sociologists, including John Kenneth Galbraith, Ralf Dahrendorf and Talcott Parsons, have adopted this interpretation, although it has fewer adherents in Canada.

The theory of internal control has been criticized from two points of view. Some neoclassical economists, while accepting the inevitability of the trend towards internal control, have criticized the "managerialists" for deficiencies of economic theory. According to these critics, the managerialists have failed to explain how resources are allocated, productive factors receive income or prices are determined in a system consisting of oligopolistic, internally controlled enterprises.[11] Marxists and radicals, on the other hand, have tended to deny that stock dispersal has proceeded as far as the managerialists maintain. They argue that, on the contrary, stock ownership remains highly concentrated, and that many cases of "internal control" are really companies in which control by a family or individual is a well-kept secret.

In *The Economy of Canada*, all the available sources on the control of corporations in Canada were brought together in order to test the hypothesis of managerial power. First, subsidiaries of foreign companies were eliminated, since these companies are ultimately controlled from outside the country and considering them would have led to an analysis of the power structure in American, British, French and Belgian multinational corporations. Information was then compiled on the control of 136 Canadian corporations with total assets of more than $100 million at the end of 1975. The list thus comprises the largest Canadian corporations and includes companies operating in all sectors of economic activity. Broken down by sector, the list includes: fifty companies in the industrial sector, sixteen in the commercial sector, fifteen in transportation and services and fifteen in real estate, as well as the eleven largest trust companies, the ten largest life insurance companies, the nine largest holding companies and ten other financial institutions (the largest mortgage loan, finance and investment companies and the leading brokerage house).

The $100 million minimum ensured that the list would be of manageable size and that the companies on it would be substantial in scale. The most serious omissions from the list are the chartered banks, whose stockholders are not required to divulge their holdings to any public source. Government-owned corporations were also excluded, since if a process of dispersal of stock ownership has indeed taken place, these companies would not be touched by it. Finally, information was not available on two groups of private corporations — the Richardson group, based in Winnipeg, and the Toronto-based holdings of Thomas Bata — and these groups also could not be included.

Data on a company's assets come from its last balance sheet in 1975. Data on share distribution were taken from the *Monthly Bulletin* of the Ontario Securities Commission, the *Weekly Bulletin* of the Quebec Securities Commission, the *Financial Post* surveys and Moody's manuals for 1976 (which publish data for 1975) and financial periodicals. All data on control refer to December 1975.

Four levels of control were defined: virtually absolute (80 to 100 per cent), majority (50 to 79 per cent), minority (5 to 49 per cent) and internal (0 to 4.9 per cent). The first three levels were divided into two types of control — family control and control by an individual or partnership — to test the managerialist hypothesis of stages of control. Companies with assets of more than $100 million that are wholly-owned subsidiaries of Canadian corporations were eliminated from the list if their balance sheets are consolidated with those of their parent companies.

The results obtained from these data contradicted the hypothesis of internal control in the Canadian context in several respects. First of all, only a third of all large Canadian-owned corporations appeared to be under the control of professional managers. To be sure, these corporations were among the largest in Canada, and accounted for 57 per cent of the assets of the companies on the list. The forty-four companies under internal control included almost all the companies in the transportation and service sector and 38 per cent of the industrial corporations, but only 22 per cent of the companies in the financial sector and 12 per cent of those in the commercial sector. None of the real estate companies was under internal control.

Several companies were under internal control not as a result of a gradual process of share dispersion but because of charter provisions or internal company regulations. In this category were six mutual life insurance companies; these had no share capital and their boards of directors were elected by the policyholders.[12] For all practical purposes, these directors do not have to account to anyone, since the policyholders do not come to annual meetings and vote by proxy, if at all. United Grain was another company in which dispersal of control is written into the statutes. No stockholder is allowed to own more than twenty-five shares, and every stockholder present at an annual meeting has one vote, regardless of the number of shares he owns. There was also Alberta Gas Trunk Line, whose 1,699 voting shares, class B, were deliberately dispersed among hundreds of shareholders when the company was founded. These are examples of internal control established as a result of legal procedures, and not as the outcome of a long process of stock dispersal.

The managerialist hypothesis of three stages of corporate control does not stand up to examination either. In all sectors, there were companies under individual or family control that were at least as old as companies under internal control. Royal Trust and National Trust appeared to be ultimately under internal control and were founded in 1892 and 1898 respectively, while Montreal Trust, under the control of Paul Desmarais, was founded in 1889. The largest holding company in Canada, Canadian Pacific Investments, was incorporated only in 1962 and, as of 1975, was ultimately under internal control. But Brascan Ltd., incorporated in 1912, was in 1975 under the control of John H. Moore and his partners*, while Power Corporation, incorporated in 1925, was controlled by Paul Desmarais. Among industrial corporations, the oldest are Molson Companies (1782) and Hugh Russel Ltd. (1818), and they were under the minority control of the Molson and Russel families respectively. Among companies in the commercial sector, the T. Eaton Co. (1867) was in 1975 under the absolute control

---

*Brascan was taken over by Edward and Peter Bronfman in 1979.

of the Eaton family, and the Hudson's Bay Company (1670) was under the minority control of John H. Moore and his partners through Brascan Ltd.

An element of family influence was also found in a number of corporations classified as being under internal control; access to a complete list of stockholders might have revealed these companies to be under minority control. This was the case for Alcan Aluminium Ltd. (Davis family), Canada Packers (McLean family), Hiram Walker-Gooderham & Worts (Hatch family), Dominion Textile (Gordon and Sobey families), Dofasco (Sherman family) and Abitibi Paper (Thomson Newspaper group). In every one of these cases, except for Abitibi Paper, a key position on the board of directors has passed from father to son for two or three generations, but the most recent representative of the family on the board held less than 5 per cent of the company's stock. These directors may have represented other family members who held securities in the companies in question, and family influence may thus be greater than it appears, but hard information is lacking.

The most serious threat to the independence of companies under internal control is not a takeover by bankers or financiers but rather the postwar formation of conglomerates. The four major Canadian conglomerates (Canadian Pacific Ltd., Power Corporation, Argus Corporation and Brascan) either were founded or became diversified after the Second World War; their major acquisitions have been companies under internal control. The founder of Argus Corp., E.P. Taylor, expressed this strategy in the following terms: "I look for companies where no very large shareholder exists. With my partners, I buy enough stock to give us effective control. Then the company holds our view."[13]

The reshaping of Brascan Ltd. into an instrument for controlling Canadian corporations, and the reorganization of Power Corp. between 1960 and 1968 were accomplished through the absorption of companies under internal or minority control.

Furthermore, family-controlled capitalism is alive and well in Canada. Thirty-seven companies on the 1975 list were under family control. Under absolute family control were such companies as the T. Eaton Co. (Eaton family), the London Life Insurance Company (Jeffery family), Kruger Paper (Kruger family), Oshawa Group (Wolfe family) and Steinberg's Ltd. (Steinberg family). The list of companies under majority family control included George Weston Ltd. (Weston family), Canadian Tire Corp. (Billes family), Bombardier Ltd. (Bombardier family) and Wood Gundy & Co. (Gundy-Scott family). Notable companies under minority family control included IAC Ltd., Seagram Co. and Cadillac Fairview Corp. (all Bronfman family), Woodward Stores (Woodward family), Molson Companies (Molson family), Maclaren Power & Paper (Maclaren family), Ivaco Industries (Ivanier family),

Feaeral Industries (Searle-Leach family), Canadian General Investments (Meighen family), Prenor Group (Lorne C. Webster and family),
Bow Valley Industries (Seaman family), The Southam Press (Southam
family), and M. Loeb & Co. (Loeb and Weston families). Members of
these families not only sat on the boards of directors of the companies in
question, but often held the key positions: president, chairman of the
board, executive vice-president, etc.

A look at the companies under individual or group control makes the
future of Canadian professional managers appear even less bright.
They included seven very new real estate companies — including
Campeau Corp. (Robert Campeau), Deltan Corp. (R.J. Prusac), S.B.
McLaughlin Associates (S.B. McLaughlin) and Unicorp Financial Corp.
(G.S. Mann) — but also three of the largest and most dynamic Canadian
conglomerates: Power Corp. (Paul Desmarais), Argus Corp. (controlled
since 1978 by the Black brothers) and Brascan Ltd. (Edward and Peter
Bronfman since 1979). In all, forty-four corporations were ultimately
under the control of an individual or group, including the eight subsidiaries of Power Corp., the eleven subsidiaries of Argus and the seven
Canadian subsidiaries of Brascan that had assets of more than $100
million.

The evidence suggests, then, that while the hyrothesis of managerial
control does apply to many companies, it is not universally applicable in
the Canadian context.

The Economic or Corporate Elite

The theory of elites has often been used in Canada to describe the control of large corporations. It is C. Wright Mills' radical version of the
theory that has served as the basis for Canadian studies of corporate
control.[14]

Originally published in 1956, Mills' book *The Power Elite* became the
basis for a radical school that questioned previous analyses of power in
large joint-stock companies. This school has had significant influence
not only in the United States but also in England, France and other
countries,[15] and it is well represented among sociologists and historians
of Canadian industry. Mills rejected the concept of "ruling class," a
central idea in Marxist studies of the control of large corporations and
the state. He argued that class is an economic concept, and that the term
implies that an economic class governs, directs or is dominant in society
as a whole. In Mills' view, on the other hand, the state has become increasingly independent of the group that holds economic power during
the twentieth century.

While maintaining that the economic, political and military elites are
relatively autonomous, Mills also postulated the internal unity of the

economic elite, which he saw as being composed of two major groups
with similar interests: the corporate rich and the chief executives. On
the one hand, Mills argued, as a result of the dispersal of stock ownership, the power of the corporate rich had been reduced somewhat, while
on the other hand, stock purchases by the chief executives had made
them stockholders of some importance. As a result, he concluded, the
two groups formed a unified elite.

A number of aspects of the Mills hypothesis have been criticized.
According to Ferdinand Lundberg, Mills exaggerated the internal unity
of the economic elite, confusing the capitalist with his administrative
employees. Paul Sweezy has noted that Mills did not explain how the
social hierarchies that support the economic elite were formed. He also
maintains that, according to Mills' own data, American politics is in the
hands of extremely wealthy businessmen.[16]

In a study dealing with the share ownership of corporations, it is
impossible to examine critically all the elements of the theory of elites,
with respect to Canada. But it is possible to disaggregate the economic
or corporate elite into two major groups: large stockholders and
advisers.

Towards this end, the members of the boards of directors of the 136
dominant companies under Canadian control were classified into four
groups: legal advisers (lawyers who are members of a law firm);
financial advisers, accountants and technicians (management consultants, brokers, consulting engineers, etc.); managers (salaried employees whose careers and main occupations are within the company);
and large stockholders. The main occupation of each director was taken
to be the position listed first in his *Financial Post Directory of Directors* entry
for 1976.

Directors in the first two groups owned very few shares of the
companies on whose boards they sat, and in 1976, companies paid out
total sums ranging from $3,000 to $8,000 in remuneration to these
"outside" directors. They had no preferential stock purchase plans or
fringe benefits. Lawyers were the largest group among them, with an
average of 1.7 lawyers per board of directors. Smaller companies dealt
with only one law firm. Thus, for example, the Oshawa Group, 100 per
cent controlled by the Wolfe family, used the services of a single
Toronto firm, Shiffrin, White & Spring; two members of this firm, A.
Shiffrin and L.B. White, sat on the board of directors of the company
but held no voting shares in it.

Conglomerates, by contrast, use several law firms. Lawyers from
eight different firms sat on the boards of Brascan Ltd. and its subsidiaries. Among these, A.J. McIntosh of the Toronto firm Blake,
Cassels & Graydon held an especially privileged position; he sat on the
boards of the parent corporation and four subsidiaries on the list: John

Labatt, Ogilvie Mills, Hudson's Bay Company and Markborough Properties. Bronfman family companies used the services of some ten law firms, but one of these, Phillips and Vineberg of Montreal, maintained a special position. Philip F. Vineberg was on the boards of the Seagram Co., Cadillac Fairview Corp., Cemp Investments and Edper Investments; Lazarus Phillips was a director of Cemp Investments and Trizec Corp.; and James A. Soden, another partner in the same firm, was president of Trizec. A similar situation pertains with respect to financial consultants and accountants, except that they are not as numerous as the lawyers. Since all these advisers participate only nominally in share ownership, and since the compensation they receive is modest, it would be a distortion to mix them up with the bourgeoisie, as Mills does.

On the other hand, career managers are paid much more substantial salaries. In 1975, the officers of companies in the United States equivalent to those on the list made between $170,000 and $416,000 a year. They also frequently accumulate stock. The top managers on the boards of directors of the 136 companies on the list held an average of $250,000 worth of shares of the companies they worked for. This places them on a significantly lower level than the multimillionaires who control these same companies, but taking their salaries into account, it is possible to consider them a dependent and subordinate section of the Canadian bourgeoisie.

Conclusion

The first conclusion that can be drawn from the foregoing is that none of these three theories fully explains the Canadian situation. All three are based on the observation of real changes in the control of large corporations taking place in the monopoly stage of capitalism, but generalize unduly from that starting point.

But the data also hint at the existence of an indigenous ruling class, a bourgeoisie that was formed in Canada during the nineteenth century and the first third of the twentieth. This class is still permeable and admits to its ranks new members from the middle bourgeoisie and the group of top executives. Almost all the families, individuals and partnership groups in control of large Canadian corporations have their roots in the nineteenth century or the period of economic expansion that lasted from 1896 to 1929.[17] Canada does not belong only to foreign capital; each year, between two thirds and three quarters of the investments made in the country are made by companies controlled by the Canadian bourgeoisie.

CHAPTER 2

The Formation of the
Canadian Bourgeoisie

The economic history of social classes in Canada (and thus of the bourgeoisie) has not yet been written. But the present state of research
makes it possible to delineate the main factors that have influenced the
formation of the capitalist class, and to divide the history of the bourgeoisie into chronological segments which are also applicable to
Canadian economic history as a whole. In this way, an economic and
social sketch will be drawn of the group of people that dominates
Canadian society and of the ways in which it is produced and reproduced.

It would be a mistake to think of the bourgeoisie as a social entity that
does not change from generation to generation. On the contrary, it
expands with the diversification of the economic structure which it both
supports and benefits from; and it contracts during the waves of
mergers and economic concentration that centralize industrial ownership and control. The bourgeoisie reflects (although with enormous
delays and distortions) demographic changes in the population as a
whole, such as changes in ethnic composition or geographic distribution. And finally, it is susceptible to government intervention in the
economy or in society as a whole, and, consequently, is affected when
the government promotes the development of specific economic activities or favours one ethnic group at the expense of another.

It is thus important to clarify the main economic, political, social and
demographic factors that have operated in the formation of the
Canadian bourgeoisie. This historical sketch will provide a context for
the profiles of the contemporary bourgeoisie presented in the following
chapters.

The Main Factors in the Development of the Bourgeoisie

Since the capitalist class has its roots in the economic system, changes in
production and exchange have a particular effect on its structure. Thus

it is worthwhile at the outset to consider the long-term tendencies in the capitalist economy that affect the composition of its dominant class. The most important of these tendencies are the following:

The Destruction of Independent Commodity Production

Strictly speaking, the only pre-capitalist mode of production Canada has experienced is independent commodity production. This mode, especially important in agriculture in the form of small farmers, was also represented by craftsmen, small manufacturers and small tradesmen. Throughout the nineteenth century, as H.C. Pentland and Leo Johnson have amply shown, independent commodity producers, with few if any wage-earning employees, were an essential element of the Canadian occupational structure.[1] Their decline began to accelerate during the nineteenth century with the introduction of machines in industry and the mechanization of agriculture.

An essential element in the destruction of this group of independent workers was the formation of a labour market. The work of H.C. Pentland provides a good description of how this process operated in Canada. But while most of the independent commodity producers swelled the ranks of wage-earning labour, there was still a minority that managed to raise itself to the level of capitalists. The concentration of the retail industry in the twentieth century provides numerous examples of grocers who have become distribution magnates. The stories of the Steinbergs, who began with a grocery store in 1917, and the Préfontaines, who started their auto parts shop in 1928, are good illustrations of the passage from craft to capitalist forms of business organization. After the Second World War, craft production in residential construction gave way to large real estate corporations, and a number of small builders, such as Robert Campeau, became rich urban developers.[2] In other words, independent commodity production is a nursery for potential capitalists, and it provides the craftsman, farmer or small merchant with the possibility of rising to the upper class, even if that possibility is a remote one and varies from industry to industry.

Economic Concentration

While the elimination of independent producers is swelling the ranks of the upper class, another process is also at work: economic concentration. It was Marx who discovered this fundamental tendency of capitalist economies. The tendency towards concentration of ownership and control is not a simple movement in one direction but the overall affect of simultaneous centralizing and decentralizing forces. Among the centralizing forces worth noting are the economies linked to the use of large-scale technologies, price and market control which only large companies can exercise, advertising, patents, the monopolization of natural resources, tariff protection, urbanization and the concentration of government purchasing. The decentralizing forces include new technologies that tend towards industrial deconcentration (such as electrical energy, road transport, production based on plastics), the administrative diseconomies of large companies, and innovation.[3]

In the Canadian economy, centralization and concentration have had the effect of reducing the number of capitalists in each sector of economic activity and increasing the power of those who remain. The following are a few examples to illustrate this phenomenon. According to the Taschereau Commission on the alleged combine in the paper industry, in 1902 there were twenty-six independent pulp and paper producers in Canada. After a process of development and merger that was completed in 1931, five companies held 75 per cent of the newsprint production capacity.[4] In the primary iron and steel industry, competition among several dozen producers prevailed until the beginning of the twentieth century; the wave of mergers that lasted from 1900 to 1917 left only four major producers — Stelco, Dofasco, Dosco and Algoma Steel — plus a few marginal ones.[5] In the automobile industry, which got underway at the beginning of the twentieth century, competitive development took place from 1900 to 1930. During the Depression, mergers and plant closings left the three American automobile giants with more than 90 per cent of car production and between 75 and 90 per cent of truck production.[6]

The Diversification of Industry

If the evolution of the capitalist economy could be reduced to a simple process of industrial centralization and concentration, then Marx's predictions would have long ago been realized and a handful of capitalists would control the whole range of production and exchange activities. However, simultaneously with the tendency towards centralization, a process of industrial diversification creates new goods and services and produces a counterweight to the overall concentration of the economy.

The Canadian financial system provides a good example of this process of diversification. From Confederation to 1920, the chartered banks amassed more than 50 per cent of the assets of all the financial institutions in Canada, and during the first three decades of the twentieth century the number of banks in operation was reduced from thirty-six to eleven. If the financial system had not been diversified, bankers' power would be even more immense than it actually is. The reason this has not happened is that since 1900 a number of other types of financial intermediaries have developed: trust companies, brokerage houses, finance companies, caisses populaires, and the like. In 1970 the chartered banks held only 28 per cent of the assets of the

Canadian financial system and this percentage is on the decline.[7] The new financial institutions did not necessarily develop under the aegis of the old ones. New enterprises (and new entrepreneurs) developed most of the brokerage houses and trust companies. Men such as A.J. Nesbitt and P.A. Thomson, James H. Gundy, and René T. Leclerc founded brokerage houses with little except the experience they had acquired as salaried employees in the trade.

Similarly, in the manufacturing sector the development of a new product can turn a workshop into a large company, although this is happening less and less frequently. The case of Bombardier Ltd., created in 1942 to exploit its founder's invention, demonstrates that even in our time not all technological research and development is in the hands of large corporations. In new industries, the technical, financial, commercial or legal barriers to the entry of new competitors are not so great as to prevent small companies from growing, and the capitalist class is broadened as a result.

The Mobility of Capital

In the *18th Brumaire*, Marx was still able to identify the principal lines of cleavage in the capitalist class as being those that divided it into industrial, commercial and financial sections. This division, however, properly belongs to the competitive phase of capitalism, in which the mobility of capital from industry to industry is very weak. In Canada, capital has always been highly concentrated and able to move from industry to industry. This does not happen through investment by the oldest corporations in a brand new industry at the outset. Rather, capital is sufficiently mobile (within the sectors under Canadian control) that some new industries at each stage fall under the aegis of already existing companies. This is what happened, for example, with the control of railways by bankers and merchants, and of pulp and paper concerns by railway magnates. But despite the mobility of capital, independent enterprises and new foci of accumulation were formed at each stage and new members of the subordinate classes were incorporated into the capitalist class. In other words, the advantages derived from class position are not absolute (as they are in a caste or a guild) and there are always new avenues of entry to the upper class.

The State and the Capitalist Class

In Marxist literature the state has often been presented as an exclusive instrument of the capitalist class. This description is not false, but it is plainly incomplete. For the state also has the power to set the guidelines of a social group's path to capitalist economic development; through this process, some social classes are created while the growth of others is stunted. The colonization of Canadian lands by the feudal French state produced a seigneurial class, while a century later the capitalist British state created an agrarian petty bourgeoisie in Ontario. In giving oil concessions to American and Canadian capital after the Second World War, the Alberta government developed a comprador and a local bourgeoisie, while the legal restrictions passed in 1967 affecting the foreign ownership of chartered banks were brought in to support the indigenous financial bourgeoisie.

The state can also contribute to the concentration of capital by a variety of means. As a result, there are fewer corporation heads and the power of those who remain is increased. The concentration of government purchases, subsidies, direct and indirect protection and patent policy are some of the means by which the state can favour some enterprises (large corporations rather than small or medium-sized ones, domestically-owned corporations as opposed to foreign-owned ones, corporations owned within a particular province rather than outside that province) and, as a result, some businessmen at the expense of others.

Ethnic and National Barriers

Ethnic and national divisions are among the most important demographic features affecting the internal unity of capitalist classes. It has often been observed that in multinational or ethnically diverse states, the majority group is overrepresented among the capitalist classes. This was the case in Tsarist Russia, Great Britain and Switzerland, where the owning classes were made up almost exclusively of Great-Russians, Englishmen and German Swiss respectively. But in the countries of white European settlement, the order of arrival of the various migratory waves often defined the ethnic composition of social hierarchies. This is the case in the United States, where the largest (and richest) part of the upper class comes from old Anglo-Saxon Protestant stock.[8]

In Canada, however, these two general laws do not apply. For a century after the British Conquest, the oldest settlers, the French Canadians, constituted a majority of the population. But as a result of the Conquest and the concentration of state power in the hands of the British merchants, the French Canadians held only a secondary position in the capitalist classes. Until the Second World War the Canadian bourgeoisie was almost exclusively Anglo-Saxon and Protestant, and a large proportion of important businessmen in Canada were born in Britain.

The underrepresentation of non-British ethnic and national groups did not apply to French Canadians alone. While in the United States at the turn of the century there were significant financial, commercial and industrial enterprises under Jewish control (for example, Salomon

Brothers, Kuhn Loeb and Lazard Frères among the brokerage houses), the rise of a Jewish establishment in Canada took place only after the Second World War, although certain families (notably the Bronfmans and the Steinbergs) were already rich before the war. And the 30 per cent of the population that is not British or Jewish or French is hardly represented at all in the Canadian establishment, although a few English-speaking business families come from eastern Europe (such as the Batas of Bata Shoes and Stephen Roman of Denison Mines).

Regional Divisions

In a country that is sharply divided into fairly distinct economic regions, the existence of regional bourgeoisies is no surprise. Until the Second World War, Montreal was unquestionably the metropolis of Canada, and the Canadian bourgeoisie was that of Montreal. As the twentieth century wore on, however, the country's industrial and commercial activity gradually shifted to the Great Lakes region, the new economic centre of the United States and Canada. A portion of the Montreal bourgeoisie followed this economic and demographic relocation. But a Toronto bourgeoisie was also formed to take advantage of the new economic opportunities. As the Canadian West was settled, the population of the western provinces and territories increased from 11 per cent of the Canadian total in 1901 to 28 per cent of the total in 1921.[9] The grain trade, finance, the paper industry, etc., fuelled the growth of regional bourgeoisies, even though partial control of these activities remained in the hands of older central Canadian interests. Later, the Alberta oil boom provided new Alberta capitalists with sure-fire opportunities in the development of real estate and resource extraction in the province.

Foreign Investment

Since the last quarter of the nineteenth century, Canada has been the recipient of a significant amount of direct foreign investment, at first largely British, then (after the First World War) mostly American. There can be no doubt about the privileged relationship of American capital with the Canadian economy in the twentieth century. Around 1914, Canada and Newfoundland surpassed Mexico in the volume of American investment received. Canada has remained the principal area of investment for American companies ever since, although this privileged status has been eroded somewhat since the Second World War. In addition, in the 1920s the United States replaced England as the principal source of direct foreign investment in Canada.

This influx of foreign capital, notably in the manufacturing and mining sectors, has taken two forms: the creation of new subsidiaries by foreign corporations and the absorption of Canadian-controlled companies. In both cases, the management of a subsidiary is subject to directives from head office. The core of managers of these subsidiaries forms the Canadian comprador bourgeoisie, a clearly defined sector of the capitalist class whose characteristics are examined in chapter 5. It suffices to say here that the expansion or contraction of foreign direct investment has an immediate influence on the evolution of the comprador bourgeoisie, and that any government measure tending to block or restrict foreign investment is inimical to its interests. The relationship between the comprador bourgeoisie and the indigenous bourgeoisie is also explored in chapter 5.

From the by no means exhaustive list of considerations just presented, it is clear that the capitalist class should not be looked at as a homogeneous and coherent group, bounded by economic and social borders that cannot be crossed. On the contrary, the bourgeoisie is a restricted group, but a dynamic and changing one, constantly incorporating new elements and excluding others as economic, political and social circumstances change.

On the basis of these premises, one can construct a division of the economic history of Canadian business circles that takes into account the principal changes that have taken place since Confederation. Such a chronology must include at least four major stages.

The Major Stages

In strictly economic terms, the history of the Canadian bourgeoisie has some highly regular features and can be divided into specific periods. Within each stage one sees the appearance, the development, and finally the growing monopolization of one or a few key industries. Each stage begins with a more or less short-term reorientation of the economy towards these new activities and ends with diminishing opportunities for the new industries. Thus, it is possible to distinguish three clear stages in the history of the Canadian economy (and of its dominant class) and the emergence of a fourth.

(a) *1867-1914:* Domination by commercial banks, export trade and railways.

(b) *1914-1940:* Growth of the pulp and paper industry, hydroelectric power and brokerage houses. Beginnings of the comprador bourgeoisie.

(c) *1940-1970:* Development of the comprador bourgeoisie (oil and gas, mining, the automobile industry) and new sectors of indigenous capital (real estate, retail trade, new financial institutions).

(d) 1970—   : Decline of American hegemony (and of the comprador bourgeoisie) and renaissance of Canadian nationalism. Rise of regional bourgeoisies, mainly
around energy and mining activities.

These stages should not be seen as mutually exclusive. The rise of the
brokerage houses did not take place at the expense of the banks, but
created new foci of accumulation distinct from the earlier ones, and a
new bourgeoisie grew up alongside the old. Real estate development
after the Second World War led to the creation of some fifteen companies with assets of more than $100 million, each of them belonging to
an individual or a closely-knit group of associates. These new entrepreneurs also took their place in the Canadian establishment alongside
older elements.

Nor should geographic changes be overestimated. Montreal was the
undisputed metropolis of Canada between 1867 and 1914 because of its
port. The chief sources of wealth in Canada were the profits derived
from trading in, transporting and financing the trade in grain, wood,
furs and other raw materials bound for Britain. Montreal was the
centre for these activities and for the large companies and rich stockholders they spawned. But towards the end of the nineteenth century
Toronto began to narrow Montreal's lead. Southern Ontario became
the home of the Canadian steel industry and of the principal foreign
investments in industry. Also, electrical energy was plentiful. Toronto,
then, replaced Montreal as the industrial and financial centre of Canada
during the third stage (1940-1970), as a result of the influx of foreign
capital. However, this was only a partial replacement; Toronto became
dominant but Montreal remained an important secondary centre.

With these guidelines, the major stages in the development of the
Canadian bourgeoisie can now be examined more closely.

*The Era of Merchant and Finance Capital and
Railway Magnates (1867-1914)*

More is known about Canada's economic development for the period
lasting from Confederation to 1914 than for any other era. The works
of Gustavus Myers, Tom Naylor, Stanley Ryerson, Michael Bliss and
T. Acheson; the numerous histories of the Canadian Pacific Railway,
the Hudson's Bay Company and the principal chartered banks; the biographies of the officers of these companies and studies of Canada's
economic structure give us an accurate picture of Canadian business
activity from Confederation to the First World War. But before pro-
ceeding, an explanation of the limits of this stage is in order.

The period was marked by the construction of three transcontinental
railways and ended abruptly in 1914 with the completion of the last two

of these lines and the closing of the London financial market as a result of the war. After 1914 there were few new railway lines built, and subsequently, Canada was no longer dependent on loans from London for its development.

Along with the railways, export trade and commercial finance were the royal roads to fortune during the period. The companies that best symbolized these types of activity were the Hudson's Bay Company, the Bank of Montreal and Canadian Pacific. The mobility of capital among these three sectors was very great: the Bank of Montreal lent money to Canadian Pacific and the Hudson's Bay Company, which had their accounts at the Bank of Montreal. In addition, the three companies were controlled by the same people, a short list of stockholders that included Lord Strathcona (Donald Smith), Lord Mount Stephen (George Stephen) and Richard B. Angus. This was an entirely Anglo-Saxon and Protestant dominant bourgeoisie, and many of its members were born in Britain. There were no significant companies under French Canadian control.

The federal and provincial governments were to a large extent the guiding spirits of this ruling class. Myers calculated in 1913 that assistance to railways in the form of cash subsidies and bond guarantees had cost the public treasury some $485 million, while governments had distributed 56 million acres of free land to these same railway companies.[10] Just as the British government created a cohort of capitalists in chartering the Hudson's Bay Company in 1670, Canada created a new one by incorporating railway companies and granting them subsidies and lands.

Mobility of capital was not limited to these three key sectors. With the help of land concessions, railway companies were often able to enter the mining and forest industries. As early as 1905, the largest and most profitable of the three dominant Canadian railway companies, the CPR, created a mining subsidiary, Cominco, that became one of the largest extraction conglomerates in Canada. Stimulated by demand from the expanding railways, the iron and steel and railway equipment industries also grew. This growth was accomplished in part with capital which came from the railways themselves. Finally, even the Canadian-controlled textile and food and beverage industries were connected to the banks by a number of links. The Molson brewing family, for example, sat on the board of the Bank of Montreal; in 1856 the Molsons founded their own bank which merged with the Bank of Montreal in 1925. The Maclaren pulp and paper interests were represented on the board of the Bank of Ottawa, while the Redpath sugar refiners were linked to the Bank of Montreal.

By the end of the period, the dominant sectors in finance, industry, trade and transportation were highly concentrated. While in 1867 there were thirty-three chartered banks, by 1914 only twenty-two remained and the five largest accounted for 50 per cent of the assets of all commercial banks in Canada.[11] Railways were similarly concentrated; three companies, the CPR, Canadian Northern and Grand Trunk, controlled almost all railway lines in Canada. As for manufacturing, the cement industry had become a monopoly with the formation of Canada Cement in 1909; iron and steel was an oligopoly consisting of only four firms; and the textile industry had been dominated by Dominion Textile since 1904. Finally, the nascent hydroelectric industry was in large part under the control of Sir Herbert Holt (of the Royal Bank) in Montreal and Sir William Mackenzie and Donald Mann (of the Canadian Northern Railway) in Ontario.

Such were the dominant sectors in Canada during the first stage, 1867-1914. One should not forget, however, that regional bourgeoisies, notably those of Quebec, Ontario and the Maritimes, coexisted with these dominant industries. In Quebec, for example, the food and beverage, clothing, footwear and textile industries remained partly outside the scope of the great pan-Canadian enterprises. A large part of this independent capital would be absorbed during the great merger wave of 1925-1931. During this period there were also a number of banks, mortgage companies, hydroelectric corporations and independent commercial enterprises tied to these regional industries. These too would disappear during the next stage.

The Rise of the Brokerage Houses; the Growth of the Pulp and Paper, Mining and Hydroelectric Industries (1914-1940)

As a result of the closing of the London financial market, a Canadian financial market was created, a minority of Canadian loans were floated in the United States and loans from London almost completely disappeared. Thus, between 1904 and 1914, sales in Britain accounted for 73 per cent of the value of Canadian bonds issued, as compared with 18 per cent in Canada and 9 per cent in the United States. Between 1915 and 1920 these proportions were 3, 67 and 30 per cent respectively, and between 1921 and 1930 they were 2, 58 and 40 per cent.[12]

By that time, the Canadian securities industry was well established and under domestic control, as almost all the new bankers and bond dealers (who organized themselves into an association in 1916) were Canadians. This industry, too, needed help from the government to get started. The first three war loans floated on the Canadian market, between December 1915 and March 1917, attracted only between 25,000 and 41,000 subscribers. The funds raised were not enough to finance the war effort and the Canadian securities market remained extremely limited. For the fourth loan, the Canadian minister of finance and the Bond Dealers Association of Canada together conceived and set up a cross-Canada organization to increase the sale of bonds. With the help of this mechanism, 820,000 Canadians subscribed to the issue and it attracted almost three times the anticipated amount of money. The government also set up a committee of bond dealers with the authority to fix prices. Since the bond houses were private companies, figures for their profits during the war are not available, but they were without doubt very high.

During the 1920s, the bond dealers invested their profits in other sectors. Nesbitt Thomson created Power Corporation in 1925 as a holding company for a number of hydroelectric concerns it had acquired since 1918. New investment companies were formed by bond houses such as Wood Gundy, Nesbitt Thomson and Cochrane Hay.[13] A number of bond dealers gained control of consolidated companies created during the 1925-1931 merger wave and became full members of the Canadian bourgeoisie.[14]

The pulp and paper industry, which had been in existence since 1867, began to flourish after 1913. Ontario imposed an embargo on the export of pulpwood cut on crown lands in 1900, and Quebec followed suit in 1910. In 1913, under concerted pressure from the Canadian provinces and the great American newspaper chains, the American government put newsprint on the list of duty-free commodities. Canadian production surpassed that of the United States in 1926 and Canada became the largest producer and exporter of newsprint in the world. Consequently, the pulp and paper industry became the largest manufacturing industry in Canada. Part of this growth was due to northward movement by great American companies, notably International Paper. But another part was the result of the expansion of Canadian firms such as Consolidated Paper (the product of a 1928 merger) and Price Brothers. The new industry grew under the protective wing of the government, which generously distributed timber berths and hydroelectric concessions and helped the industry both by supporting it in the embargo and tariff struggles early in the century and by regulating the market when prices collapsed between 1931 and 1936.[15]

Hydroelectricity was a sector in which new fortunes were made. Although most of the great hydroelectric companies were founded before 1914, their expansion took place after that date: Canadian hydroelectric production quadrupled between 1915 and 1939. The Ontario government took over the industry between 1905 and 1925, but Quebec (representing between 40 and 50 per cent of Canadian production) and British Columbia (10 per cent) remained fiefdoms of private enterprise.[16]

The new sectors of activity quickly became concentrated. In 1927 five houses — Wood Gundy, Nesbitt Thomson, A.E. Ames and Co., Dominion Securities and Royal Securities — underwrote almost 50 per cent of all bond issues in Canada, either independently or as lead firms in underwriting syndicates. Concentration in this industry has not diminished subsequently. In addition, Nesbitt Thomson and Wood Gundy controlled the major investment companies in Canada; the Montreal bond dealers controlled a large part of the hydroelectric industry through Power Corporation; and J.H. Gundy held positions of control in Massey-Harris, Simpsons and Consolidated Paper, among others.

In mining, the principal developments occurred under foreign control. Nickel was under the almost exclusive control of International Nickel from 1902; asbestos was controlled by American and British companies (except for Asbestos Corporation at the time); copper was controlled by large foreign companies (such as Inco and Noranda Mines, which was then under American control); and similar patterns prevailed for other minerals. Canadians had neither the technology nor the access to markets needed to develop this industry, which quickly fell under American or European control and became just as concentrated as Canadian-controlled industries. Government participation was as determining a factor in mining development as in other sectors. In this case, concessions on crown lands, subsidies and bonuses, and the building of infrastructure in the form of roads, railways or harbours facilitated and stimulated the growth of foreign capital and the comprador bourgeoisie.

During this stage, the outlines of the split between the indigenous bourgeoisie and the comprador bourgeoisie became apparent. Foreign direct investment, most of which came from the United States, had few if any ties with Canadian capital. Nationality of control was not the only difference between the foreign mining companies and Canadian firms. Since foreign-controlled companies produced for the world market, they were not highly integrated into the Canadian economy, and many of them did not issue securities in Canada. As a result they had only limited contact with the Canadian financial system. The branch-plant manufacturing industries were of course more integrated into the Canadian economy, as they produced for the internal market.

During this period, the Canadian economy became more diversified but remained in essence externally-oriented. The dynamic sectors were the new "staples" (paper, aluminum, minerals) and were largely under foreign control. The Canadian bourgeoisie gained new ground in finance, public service and industry, but yielded to foreign interests in more technologically advanced sectors.

The Comprador Bourgeoisie, Real Estate Developers and the New Merchant and Financial Bourgeoisie (1940-1970)

The Second World War altered the Canadian economy's relations with the outside world, and, consequently, its internal structure as well. During and after the war, integration into the American economy accelerated. The great iron ore deposits of northeastern Quebec, discovered just before the war, were exploited by the large American steel producers (in some cases with minority Canadian participation) after 1950. Canada became one of the great world exporters of iron ore. The discoveries of oil and natural gas in Alberta in 1947 stimulated production under foreign control.

Manufacturing development also took place increasingly through the medium of branch plants: the automobile industry underwent unprecedented growth after the signing of the Auto Pact in 1965; war industries developed under the impetus of a series of agreements, which began with the Hyde Park declaration of 1941 and was completed by the Defence Production Sharing Agreement in 1959. Foreign ownership of Canadian manufacturing increased from 42 per cent in 1939 to 53 per cent in 1970; in mining, foreign ownership increased from 40 per cent to 69 per cent in the same period. Meanwhile, in other sectors foreign ownership and control declined appreciably.[17]

New sectors which had previously been the domain of small and middle-sized business became concentrated after the war, and this process took place under Canadian control. Real estate is the most striking example. Urbanization, industrialization and the growth of service industries led to an increased demand for houses, office complexes and industrial and commercial buildings. Huge companies were built up to meet this demand. Real estate provided an opportunity for entrepreneurs who were not of Anglo-Saxon origin to become the heads of large companies. Campeau Corp. and Allarco Developments (French Canadian), Trizec and Cadillac-Fairview (Jewish Canadian), and Orlando Corp. (Italian Canadian) are examples of the rise of ethnic minorities in Canadian big business after the Second World War. In the retail business, where concentration took place very late, the same phenomenon occurred, and the market shares of Jewish (Oshawa Group, Steinberg's Acklands) and French Canadian (Provigo, UAP Inc.) businesses became significant.

A similar process can be seen in the financial sphere: Jewish and French Canadian firms developed very rapidly. Among the Jewish-owned companies are IAC Ltd. (which became the Continental Bank of Canada in 1979), Central and Eastern Trust Corp., First City Financial Corp., and most recently Brascan Ltd., which fell under the control of the Bronfman family in 1979. French Canadian interests own the Desjardins and La Laurentienne insurance groups, the Caisses Populaires Desjardins, the financial institutions in the Power Corp. group and others. There has, however, been a marked difference between the rise of ethnic minorities in finance and their rise in other sectors. In finance, with a few exceptions, Jewish and French Canadians have made their entry through the purchase of existing institutions. This was the case with the Bronfmans in IAC Ltd. and Brascan, with Paul Desmarais in Power Corp., with Cohen and Ellen in Central and Eastern Trust, etc. And almost invariably, the takeovers of old Anglo-Saxon financial institutions have been preceded by virtual pitched battles, the most recent being that which surrounded the purchase of Brascan by Edward and Peter Bronfman in 1979.

Government ensured the expansion of foreign investment through measures such as agreements establishing a common market in munitions, the Auto Pact, oil concessions, and the construction of the St. Lawrence Seaway so that iron ore could be exported to the United States.[18] It also contributed to the development of large real estate companies through the concentration of government purchases, appropriate legislation and financial aid to the developers' large-scale projects. The land grants given to railway companies in the nineteenth century have allowed some of them (notably Canadian Pacific and Canadian National) to become owners and developers of urban land. In 1963, Canadian Pacific established a real estate subsidiary, Marathon Realty, to which it transferred a million acres of land, half of which was in urban areas. In this way government in the nineteenth century contributed towards the formation of today's real estate industry.

Mobility of capital between the old Canadian-controlled sectors and the new ones has been fairly extensive. The example of Canadian Pacific entering a new industry, real estate, has just been cited. The largest banks and insurance companies, too, have created subsidiaries in this lucrative area. But the postwar era has also seen mobility of capital become more significant with the appearance of conglomerates such as Argus Corporation (founded in 1945), Power Corp. (turned into a conglomerate between 1960 and 1968, when it sold its hydroelectric interests) and Brascan Ltd. (restructured as a conglomerate through acquisitions in Canada since 1967). This development has allowed large amounts of capital to circulate more freely among different spheres, to the extent that the distinctions among the "industrial," "commercial" and "financial" bourgeoisie have lost some of their utility. The great families of the Canadian establishment are in control of companies in several sectors. Mobility of capital between the Canadian and foreign-controlled sectors is, however, very low, and accumulation by each group of companies takes place in some sense within a closed system.

The distinction between "indigenous" and "comprador" sectors has therefore lost none of its cutting edge during this stage.

One last process that took place during this period is worth noting. In addition to industrial concentration, there was during the Second World War and the subsequent quarter-century a geographic concentration of economic activity. Ontario became both the centre of foreign investment and the pole of attraction for indigenous capital. At the same time, regional bourgeoisies (notably in Quebec, Alberta and British Columbia) developed as a result of the general prosperity. These regional groups, supported by provincial governments, would start to resist (in Quebec after 1960, in Alberta after 1971, and in British Columbia after 1975) the process of concentration that was displacing Canadian industry to the benefit of Ontario.

Decline of American Hegemony
and Renaissance of Canadian Nationalism;
Rise of the Regional Bourgeoisies (1970-1980)

The 1970s marked a new period in Canadian-American relations. In 1968, the American economy entered a stage of slow growth accompanied by inflation. The decline in the international liquidity of the United States forced the Nixon administration to implement a new economic policy involving an increase in tariffs and an attempt to bring home foreign investment as a means of checking rising domestic unemployment. Finally the gradual disengagement from the war in Indochina reduced American military spending, and the benefits that had accrued to the Canadian economy were curtailed. In this context, it is not surprising that the nationalist preaching of Walter Gordon and other minority elements in Canadian business fell on more receptive ears. In the early 1970s the government established the Gray commission on foreign investment, revived its proposal to create a Canada Development Corporation (CDC), and established the Foreign Investment Review Agency. The CDC bought Texasgulf Corp. in 1973, and in 1975 Ottawa created Petro-Canada to bring two large American oil companies (one of them including a major subsidiary) under public control.* Canadair became the property of the federal government in 1975. The Canadian private sector benefited from the new legislation. Two of the largest foreign-controlled real estate companies were bought by Canadians, as well as several substantial industrial and financial corporations (tables 2-1 and 2-2).

---

*A third major Petro-Canada acquisition, that of Petrofina Canada, took place in 1981.

The provinces also took part in this process. Taking advantage of postwar prosperity, regional bourgeoisies had begun to grow and had challenged the movement of economic activity towards Ontario. In 1967-68, Nova Scotia and Quebec bought the steel manufacturing capacity of Dosco, a financially-troubled subsidiary of a British company. For its part, the Quebec government's aim was to build its steel company, Sidbec, into an integrated steel manufacturer. This was later achieved when Sidbec bought part of Quebec Cartier Mining's holdings in the iron mines of northeastern Quebec. In 1976, the Quebec government announced its intention to buy a majority of the shares of the Asbestos Corporation and in 1978 it intervened in a transaction in which the Crédit Foncier Franco-Canadien came under French Canadian control. In 1978, the Alberta government gave the green light to Alberta Gas Trunk Line, a joint public-private company, to buy Husky Oil, while between 1976 and 1979 the NDP government of Saskatchewan bought half the province's potash industry from foreign interests.

Nationalism has not been the only force behind provincial moves, as the regional bourgeoisies have also tried to maintain or enlarge their

TABLE 2-1

Value of Assets under Foreign Control as a Percentage of Total Assets of Declaring Corporations, 1970 and 1978

Sector	1970	1978	Difference
Agriculture	13%	6%	-7%
Mining	69%	47%	-22%
Manufacturing	58%	52%	-6%
Construction	16%	10%	-6%
Utilities	8%	6%	-2%
Wholesale trade	27%	26%	-1%
Retail trade	22%	15%	-7%
Services	22%	18%	-4%
Total, non-financial industries	36%	29%	-7%

N.B.: 1) The most recent data available are for 1978, which makes it impossible to see how the process has continued since then.
2) Assets under foreign control reached their maximum point in 1968, at 38 per cent, while positive taxable income declared by subsidiaries of foreign companies reached its maximum in 1969 at 49 per cent, the same figure as in 1976.
Source: Statistics Canada, *Companies and Labour Unions Returns Act. Part I: Corporations* (Cat. 61-210), 1970-1980

spheres of influence through interprovincial struggles. In 1975-76 the Alberta government bought Pacific Western Airlines and transferred its head office to Calgary, over the protests of the government of British Columbia. Quebec intervened in 1977 to support a group of French Canadian businessmen who opposed Nova Scotian interests that were trying to take over Provigo, and acted again the following year to prevent the purchase of the Crédit Foncier by another Nova Scotian group. In July 1979, the Caisse de Dépôt et Placement du Québec gained control of Domtar, while the British Columbia Resources Investment

TABLE 2-2

Major Subsidiaries of Foreign Companies Purchased by Canadian Interests, 1968-1981*

Company	Year of Purchase	Buyer
Dosco	1967-68	Govts. of Quebec and N.S.
Canada Steamship Lines	1972	Power Corp.
Texasgulf	1973	CDC
Algoma Steel	1974	Canadian Pacific
Dominion Bridge	1974	Canadian Pacific
Canadair	1974	Federal Government
De Havilland	1975	Federal Government
Atlantic Richfield	1976	Petro-Canada
Trizec	1976	Bronfman Family
Abbey Glen Property Corp.	1976	Private group, Toronto
Zeller's	1976	Private group, Vancouver
Maple Leaf Mills	1978	CP Enterprises
Pacific Petroleums	1978	Petro-Canada
Westcoast Transmission	1978	Petro-Canada
Husky Oil	1978-79	Alberta Gas Trunk Line
Several companies, potash	1976-79	Govt. of Saskatchewan
Kaiser Resources	1980	B.C. Resources Investment Corp.
Brinco	1980	Olympia & York
Canadian Utilities	1980	Atco Industries
Hudson's Bay Oil & Gas	1981	Dome Petroleum
Petrofina Canada	1981	Petro-Canada
Canadian Int. Paper.	1981	CP Enterprises
Aquitaine of Canada	1981	CDC

*Entries for 1980 and 1981 have been added to the original table.

Corporation was preparing to buy MacMillan Bloedel, the largest Canadian pulp and paper producer. MacMillan Bloedel had also been the target of a Canadian Pacific takeover bid at the beginning of the same year.*

Nationalism and regionalism — these are the two constants of the period that began in 1970. Under the constraints of slower growth, the conflicts between the comprador and indigenous bourgeoisies became more acute, and additional conflicts occurred between the indigenous centralizing bourgeoisie and its regional challengers. The federal-provincial conflict does not pit the Canadian bourgeoisie against the multinationals (a theory which the New Democratic Party and the nationalist wing of the Liberal Party of Canada find attractive). Rather it is a question of the emerging regional bourgeoisies being pitted against the indigenous bourgeoisie, which is becoming increasingly concentrated in Ontario.

Finally, the growth of publicly-owned corporations does not give rise to a "state bourgeoisie." The very existence of these corporations requires that they be managed by Canadian businessmen, and thus they are not an autonomous source of power. They are quasi-private corporations and Canadian capitalists take turns ensuring they are managed soundly and profitably for everyone. This question is examined in chapter 4.

Conclusion

By dividing the study of the Canadian bourgeoisie into chronological periods, one discovers that it is composed of successive strata contributed by new industries, each of which in turn acted as an engine of economic development. The oldest of these layers consists of the great merchants, bankers and railway magnates of the era of consolidation of Canadian capitalism (1867-1914). Next come those who acquired wealth from pulp and paper, hydroelectricity, and brokerage. The Second World War and the postwar period brought massive foreign direct investment. These years also saw the rise of Canadian real estate developers and organizers of conglomerates and the new merchant class — to which should be added the owners of the new mass media. Some elements of the older strata became part of the newer ones, and thus in recent years large distillers have become real estate developers, just as earlier bankers became pulp and paper industrialists or railway magnates became owners of hydroelectric companies.

---

*The BCRIC bid for MacMillan Bloedel was unsuccessful, and a majority interest in the pulp and paper giant was purchased by the Noranda group of Toronto in 1981.

Nevertheless, new industries created new paths to fortune, and the Canadian capitalist class, at one time exclusively Anglo-Saxon and Protestant, has had to adapt to the arrival of Jewish and French Canadian newcomers. These *nouveaux riches* have, however, not been well received by the older members of the bourgeoisie, and they have fought their exclusion from the circles of the social elite through their position of influence in the party of the non-WASPs — the Liberal Party of Canada. After the comprador-indigenous conflict, the ethnic split is the most important division in the Canadian capitalist class. The regional bourgeoisies are at this point composed essentially of small and middle-sized business, but their ability to influence provincial governments is at the root of Canadian "provincialism."

CHAPTER 3

The New French Canadian Bourgeoisie

There is wide recognition of the inferior position of the French Canadian bourgeoisie with respect to its English-speaking counterpart, just as there is of the economically inferior status of the French Canadian population as a whole with respect to English-speaking Canadians. What is of interest here is not Quebec's economic "lag" or the fact that per capita income is 10 per cent lower in Quebec than in Ontario, but rather the unequal distribution of jobs and incomes across Canada. Both in Quebec and in the other provinces, French Canadians occupy the lowest-skilled, lowest-paying jobs.

Different writers have advanced economic, political and cultural explanations for this phenomenon; these are presented as mutually exclusive and often incompatible factors. However, it is not difficult to demonstrate how many of these explanations are historically and sociologically complementary.

Maurice Séguin's conquest thesis probably accounts for part of the phenomenon.[1] After 1760, the new regime favoured commercial and financial links with England. For a century and a half, British-Canadian trade, transportation and commercial finance were the leading economic activities in Canada. These activities were mainly controlled by the Anglo-Saxon bourgeoisie, which had all the advantages it needed to assure itself of a dominant position — language, contacts, knowledge of the British market and the laws and customs of the mother country, etc. There does not appear to have been a class of substantial francophone entrepreneurs in Canada at the time of the conquest, and the presence of a new English-speaking bourgeoisie prevented such a class from developing. French Canadians, then, were not "driven back" ("refoulés": Séguin's term) into agriculture but simply left there, and hence the formation of an indigenous bourgeoisie, such as the one that emerged in Latin America, was prevented.

Nevertheless, between 1760 and the end of the nineteenth century, a French Canadian petty and middle bourgeoisie developed. It controlled several banks, as well as companies in the industrial (food and beverages, textiles, footwear, clothing, paper), commercial and transportation sectors. But the years between 1900 and 1930 saw the disappearance of French Canadian-controlled companies in the banking, manufacturing and service sectors. Paul-André Linteau has offered the plausible suggestion that the merger waves of this era were responsible for this loss of position.[2] Meanwhile, a substantial majority of French Canadian heads of household remained tied to agriculture. However, under the capitalist system of production, agriculture — especially small family farming — is marginal compared to more dynamic and concentrated urban activities such as trade, finance and industry.

Between 1930 and 1940, the Depression prevented capitalists from venturing into new sectors and few new companies were founded. After 1940, wartime demand stimulated economic growth and the development of new branches of industry. This was the time when the Simard family of Sorel presided over the growth of Marine Industries, Sorel Industries, Sorel Steel Foundries and other companies.[3] However, in this era the Simards still represented an exceptional case. To explain the "lag" in the creation of a French Canadian bourgeoisie between 1930 and 1960, cultural and political factors must be taken into account. Before 1960, the Quebec government did not act as the promoter of the French Canadian bourgeoisie. This was clearly not one of its political goals, and it did not endow itself with the means to achieve it. Under Premier Maurice Duplessis, the government intervened in favour of big business — English Canadian or foreign — while espousing a conservative and clerical version of French Canadian nationalism.

Institutions of higher learning had always been geared to training clerics, members of the liberal professions and men of letters. Science, technology, management and economics were almost completely ignored. Profitability was the criterion used by both the federal and the provincial government in promoting industrial development, and this favoured American, European and English Canadian business. Errol Bouchette, at the beginning of the twentieth century, was the first to stress the role that the Quebec and Canadian governments should play in promoting French Canadian industry.[4]

Another characteristic of turn-of-the-century French Canadian business that contributed to its fragility was its provincial nature. The francophone bourgeoisie that was marginalized in the merger waves of 1900-1930 was a local Quebec group. The Sénécals (railways), Boivins (footwear), Barsalous (soap), Dupuis (retailing), Béiques (hydroelectricity), Forgets (finance, paper), Leducs (sawmills), Rollands (paper), Desjardins and Beaudrys (banking) operated almost exclusively in the Quebec market. For whatever reason, their enterprises never grew beyond the borders of the province, and they could not hope to become dominant corporations in Canada as a whole. For the most part, they were doomed to absorption by their English Canadian or American competitors.

Other theories that have been advanced appear to treat the consequences of French Canada's economically inferior situation as its cause. The family nature of French Canadian business (Jacques Melançon, Norman Taylor) and the conservative mentality of French Canadian business (Fernand Ouellet) were, in this writer's view, only peripheral effects of French Canada's situation of socio-economic inferiority.[5] This inferiority is better accounted for by dependent economic and political structures than by the educational system which they produced. In addition, the causes of the economic inferiority of French Canadians (and of their bourgeoisie) were probably not the same from century to century, and the factors that once shaped the French Canadian condition have diminished in importance. The dynamism of postwar Canadian capitalism has allowed a new French Canadian bourgeoisie to emerge, in the context, however, of an economy and a society dependent on the United States.

A New Bourgeoisie

The rest of this chapter is devoted to demonstrating that since the Second World War, a new francophone bourgeoisie has grown up in Canada, consisting primarily but not exclusively of Quebec businessmen. This thesis was outlined in a two-page article entitled "A Proud New French Canadian Bourgeoisie" by two journalists, Richard Daignault and Dominique Clift, that appeared in the Montreal magazine *Commerce* in September 1964. They wrote in part:

> The so-called Quiet Revolution in Quebec, born of a young and dynamic French Canadian bourgeoisie, is about to expire. The revolutionary phase, the phase of great reforms, is almost over. It is being replaced by an era of bourgeois consolidation, an era that has already begun.... The French Canadian bourgeoisie is a well-defined group of enterprising men, already quite successful, who are graduating from small to big business and who won't stand for any more of what is called "fouillis et brouillon" (muddle and mess). A taste for well-done, well-organized, neat, effective work is one of the characteristics of a big bourgeoisie .... This bourgeoisie is consolidating its position on all fronts. Consolidation has become the

main preoccupation of the leaders of the bourgeoisie in both government and industry. If, as we noted earlier, consolidation has already begun, it is by no means assured of success. North America's other big bourgeoisies are old and rich, and the Quebec bourgeoisie has a lot of catching up to do. Its primary goal is to consolidate its material base.

In their short article, Daignault and Clift saw the beginnings of "difficulties of adjustment" between the francophone bourgeoisie and members of the English Canadian bourgeoisie. The article offered no explanation for the emergence of the francophone bourgeoisie, and made no attempt to estimate the scope of the phenomenon.

Twelve years later, in an unpublished paper delivered before the Learned Societies of Canada in June 1976 ("Towards a French Canadian Big Bourgeoisie"), Pierre Fournier offered a new description of the same phenomenon. Like Daignault and Clift, Fournier did not attempt to explain it, but he added some plausibility to the thesis by including some precise dates and figures. However, Fournier included the leading figures in crown corporations and the cooperative movement in the francophone bourgeoisie. Chapter 4 endeavours to show that there is little evidence for the existence of a "state bourgeoisie" in Quebec. Moreover, it is shown in this chapter that the cooperative movement is under the control of Quebec's traditional petty bourgeoisie, and not of the new francophone bourgeoisie.

This chapter's working hypothesis is thus that a francophone bourgeoisie emerged in Canada after the Second World War. There are a number of reasons for this development. First, there have been substantial changes in the economic structure of Canada as a whole and Quebec in particular, including urbanization and the concomitant growth of new sectors of activity for which there are no technological barriers to entry (real estate, retailing and wholesaling, financial services). The growth in per capita personal income, Quebec government support for French Canadian business after 1960 and, finally, the decline of religious ideologies in Quebec have also contributed to the growth of the francophone bourgeoisie.

The Contemporary French Canadian Bourgeoisie

The owners of the largest companies under French Canadian control at the end of 1975 were studied, using a threshold of $10 million in total assets. Data on assets could only be collected for public companies since private companies do not publish financial statements. As a result, the list of companies studied does not include the largest French Canadian brokerage houses (such as Lévesque, Beaubien or René T. Leclerc Inc.)

or private family companies such as J.B. Baillargeon Express or Sorel Steel Foundries. Data on assets and company histories were taken from the annual surveys published by the *Financial Post* and from reports of the Quebec Department of Consumers, Cooperatives and Financial Institutions.[6] Since 1950, *Commerce* magazine has published monthly profiles of French Canadian companies and businessmen, which help in tracing their histories. Data on stock ownership were compiled from the bulletins of the Quebec and Ontario Securities Commissions. Additional information on company directors came from the *Financial Post Directory of Directors*, the *Martindale-Hubbell Law Directory*, and the major Canadian biographical dictionaries, including the *Biographies canadiennes-françaises*, the *Canadian Who's Who* and *Who's Who in Canada*.[7]

The data collected are summarized in appendix 1. Among the companies on the list are seventeen whose total assets were more than $100 million at the end of 1975: the nine largest companies in the Power Corporation group, two real estate companies (Campeau Corporation and Allarco Developments), Bombardier Ltd., the General Trust of Canada, North West Trust, the Banque Canadienne Nationale, the Provincial Bank of Canada and the Montreal City and District Savings Bank. Provigo, a Quebec company in the commercial sector, crossed the $100 million threshold when it absorbed M. Loeb & Co. of Ottawa in August 1977.

The following are the main characteristics of these large French Canadian companies:

- In the list of the 136 largest Canadian-controlled companies as of the end of 1975, companies controlled by French Canadians account for only 12 per cent. The francophone element is thus underrepresented in the Canadian capitalist class.[8]
- Most of these French Canadian companies either were founded recently (Bombardier in 1942, Campeau Corp. in 1953, Allarco Developments in 1954, Provigo in 1969) and are still controlled by their founding owners, or else were recently taken over by French Canadians (the Power Corp. group, purchased from the Nesbitt and Thomson families by Paul Desmarais in 1968). Only the three banks on the list and the General Trust of Canada (founded in 1909) are older companies that have always been under French Canadian control.
- All these companies have interests in more than one province; they are pan-Canadian, and several are multinational. This is a significant new characteristic of today's large French Canadian companies; turn-of-the-century French Canadian companies rarely had interests outside Quebec.
- French Canadians from outside Quebec are well represented in

these large companies. Notable examples are the Franco-Ontarians Paul and Louis Desmarais (Power Corp.); Robert Campeau (Campeau Corp.), also a Franco-Ontarian; and Charles Allard (Allarco Developments), a Franco-Albertan.

It is thus reasonable to conclude that after the Second World War a French Canadian capitalist class developed, not exclusively based in Quebec, with pan-Canadian and multinational ambitions. No doubt it is underrepresented in the largest Canadian-controlled corporations, but it is dynamic and growing rapidly.

After these seventeen large companies come about thirty middle-sized companies, with assets between $10 million and $100 million (appendix 1). More than half of these companies are relatively new and date back to the immediate postwar years at the earliest. Of the four companies in the commercial sector on our list, only Dupuis Frères (established in 1868)* has been under French Canadian control for a long time. Cassidy's Ltd. (figure 3-1) was purchased from the Prentice and Yuile families by Alphonse T. Brodeur in 1953.[9] United Auto Parts was founded by Charles-E. Préfontaine in 1926 and went public in 1961. And Provigo is the result of a merger of three large grocery enterprises in 1969. Of the three transportation companies, two — Logistec Corp. and La Vérendrye — were founded after the Second World War. Seven of the eleven companies in the industrial sector were founded after 1945: Québécor, Normick Perron, Télé-Capitale, Télé-Métropole, Simard-Beaudry and Vachon Inc. In the financial sector, most of the middle-sized companies were founded after 1940. Among these are insurance companies (L'Unique, La Solidarité, L'Union Canadienne, etc.) and mutual funds. Appendix 2 gives the date and place of incorporation of the companies on the list.

The owners of these companies do not belong to the turn of the century francophone bourgeoisie, and most of them have made their fortunes within one generation. Names such as Paul Desmarais, Charles Allard, Robert Campeau, Antoine Turmel, René Provost, Marc Carrière, Jean-Louis Lévesque, Jean-Paul Tardif, Gérard Parizeau, Paul and Benoît Vachon, Michel Latraverse, Paul Gourdeau, the Perron brothers, Alphonse T. Brodeur, Pierre Péladeau and Fernand Doyon were unknown to French Canadian biographers and historians in 1940. There are a few exceptions to this rule: the Beaubien family (of Beaubran Corp. and Lévesque, Beaubien), the Rollands (of Rolland Paper) and the Marchands (of Melchers Distilleries, bankrupt in 1977).

It is difficult to estimate the degree of underrepresentation of French Canadians in middle-sized companies, but it is at least as striking as their underrepresentation in large corporations. Among the more than one thousand companies of comparable size catalogued by the yearly

---

*Now in liquidation.

FIGURE 3-1
The Cassidy's Group

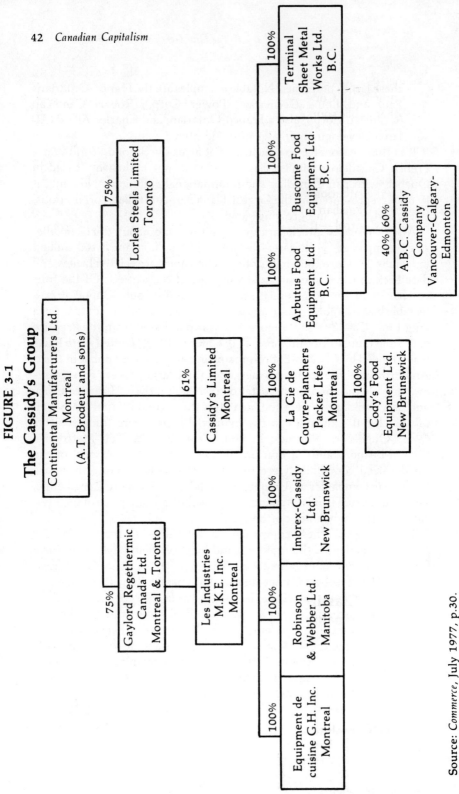

Source: *Commerce*, July 1977, p.30.

Financial Post surveys, Moody's manuals, the reports of the Quebec Department of Consumers, Cooperatives and Financial Institutions and other public sources, the almost marginal nature of French Canadian business is evident. This study's data do not include private companies that do not publish financial statements, and there are several brokerage houses, industrial corporations and transportation companies in this category. However, adding them to the list would not change the situation.

French Canadian companies tend to be tightly controlled by their owners. Control — the capacity to elect the board of directors of the company or at least a majority of its members — is conferred through voting shares issued by the company and belongs to the holder (individual, group or family) of the largest block of these shares. Jean-Marie Chevalier's classification system has been adopted here: virtually absolute control (80 to 100 per cent of the votes), majority control (50 to 79 per cent), minority control (5 to 49 per cent) and internal control (0 to 4.9 per cent).[10]

The forty-eight companies on the list were classified by level of control. Subsidiaries on the list were classified according to the level of control exercised by the parent corporation on the subsidiary or the level of control of the parent corporation itself, whichever is less. Thus for example, the F-I-C Fund was controlled by Jean-Louis Lévesque with 35.9 per cent of the votes. Alfred Lambert Inc., an industrial corporation, is wholly owned by the Fund. Albert Lambert Inc. is therefore classified as being ultimately under minority control. In this classification, the criteria used in all classic works on corporate control were followed.

The table would not change significantly if approximately twenty private companies which do not publish financial statements and a few mutual life insurance companies, of which the La Laurentienne group is the most significant, were added.

TABLE 3-1
Classification of 48 French Canadian
Companies According to Level of Control

Level of Control	Number of Companies	Percentage of Total
Internal	5	10%
Minority	8	17%
Majority	25	52%
Virtually absolute and private	9	19%
Unknown	1	2%
TOTAL	48	100%

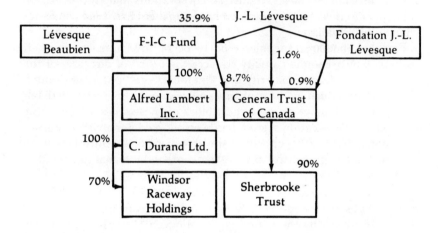

FIGURE 3-2

The Jean-Louis Lévesque Group
(Assets, December 1975: $510 million, not including Lévesque, Beaubien, Inc.)

Sources: *F.P. Survey of Industrials*, 1976; Ontario and Quebec Securities Commissions, Bulletins.

The five companies under internal control are the two French Canadian chartered banks (Banque Canadienne Nationale and Provincial Bank), the Montreal City and District Savings Bank and the two largest subsidiaries of the BCN, Imnat and Canagex. The companies under minority control are those in the Jean-Louis Lévesque group (see figure 3-2), two in the Power Corporation group (Consolidated-Bathurst and its subsidiary Dominion Glass) and Provigo. More than 50 per cent of the companies are under majority control and another 20 per cent are under virtually absolute or private control. This very high level of control can be explained to a large extent by the size of the companies, which are smaller than the companies considered in classic studies of control. It is also a result of the relative youth of the companies and of the new francophone capitalists' position as outsiders.

There is thus a new French Canadian bourgeoisie, which has evolved since the Second World War. Factors which have influenced this development are as follows:

    (a) The growth of new sectors of economic activity in which industrial technology is not required. Notable among these is real estate, whose development is a result of urbanization and the land speculation that ensued.

(b) The concentration of retail trade after the Second World War, which provided opportunities for a number of small merchants to build giant corporations in retail distribution.

(c) Higher incomes in Quebec in general and among French Canadians in particular since 1940, which provided an expanding market for local capitalists. Per capita personal income in Quebec grew from only $363 in 1926 to $655 in 1946 (an 80 per cent increase). By 1974 it had grown to $4,504 (an increase of almost 700 per cent between 1946 and 1974). French Canadians have become an increasingly affluent market since the Second World War. They have been consumers of new financial services, insurance and urban dwellings and are fully integrated into the market economy.

(d) The relative decline of religious thinking and the adoption of an ideology more suited to modern Canadian capitalist society.

(e) Quebec government support for French Canadian capitalists after 1960. The Quiet Revolution established a network of public institutions that have contributed to the development of a francophone bourgeoisie. Among these institutions are the Caisse de Dépôt et de Placement and the General Investment Corporation, which have participated as stockholders in numerous francophone Quebec businesses. In that capacity they have helped capitalize French Canadian companies, supported francophone boards of directors that were in danger of losing their companies, and placed French Canadian directors on the boards of companies in which they held stock.

The Caisse de Dépôt et Placement was founded in 1965 by the Liberal government of Premier Jean Lesage, the government of the Quiet Revolution. It is responsible for managing the Quebec pension fund, Quebec's medicare plan and the investment portfolios of a number of public and semi-public agencies. It invests both in bonds (provincial, municipal, Hydro-Quebec, hospital, etc.) and in shares of Canadian companies, which make up between 15 and 20 per cent of its assets. The list of its holdings is kept secret, but it is known that it holds large blocks of shares in Provigo, Bombardier, Logistec and other French- and English-Canadian companies.

The following are a few instances in which the Caisse has given support to French Canadian capitalists:

• In late August 1977, Provigo Ltée purchased almost 80 per cent of the outstanding shares of M. Loeb Ltd., an Ontario-based retailing multinational. As a result of this move, Provigo became a group of companies in the commercial sector with consolidated assets approaching $300 million. Two weeks later the Sobeys Stores group of Nova Scotia, then controlled by the Sobey (54 per cent) and Weston (40 per cent) families, succeeded in buying 18.5 per cent of Provigo. Provigo shares had been trading at $7 in May 1977 but the Sobey group paid $14 each for them in September. The private French Canadian group that manages Provigo held only about 18 per cent of its stock, and thus was highly vulnerable to a Sobeys takeover. However, the Caisse de Dépôt et de Placement held 24.6 per cent of Provigo's stock. It supported the existing Turmel-Provost-Lamontagne management of the company, and refused to sell to Sobeys. On September 24, 1977, *Le Devoir* was able to report that, "Provigo will remain a Quebec company .... Thanks to support from financial institutions, Provigo management is assured that control of the company will remain firmly in their hands, board chairman Antoine Turmel said yesterday."

- Conversely, when Paul Desmarais was trying to take over Argus Corporation in March and April of 1975, the Caisse turned its shares of the Toronto holding company over to Power Corp.[11]
- In April 1976 Marcel Cazavan, the Caisse's general manager, said that it had drawn up a list of French Canadians who should be elected to the boards of the large companies in which it held stock. *Le Devoir* reported:

"The Caisse de Dépôt et de Placement intends to play a larger role in naming directors to the boards of companies in which it holds stock," Marcel Cazavan, the agency's general manager, told *Le Devoir* yesterday. "With a portfolio of more than $600 million in common stock, the Caisse should have a say in choosing directors of a number of large Canadian companies .... Robert Després of the University of Quebec was recently named to the boards of Campeau Corp. and Norcen Energy, two companies in which the Caisse has a substantial interest.[12]

Clearly, the election of French Canadians to the boards of directors of companies in which the Caisse holds stock will not in itself automatically contribute to the growth of the French Canadian bourgeoisie. But through this process, some senior civil servants may become privy to the secrets of the top management of large corporations, and thus be able to learn the art of becoming millionaires.

The New Conglomerates

The new French Canadian bourgeoisie has adopted the form of corporate organization into which much of North American business has

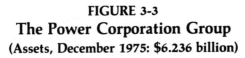

FIGURE 3-3
The Power Corporation Group
(Assets, December 1975: $6.236 billion)

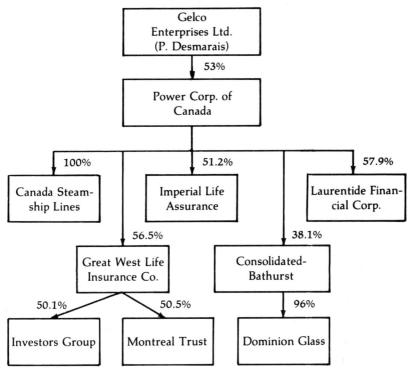

Sources: *Financial Post Directory of Directors, 1976; F.P. Survey of Industrials, 1976.*

been reshaped since 1945: conglomerate organization. Conglomerates are companies or groups of companies under unified control that produce goods and services in unrelated sectors of activity. In Canada, groups such as Canadian Pacific, Brascan Ltd. and Power Corporation, at one time active in one industry or a few related ones (primarily transportation and electricity) are now conglomerates whose interests extend to ten or more different branches of economic activity. The list of Canadian conglomerates also includes Argus Corporation, founded as a conglomerate in 1945.

The Power Corporation conglomerate (figure 3-3) was examined in *The Economy of Canada: A Study of Ownership and Control.*[13] It is worth recalling here that through its subsidiaries, acquired between 1960 and 1973, Power Corp. controls a third of the mutual funds in Canada (Investors Group), half the French-language newspaper circulation in

Quebec (Gesca Ltée), the largest Great Lakes shipping company (Canada Steamship Lines), the fourth largest insurance company in Canada (Great West Life), the sixth largest trust company in Canada (Montreal Trust), the third largest finance company (Laurentide Financial Corp.), the fourth largest pulp and paper company (Consolidated-Bathurst), the largest glass company (Dominion Glass), etc. This conglomerate was 53 per cent owned by Paul Desmarais in 1975.

Other new French Canadian groups have adopted the same forms of organization on a smaller scale. Significant companies in the group controlled by Jean-Louis Lévesque (figure 3-2) include Lévesque, Beaubien Inc., the largest French Canadian securities brokerage house, and the F-I-C Fund, a holding company whose subsidiaries manufacture shoes (Alfred Lambert Inc.), sell hardware at the wholesale and retail levels (C. Durant Ltd.) and operate a racetrack (Windsor Raceway Holdings). Lévesque also had the largest known holding in the share capital of the General Trust of Canada, which in turn controls Sherbrooke Trust. He controlled a number of other companies in the past, among them Dupuis Frères (as of 1949), and another conglomerate, Trans-Canada Corporation Fund, which was sold to Paul Desmarais in 1963 and later integrated into the Power Corporation group. It was after this transaction that Lévesque began to acquire interests in the companies that form his new conglomerate.

The Prêt et Revenu group (figure 3-4) dates back much further. The parent corporation was founded in 1928 by Alphonse Tardif under the name Corporation Prêt et Revenu, and control passed to Tardif's son Jean-Paul in 1947. Diversification began in 1953 with the founding of the St-Maurice, Compagnie d'Assurances, while in 1957 two newly-incorporated companies were added to the group: Aeterna-Vie and the Fonds Mutuel Prêt et Revenu. In 1961, the Fiducie Prêt et Revenu was founded, while new mutual funds were added to the group in 1968, 1972 and 1975. The Prêt et Revenu group, a conglomerate under family control, held total assets of about $141 million at the end of 1975.

The Sodarcan group (figure 3-5) comprises twelve companies operating in the fields of reinsurance, insurance and reinsurance brokerage, reinsurance company management, and consulting. Sodarcan Ltée was founded in 1972 to consolidate these companies financially. A majority of Sodarcan's shares is held by Robert Parizeau, brother of Jacques Parizeau, finance minister in the Parti Québécois government, and their father Gérard Parizeau. The companies in the group were all founded or purchased after the Second World War. La Nationale, Compagnie de Réassurance du Canada is the largest company in the group, with assets of $29 million at the end of 1975. It was purchased in 1965 from La Nationale of Paris, of which it has been the Canadian subsidiary. The

FIGURE 3-4
The Prêt et Revenu Group
(Assets, end of 1975: $141 million)

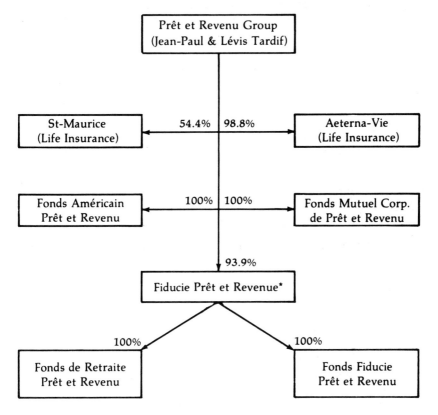

*Fiducie Prêt et Revenu administers both the Fonds de Retraite and the Fonds H Prêt et Revenu.

Sources: *Financial Post Directory of Directors*, 1976; *Financial Post Survey of Funds*, 1976; Quebec Department of Consumers, Cooperatives and Financial Institutions, Insurance Branch, *Annual Report* (Editeur du Québec 1976); *Financial Post Survey of Industrials*, 1976.

Sodarcan group has shown considerable dynamism not only in Canada but also in the United States, where it operates through its reinsurance brokerage subsidiary Intermediaries of America; it also has an Ontario subsidiary, Canadian Reinsurance Brokers Ltd., founded in 1972. Total assets of the group were $45 million at the end of 1975.[14]

FIGURE 3-5

The Sodarcan Group

(Assets, November 1975: $45 million)

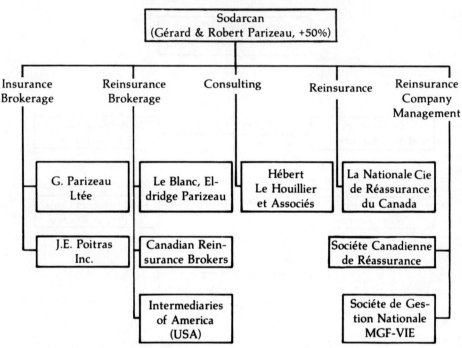

Source: *La Presse*, November 11, 1975

Finally there is the York Lambton Corp. group (figure 3-6), controlled by the Brillant family and its partners through a private company, Wellington Corp. In May 1975 York Lambton bought the Corporation d'Expansion Financière, a holding company with subsidiaries in the construction industry (Simard-Beaudry Inc.) and the manufacturing of electrical products (BFG Industries Ltd.), plastic products (GM Plastic Corp.), glass panelling (Superseal Corp.) and petroleum products (Gasex Ltd.).

Organic Intellectuals: Lawyers

The sources used in this study make it possible to identify not only the people who control French Canadian companies but also the advisers and consultants who are not owners of these companies but sit on their boards of directors.

Members of law firms and lawyers in independent practice help businessmen with a multiplicity of legal questions. However, like management and investment advisers and consulting actuaries, lawyers are not part of the bourgeoisie.

Appendix 3 is a list of lawyers who serve as outside directors of French Canadian companies under consideration. It can be seen that most of these companies use the services of at least one lawyer. Only seventeen companies (36 per cent) have no lawyers serving as outside directors on their boards. The average is 1.4 lawyers per board of directors. Companies with several lawyers on their boards select them from various firms. Thus, there are five lawyers on the board of the General Trust of Canada, four of them from different firms and the fifth (Hon. Edouard Asselin) in independent practice.

Lawyers hold very few shares in the companies they advise. In the case of the General Trust, according to the last declaration of stockholdings for December 1975, Edouard Asselin held 1,153 common shares, Lavéry Sirois held 3,533, Isidore Pollack 1,023, Marcel Piché

FIGURE 3-6

The York Lambton Corp. Group
(Assets, December 1975: $124 million)

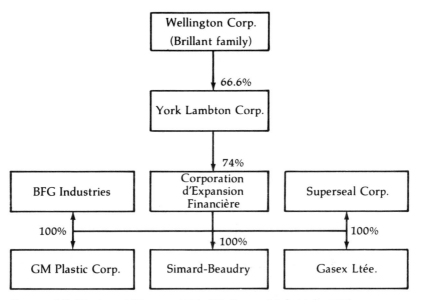

Source: *F.P. Directory of Directors, 1976; F.P. Survey of Industrials, 1976.*

1,666 and Daniel Doheny 216. In 1975, common shares of the General Trust traded at between $17.50 and $22. Control was exercised by Jean-Louis Lévesque, who directly or indirectly held 94,441 common shares, with a market value of about $2 million. The four lawyers on the board of Power Corp., Wilbrod Bhérer, Pierre Genest, Claude Pratte and Hon. John P. Robarts, held 2,500 shares, 100 shares, 5,375 shares and 100 shares respectively. Paul Desmarais held 1,353,000 6 per cent preferred shares (with ten votes each) and 1,585,058 5 per cent preferred shares (with one vote each), giving him 53 per cent of the votes at a stock-holders' meeting. One more example: Cassidy's Ltd. is 61.1 per cent owned by the Brodeur family through Continental Manufacturers, which holds 458,497 shares of Cassidy's common stock. The company's legal adviser, F.C. Cope of the Montreal firm Ogilvy, Cope, Porteous, Montgomery, Renault, Clarke and Kirkpatrick, holds 480 common shares of Cassidy's.[15]

In rare cases, a member of a law firm is also the owner or co-owner of a company. Thus Claude Pratte, a lawyer with Létourneau, Stein, Marseille, Delisle & La Rue, holds 73,864 class B shares (25 per cent of the vote) of Télé-Capitale, which he controls in conjunction with Hervé Baribeau and J. A. Pouliot, who each hold the same number of shares as Pratte. This, however, is the only example of this type on our list, al-though similar cases were found among English Canadian companies.

Lawyers on boards of directors rarely fill management positions. In nine cases out of ten, they are purely outside directors who attend monthly board meetings and receive total compensation of $2,000 to $8,000 a year, depending on the size of the company. In light of the number of shares they own and the compensation they receive, it would be a distortion to mix them up with the capitalists they advise. They are not owners, but intellectuals who are organically linked to the ruling class.

Most French Canadian companies retain francophone law firms, but this is far from being an absolute rule. The largest companies, notably those in the Power Corp. group, use the services of lawyers in English-speaking firms, such as Ogilvy, Cope, Porteous, Montgomery, Renault, Clarke and Kirkpatrick of Montreal and Aird, Zimmerman & Berlis of Toronto. English-speaking firms are also employed by some middle-sized companies, including Beaubran Corporation, Cassidy's Ltd. and Rolland Paper.

Theories of the economic or corporate elite give each director on a board equal weight. A critique of these theories has already been pre-sented,[16] but it should be stressed that in Canada these theories are not at all the exclusive property of the radical sociologists. They also have the support of Guy St-Pierre, Minister of Industry and Commerce in the Liberal Quebec government of Robert Bourassa. In a speech to the Canadian Club in Montreal shortly before his party's defeat — and his own — in the 1976 election, Mr. St-Pierre advocated the appointment of at least two French Canadian directors to the board of every company operating in Quebec, in order to broaden the base of the francophone corporate elite. "About twenty French Canadians are members of the corporate elite," he said, "and they appear on the boards of the largest and most prestigious companies according to the oft-criticized principle of musical chairs."[17] A man with the courage of his convictions, Mr. St-Pierre in October 1977 accepted the presidency of Ogilvie Mills, controlled by Brascan Ltd. of Toronto.[18]

The major law firms in Quebec have both English- and French-speaking partners and associates. This is the case for the largest law firm in Canada, Ogilvy, Cope, Porteous, Montgomery, Renault, Clarke & Kirkpatrick of Montreal, with seventy-six lawyers; the second largest firm in Quebec, Martineau, Walker, Allison, Beaulieu, McKell & Clermont, with forty-four lawyers; and the third largest firm, Weldon, Courtois, Clarkson, Parsons & Tétreault, with forty-two lawyers. Other firms, with considerably fewer partners and associates, are exclusively French Canadian. This applies to the firms of Amyot, Lesage, de Grandpré, Colas, Bernard & Drolet of Quebec City, with twenty-three lawyers; and Desjardins, Ducharme, Desjardins & Bourque of Montreal, with twenty-eight lawyers.

The largest and most prestigious firms have as their clients foreign, English Canadian and French Canadian companies. Their senior partners sit on the boards of companies controlled by groups of various national origins. For example, in 1975 the two senior partners of St-Laurent, Monast, Walkers & Vallières of Quebec City, the late Renault St-Laurent and André Monast, sat on the boards of a number of companies. These included the Canadian Imperial Bank of Commerce, Dominion Stores, Noranda Mines and Confederation Life (English Canadian), the Banque Canadienne Nationale and Imperial Life (French Canadian), IAC Ltd. (Bronfman family), Canada Cement (a subsidiary of Ciments Lafarge of France), IBM Canada and Home Oil (American-controlled), and Rothmans of Pall Mall (South African-controlled). The leading French Canadian law firms are shown in table 3-2.

The Quebec Cooperative Movement: the Petty Bourgeoisie Writ Large

The cooperative movement in Quebec appears to be well on the way to becoming a financial and commercial giant. Already, the Fédération de

TABLE 3-2

Major French Canadian and
Partially French Canadian Law Firms

Firm	Number of Partners and Associates
Amyot, Lesage, de Grandpré, Colas, Bernard & Drolet (Quebec City)	23
Bernard, Fournier, Savoie, Demers, Caron, Tanguay & Dupré (Sherbrooke)	9
Bhérer, Bernier, Côté, Ouellet, Dionne, Houle & Morin (Quebec City)	?
Blain, Piché, Godbout, Eméry & Blain (Montreal)	19
Byers, Casgrain & Stewart (Montreal)	20
De Grandpré, Colas, Amyot, Lesage, Deschênes & Godin (Montreal)	27
Desjardins, Ducharme, Desjardins & Bourque (Montreal)	28
Flynn, Rivard, Cimon, Lessard & Le May (Quebec City)	20
Gagnon, de Billy, Cantin, Dionne, Martin Beaudoin & Lesage (Quebec City)	14
Guy, Vaillancourt, Bertrand, Bourgeois & Laurent (Montreal)	11
Létourneau, Stein, Marseille, Delisle & La Rue (Quebec City)	16
Martineau, Walker, Allison, Beaulieu, Mackell & Clermont (Montreal)	44
Riel, Vermette, Ryan, Dunton & Ciaccia (Montreal)	?
St-Laurent, Monast, Walters & Vallières (Quebec City)	7
Weldon, Courtois, Clarkson, Parsons & Tétreault (Montreal)	42

Source: *Martindale-Hubbell Law Directory,* 1976

Québec des Caisses Populaires Desjardins (figure 3-7) dominates the savings and loan sector, with assets of $5.2 billion in December 1975. Its insurance, trust, management and investment subsidiaries had assets of $717 million at the end of 1975, not counting its 23 per cent share of Provincial Bank of Canada's assets of $3.059 billion or its 83 per cent share of Vachon Inc.'s $27 million. In all, the Desjardins movement and its subsidiaries held total net assets of about $9 billion in December 1975.

The Quebec cooperative movement has other components as well, but they are nowhere near the Fédération in size. They include the Coopérative Fédérée du Québec, with assets of $116 million at the end of 1975; the Coopérative Agricole de Granby ($67 million); the Fédération de Montréal des Caisses Desjardins ($48 million); the Fédération des Caisses d'Economie de Québec ($28 million); the Pêcheurs Unis du Québec, etc.

FIGURE 3-7

The Desjardins Movement
(Assets, end of 1975: $8.971 billion)

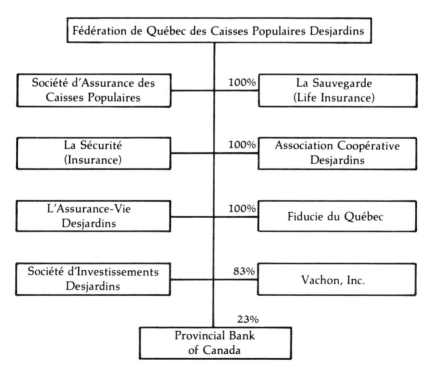

Sources: Annual reports of companies in the group.

Founded in 1900 by Alphonse Desjardins, the caisse populaire movement developed slowly in its early years. In 1920 it consisted of 113
"caisses" with 32,000 members and assets of $6.3 million. During the
1920s four regional unions were created — Quebec, Trois-Rivières,
Montreal and Gaspé — and in 1932 these unions formed the Fédération
de Québec des Caisses Populaires Desjardins. Twelve Montreal caisses
seceded from the Fédération in 1945 to form the Fédération de
Montréal des Caisses Desjardins. After the Second World War, the
Desjardins movement began to look more and more like a conglomerate. In 1943 it founded its first insurance company, the Société
d'Assurance des Caisses Populaires (SACP), on a mutual basis. In 1948
the SACP became a mutual life insurance company, and the same year
the Desjardins movement created Assurance-Vie Desjardins, another
mutual company.

In 1962, the Fiducie du Québec, a trust with share capital that
manages six mutual funds, was founded and a majority of the share
capital of La Sauvegarde, a life insurance company, was purchased from
the Ducharme family. La Sauvegarde had belonged to the Ducharmes
since its founding in 1901, and two members of the family still sit on its
board, although the company is now wholly controlled by the Desjardins movement. In 1963 La Sécurité, Compagnie d'Assurances
Générales du Canada, was bought from its French owners. That same
year the Association Coopérative Desjardins (ACD) was set up as a
non-profit holding company for a number of subsidiaries, including
La Sauvegarde, La Sécurité and the Fiducie du Québec. A majority of
shares in the ACD are held by the regional unions that constitute the
Fédération.

The Société d'Investissements Desjardins (SID) was created in 1971
as a company with share capital investing in and extending credit to new
companies in the industrial and commerical sectors on a medium- and
long-term basis. The SID's share capital is controlled by the Fédération.
In addition, during the 1960s the Desjardins movement became the
largest stockholder in the Provincial Bank of Canada, the sixth largest
Canadian chartered bank in terms of assets. In 1970 it purchased 83
per cent of the shares of Vachon Inc., the cake manufacturer that
supplies 55 per cent of the Quebec market.

From the beginning, the Desjardins movement was structured
democratically. The customers of the caisses populaires are also
stockholders and at annual meetings each stockholder has one vote.
This structure has served to prevent a takeover of the movement by
French Canadian capitalists. Also, it has encouraged the appearance and
development of a group of administrators who sit on the boards of
directors of the Fédération de Quebec, the regional unions and their
subsidiaries. This group is comprised of lawyers, notaries, accountants,

doctors, dentists, pharmacists, actuaries, owners of small businesses, engineers, etc. The vast majority of the directors of the Desjardins movement and its subsidiaries are from the petty bourgeoisie. They represent the more well-to-do customers of the caisses and come from various regions of the province. They are not, however, the private owners of the movement and they cannot use the assets of its institutions to benefit themselves or to finance the political party of their choice. It would be wrong to confuse the class that runs the Desjardins movement with the more substantial French Canadian private-sector bourgeoisie. The petty bourgeoisie has neither the economic nor the political power of the group that controls large and middle-sized non-cooperative corporations.

There is also another, very different kind of director on the boards of some of the movement's subsidiaries. For example, the board of directors of Vachon Inc. includes two members of the Vachon family, which owns 17 per cent of the company. Several French Canadian capitalists sit on the board of the Provincial Bank of Canada. Among them are Antoine Turmel (of Provigo), Marc Bourgie (Urgel Bourgie Inc.) and P.H. Plamondon (La Solidarité, Compagnie d'Assurance sur la Vie). Members of the Ducharme family, the former owners of La Sauvegarde, have become Desjardins group directors: two of them sit on the board of the old family company, while one is a director of La Sécurité. In addition, the boards of Desjardins movement subsidiaries contain a number of lawyers, accountants and actuaries who also advise the largest privately-owned companies in Canada. Among them are Louis Desrochers and Jacques de Billy, who are both law firm partners and bank directors (the firm McCraig, Desrochers of Edmonton and the Bank of Montreal in the case of Desrochers; the firm de Billy, Cantin, Dionne, Martin, Beaudoin & Lesage of Quebec City and the Toronto-Dominion Bank for de Billy). There is also chartered accountant Marcel Bélanger, who sits on the board of the Provincial Bank. Bélanger is a member of the firm of Bélanger, Dallaire, Gagnon et Associés, chartered accountants, of Quebec City, and his other directorships include John Labatt Ltd. and Provigo.

However, the French Canadian bourgeoisie and its lawyers, accountants and actuaries are only a small minority on the boards of Desjardins movement subsidiaries and are not represented at all on the board of the Fédération de Quebec. The French Canadian petty bourgeoisie still controls the Desjardins movement, and uses it as an instrument of advancement.

An analysis of the other components of the Quebec cooperative movement leads to the same conclusions. The Coopérative Fédérée du Québec was the product of a merger of three Quebec agricultural cooperatives in 1922. By 1972, it had 52,000 members and sales of $255 million. The Coopérative Fédérée is a conglomerate and in 1975, farm supplies accounted for 42 per cent of its sales, dairy products for 35 per cent, and meat for 23 per cent. It has been growing rapidly and has acquired a number of Quebec dairy operations, farms and poultry processing plants, including Quebec Poultry, purchased in May 1975. The Coopérative Fédérée's registered capital is made up of qualifying common shares subscribed by its members and common and preferred shares issued by the Coopérative. The rule at stockholders' meetings is "one man, one vote." This democracy, of course, extends only to the owners of the Cooperative, the farmers who constitute its membership, and not to its wage-earning employees, who have no say in decision-making. Decisions concerning wages, working conditions and the opening and closing of factories are made according to capitalist profitability criteria. A Confederation of National Trade Unions publication summed it up well when it said that the Coopérative Fédérée is capitalist in its operation.[19] In effect, it is a cooperative controlled by the Quebec agricultural petty bourgeoisie.

The Coopérative Agricole de Granby was founded in 1938 and specializes in the production and marketing of milk and dairy products. It also supplies farmers with machinery, tools and raw materials. Its subsidiary Québec-Lait, of which it owns 70 per cent, realized sales of $52 million in 1975. The Coopérative also runs twelve industrial plants, five dairies and a granary. It dominates the Quebec milk market and its share of related sectors (powdered milk, butter, etc.) is growing. Farmer-run, the Coopérative Agricole de Granby, like the Coopérative Fédérée, is an instrument for the economic advancement of the agricultural petty bourgeoisie.

Although they have more limited means, Quebec's other cooperative institutions, such as the Fédération de Montréal des Caisses Desjardins, the Fédération des Caisses d'Economie de Quebec, the Pêcheurs Unis du Québec (which accounts for 50 per cent of the province's fisheries by value) and the forest cooperatives, are also organizations through which the Quebec petty bourgeoisie resists the process of industrial, commercial and financial concentration that threatens its existence as a class.

Politics and the French Canadian Bourgeoisie

The political power of the francophone bourgeoisie is necessarily limited. After all, its members are few; its base for accumulation, the Quebec market, is small; and its larger fortunes are historically very new. On the whole, it is federalist and mostly Liberal. The reason for this is simple: as soon as they attain a relatively large scale of production,

French Canadian companies look to the Canadian market as a whole. Provigo acquired an Ontario subsidiary, M. Loeb Co., in August 1977, and became one of Canada's retailing giants. Vachon cakes supply 35 per cent of the Ontario market. Rolland Paper has a plant in Scarborough, Ontario. One of the subsidiaries of the F-I-C Fund, Windsor Raceway Holdings, is in Ontario. All the companies in the Power Corporation group are Canada-wide. Bombardier Ltd. sells snowmobiles and railway cars all over Canada. Campeau Corporation has its head office in Ottawa and does business in Quebec and Ontario. Allarco Developments operates from a head office in Edmonton. Cassidy's Ltd. is established in several provinces. Normick Perron has a factory in Cochran, Ontario. *In sum, if Quebec separated, the French Canadian bourgeoisie's principal market would be divided, its companies would have to be reorganized and it would be weakened on the Canadian and international levels.*

The French Canadian bourgeoisie is Liberal. It is well known that the major media outlets controlled by French Canadians — Paul Desmarais's newspaper chain, Télé-Capitale, Télé-Métropole — support the Liberal Party at both the federal and the provincial level. Paul Desruisseaux, the owner of Melchers Distilleries, is a Liberal senator, and the Simard family has long-standing ties to the Quebec Liberal Party. These are only a few examples of the closeness that exists between the francophone establishment and the Liberal Party.

Since the late nineteenth century, the Conservative Party has been less amenable to the promotion of French Canadian interests. At one time, it advocated a centralist form of federalism that Quebec never accepted; also, the Conservatives have never had a French Canadian leader. There are, of course, exceptions to the absence of French Canadian representation in the Conservative Party, the most notable being the Beaubien family (of Beaubran Corporation; Lévesque, Beaubien; etc.). For four generations this family of businessmen has provided Conservative governments with a steady stream of senators, provincial cabinet ministers and funds.

The French Canadian bourgeoisie is unreceptive to the New Democratic Party, with its ties to labour, and except for some very special cases, is not attracted by the Parti Québécois. The presence of Jacques Parizeau and Guy Joron in the PQ cabinet did not herald a change in the political allegiance of the francophone bourgeoisie. The Parti Québécois has been and remains a party run by people whose professions involve language: journalists, lawyers, publishers, writers, artists, teachers, notaries. The PQ government's priorities are not at all those of the bourgeoisie, nor are they those of workers. Rather they are those of people who make a living by manipulating symbols, and whose interests and ideological positions are most directly threatened by the assimilation of the Quebec nation.

This study agrees in part with Gilles Bourque and Nicole Frenette's classic analysis of the francophone bourgeoisie, but it also, in part, contradicts that analysis.[20] Bourque and Frenette maintained that the dominant position of the English-speaking establishment left French Canadian businessmen only a subordinate role as a petty bourgeoisie. This petty bourgeoisie, they stated, could be divided into two major sections: a traditional group (farmers, small merchants and members of the liberal professions), represented by the Union Nationale between 1936 and 1960, and a modern, urban, industrial group, represented by the Quebec Liberal Party between 1960 and 1967. Within this latter group, two sub-sections became progressively more distinct: a private sector group, still represented by the Liberal Party, and a technocratic group (managers of crown corporations, civil servants, etc.).

It seems that Bourque and Frenette underestimated the importance of the francophone bourgeoisie and its potential for growth. Now that there are several French Canadian groups that control giant corporations, it can be said that the French Canadian element in the private sector in Quebec and in Canada as a whole constitutes something considerably more substantial than a "petty bourgeoisie." Also, it appears that the Parti Québécois represents part of the traditional petty bourgeoisie of the liberal professions as well as a majority of teachers and civil servants. But its program can attract only the most backward sectors of Quebec agriculture and industry, those which need protection from extra-provincial competition. The analysis advanced here coincides with Bourque and Frenette's in that it views the federal and provincial Liberal parties as the most likely instruments for channelling the interests of the new francophone bourgeoisie.

Quebec or French Canadian Bourgeoisie?

Is the network of companies that has been just outlined a Quebec network or a French Canadian one? This writer maintains that it is clearly the latter. The political allegiances and economic ambitions of Canada's francophone bourgeoisie are not limited to Quebec alone. In an article commenting on a preliminary version of this chapter, Pierre Fournier takes issue with this point of view.[21] Within the francophone bourgeoisie, he distinguishes between a dominant "Canadian" segment (which would include Power Corp., for example) and a majority "Quebec" segment made up of provincial crown corporations, the cooperative movement, some privately-owned companies and small and middle-sized businesses controlled by francophone Quebecers.

The criterion Fournier uses to distinguish the "Canadian" segment of the francophone bourgeoisie from the "Quebec" segment is the financial network to which each segment belongs. He uses seven indicators to determine which financial network a company belongs to: the principal market for its products, the government on which it depends for support, whether or not it is in conflict with the non-francophone Canadian bourgeoisie, the composition of its board of directors, the actual locus of ownership and control, where it is financed, and where it purchases the legal, financial and other services it needs. Thus the "Quebec" bourgeoisie is composed of companies for which Quebec is the principal market, which depend primarily on the Quebec government for support, are in conflict with the non-francophone Canadian establishment, have boards of directors made up mostly of Quebecers, are owned and controlled in Quebec and receive their financing and related services from Quebec firms. The Banque Canadienne Nationale, Provigo, the Desjardins movement and Hydro-Quebec are part of the "Quebec network," while Power Corp. and Rolland Paper are part of the "Canadian network."

According to the Fournier thesis, then, there are two networks into which most, if not all, French Canadian companies can be classified. But the reality of the situation is very different. Take the case of Bombardier, which would be in the "Quebec" network. According to Fournier himself, markets outside Canada account for more than 50 per cent of Bombardier-MLW's production.[22] The same firm not long ago asked the Quebec government for support in the form of a contract, but in December 1977 the government awarded the contract in question to General Motors instead. And its chief executive officer, Laurent Beaudoin, is on the boards of companies with Canada-wide interests such as the Canada Development Corporation and Petrofina Canada.

To take another example, Campeau Corporation has its principal market in Ontario and Quebec, and on its board of directors sit eight anglophones and eight francophones, apart from Robert Campeau himself. As for Rolland Paper, its board of directors, apart from Lucien G. Rolland, is made up of eight francophones and five anglophones, but it produces primarily for export markets. Lucien G. Rolland, the head of the family and chief executive officer of the company, sits on the boards of companies such as the Bank of Montreal, Canadian Pacific and Bell Canada. He is also a director of "Quebec" firms such as UAP, Inco and Donohue Ltée.

Fournier's criteria seem to lead to an extremely dubious division. How does one account for all the francophone capitalists who sit on the boards of federal crown corporations, even though they are classed as "Quebec" capitalists by Fournier and thus in opposition to the federal government? These capitalists include: Camille A. Dagenais, the head of SNC, a Montreal firm of consulting engineers (on the board of the Bank of Canada), C.C. Frenette of Melchers (Federal Business Development Bank), Laurent Beaudoin of Bombardier, Philippe de Gaspé Beaubien of Télémedia, Pierre Côté of Laiterie Laval and R.B. Casgrain of Casgrain et Cie (Canada Development Corporation), Yvon F. de Guise of Hydro-Quebec (Atomic Energy of Canada), Pierre Des Marais II of P. Des Marais Inc. and the General Trust (Canadian National and Air Canada), G. St-Germain of the Commerce insurance group (Teleglobe Canada), and others.

"Quebec" capitalists also frequently sit on the boards of "Canadian" companies in the private sector: Jean-Paul Gignac of Sidbec (Power Corp.), Camille A. Dagenais (Royal Trust), Claude Castonguay of La Laurentienne (Imasco), R. Lavoie of the Crédit Foncier and the Caisse de Dépôt et de Placement (Bank of Montreal), Pierre Côté (Bank of Montreal and Mutual Life), Philippe de Gaspé Beaubien (Dominion Bridge).[23] Roland Giroux, the very prototype of Fournier's "Quebec" capitalist, soon after resigning as president of Hydro-Quebec, accepted the presidencies of Consolidated-Bathurst (Power Corp. group) and the Canadian Commercial Corporation (a federal crown corporation) — both "Canadian" companies in Fournier's schema.

There are also cases of Quebec government support for French Canadian-run companies that Fournier classifies as "Canadian." Already mentioned was the Caisse de Dépôt et de Placement's support for Paul Desmarais in his attempt to take over Argus Corp. in March 1975, and one might add that in late 1978 the *Financial Post* learned that the Caisse was intervening in Desmarais's favour in his attempt to buy Abitibi Paper.[24] In addition, when this "Canadian" capitalist, Paul Desmarais, in the process of effecting a major reorganization of his conglomerate, disposed of large companies he no longer wanted, he sold them exclusively to French Canadians. He sold Imperial Life to Jean-Marie Poitras and Claude Castonguay of La Laurentienne, and Davie Shipbuilding to a group of former Marine Industries executives (including L. Rochette, M. Lafrance and M. Provencher). Power Corp. and Rolland Paper (which, incidentally, receives its timber berths from the Quebec government) have their head offices in Quebec.

As for financing, it is well known that Hydro-Quebec has been going outside Quebec for more and more of its financing — to English Canada as well as the United States, Europe and Japan. In December 1977 the *Financial Post* reported:

Even before the separatist Parti Québécois came to power last November, Hydro followed a policy of straddling several financial markets. Japanese, Saudi Arabian, Swiss and German bankers, among others, have played their part in feeding the provincial utility's massive financial hunger. This month Hydro-Quebec diversified its borrowing program further by signing up with seven

Canadian chartered banks for a $1.25 billion medium-term Euro-dollar loan.... The banks arranging the financing are Banque Canadienne Nationale, Banque Provinciale du Canada, Canadian Imperial Bank of Commerce, Bank of Nova Scotia, Royal Bank and Toronto-Dominion Bank.[25]

It can be seen that Fournier's two-network thesis is not supported by the evidence. *All* francophone capitalists, it would seem, seek the support of the Quebec government to some degree. It is in their collective interest to strengthen the Quebec government, but not to the extent of separating from the rest of Canada. And while francophone capitalists are nationalists, they are Canadian nationalists.

Pierre Fournier links his two-network thesis with what he regards as control of industry by the banks. "Power Corp. and its subsidiaries are in the financial orbit of the Royal Bank," he writes, "and to some degree Power is the bank's operating arm. A significant number of the conglomerate's expansion and takeover projects were approved and financed — if not piloted — by this largest of Canadian banks. Power's takeover bid for Argus Corporation of Toronto was among these."[26]

In other words, the financial networks are headed by banks. Fournier offers no hard evidence for this assertion, however. A critique of what might be called the myth of the control of Canadian industry by the banks has already been outlined. It is worth recalling here that with 53 per cent of the votes in 1976 and almost 75 per cent in 1979, Paul Desmarais is unquestionably the owner of Power Corp. and the Royal Bank's only role is to provide financing. In that role, the bank obviously does have to "approve" Desmarais's projects (just as it approves a mortgage or personal loan) but in so sense is it the initiator of those projects or the driving force behind them.

The situation described by the two-network thesis is simply that the larger a corporation is, the more it is likely to do business across Canada, and the more it will have to deal with capitalists and companies in other regions if it doesn't want to be seen as an "enclave" of Montreal or Toronto interests. But within the same region, capitalists sit on each other's boards of directors and make use of financial and legal services that are available locally. This is why Quebec capitalists sit on the boards of directors of other Quebec companies. There are also distinct ethnic cleavages: WASPs generally invite other WASPs to sit on their boards, Jews invite other Jews, and French Canadians other French Canadians. Both A. Sales[27] and this writer have dealt with this phenomenon with respect to French Canadians, and it is not necessary to elaborate here. Yet, it follows that the larger a corporation is, the less it wants to be identified with an ethnic group. This is why Seagram's appears less Jewish than Steinberg's, and Power Corp. less French Canadian than Sodarcan.

Growth and Consolidation of the Francophone Bourgeoisie Between 1975 and 1979

Between 1975 and 1979, the process of development and consolidation of the new francophone bourgeoisie took on unprecedented proportions. A look at the main aspects of this process is in order.

First of all, the francophone bourgeoisie gained control of a number of large companies that were formerly under English Canadian or foreign control. Mention has already been made of the case of M. Loeb and Co., an Ontario company in the commercial sector; the majority of its shares were bought by Provigo in July 1977. In December 1978 and January 1979, the Montreal City and District Savings Bank gained control of the Crédit Foncier Franco-Canadien, one of the largest foreign-owned financial institutions in Canada.[28] In August 1979, Alfred Hamel bought a majority of the shares of Quebecair, the second largest regional air carrier in eastern Canada, from the English Canadian financier Howard R. Webster. Webster had bought it fifteen years earlier from the Brillant family of Rimouski. Hamel bought Quebecair with an eye to reorganizing the three eastern Canadian regional airlines (Quebecair, Nordair and Eastern Provincial Airways) under Quebec control, and at the time there was a prospect of other French Canadian takeovers in this sector.[29] In 1979 the York Lambton group gained control of Canadian Admiral, a former subsidiary of the American-based Rockwell group. In November 1978 the transfer of all the shares of Multiple Access and the Montreal television station CFCF-TV for $26 million from the Charles Bronfman family to Jean A. Pouliot, the former president of Télé-Capitale, was made public.[30]

In the forest products sector, the Caisse de Dépôt et de Placement bought 19 per cent of the shares of Domtar in July 1979, a few months after a consortium of companies in the Power Corp. group bought 15 per cent of the share capital of Abitibi Paper. In June 1979 the Montreal-based engineering group Lavalin confirmed that it intended to buy Gaz Métropolitain of Montreal, a subsidiary of Norcen Energy Resources of Toronto.[31] These are only the major instances of French Canadian firms expanding by absorbing their competitors. They show that large and middle-sized companies, English Canadian or foreign, are no longer safe from a takeover bid by one French Canadian company or another.

Second, French Canadian companies have also demonstrated remarkable "internal" growth (through the accumulation of undistributed profits). If the 1978 assets of the entries on the list of large French Canadian companies are compared with their 1975 assets, it is in the financial sector that French Canadian companies have performed best. In the three-year period, assets of the Banque Canadienne Nationale grew by 62 per cent and those of the Provincial Bank by 63 per cent. The most spectacular growth was that of Imnat, a mortgage loan company owned by the BCN, with a 279 per cent increase in three years. North West Trust, a company in the Charles Allard group, followed with growth of 100 per cent.

Growth rates in the industrial sector were less spectacular. Quebecair, Télé-Capitale and Télé-Métropole had the highest rates — 74 per cent, 64 per cent and 59 per cent respectively — followed by Bombardier with 48 per cent. Some companies experienced almost no growth, including Rolland Paper (2 per cent) and Alfred Lambert (5 per cent). And there were even a few failures, including Sorel Steel Foundries, a Simard family company that went bankrupt in 1978, and Melchers Distilleries, which failed in 1977. In the commercial sector, the spectacular growth of Provigo (186 per cent) and other companies in the food business was balanced by the failure of Dupuis Frères in February 1978. In the transportation sector, La Vérendrye grew by 181 per cent in three years, but other companies had growth rates bordering on stagnation, such as Logistec (5 per cent). To summarize, it is in the financial sector and the mass media that French Canadian companies experienced the most rapid growth in assets.

Third, there were major reorganizations and mergers during the late 70s. The Power Corporation group was extensively reorganized. In 1977 it sold Imperial Life to the La Laurentienne group, controlled by Jean-Marie Poitras and Claude Castonguay. In 1978 it sold Laurentide Financial Corporation to the Provincial Bank, while Davie Shipbuilding was turned over to a partnership of former Marine Industries executives. Power Corp. also merged Domglas with Consolidated-Bathurst, and Canada Steamship Lines with the parent corporation. Desmarais increased his participation in Power from 53 to 73 per cent.

A number of other mergers took place during the same period. In 1977, the Provincial Bank absorbed the Unity Bank to strengthen its presence in western Canada, and in 1979 it merged with the BCN to form the National Bank of Canada, with consolidated assets of close to $14 billion. In the investment sector, two of Quebec's oldest brokerage houses, Geoffrion Robert et Gélinas and René T. Leclerc, merged in October 1979. The new company was called Geoffrion, Leclerc and it was to handle nearly 25 per cent of the province's municipal bonds.[32] French Canadian brokerage houses have grown spectacularly in the last few years. In 1979 they accounted for 95 per cent of the municipal bond market in Quebec and held a dominant position in the provincial bond market, due in part to the "Quebecization" of the province's financial syndicate effected by the Parti Québécois government in January 1978.

The Jean-Louis Lévesque group was dismantled during this period. Lévesque sold his stock in Lévesque, Beaubien (the leading French Canadian brokerage house) to executives of the firm. He turned the F-I-C Fund over to La Laurentienne in March 1979, giving La Laurentienne an 8 per cent share of the General Trust of Canada, enough for joint control along with the Simards, who hold 12 per cent.[33]

Fourth, even if relations between the PQ government and French Canadian business circles are much less strained than they were in 1976-77, business has not softened its federalism. Thus in October 1979 it was learned that a number of firms with francophone owners had contributed funds to the Pro-Canada Committee, which was organizing the pre-referendum campaign against the PQ's constitutional option. These companies included three subsidiaries of Power Corporation as well as Bombardier, Provigo, the Banque Canadienne Nationale, the Provincial Bank (controlled by the Desjardins movement), Télé-Métropole and Rolland Paper.[34] The Conseil du Patronat du Québec, the province's leading employers' association, also took part in the referendum campaign on the federalist side.

As for the PQ government itself, its speeches before business audiences took on an increasingly moderate tone. The first two PQ budgets were not well received by business organizations,[35] but the government's third budget, in 1979, elicited their approval. The government also gave up its initial idea of the state as the main engine of the economy in favour of the primacy of the private sector. Early in its term the government was willing to intervene in the economy, as it did in converting the automobile insurance industry to public ownership, even if it meant that private companies would lose hundreds of millions of dollars in premiums. But it later refused to interfere in the public (or private) sector in air transport — unlike the government of Alberta, which established a partnership with local businessmen in that field. The negotiations for the purchase of the Asbestos Corporation were drawn out, as compared with the rapid takeover of the potash industry in Saskatchewan between 1976 and 1979. In 1979 the PQ government promised an investment corporation and an export finance corporation, but it certainly did not proceed with these projects with undue haste.

On the whole, it seems the government wanted to mollify the French Canadian business circles which it in no sense represented. With their close ties to the federal and provincial Liberal parties, the stance of these circles towards the PQ's constitutional option in the referendum was predictable. It was equally evident that by intervening sporadically in support of French Canadian companies (as when it blocked the sale of Crédit Foncier to a Nova Scotian group in December 1978, or constituted a French Canadian financial syndicate in January 1978), the PQ cabinet would not succeed in bridging the gap that separated the government from business.

Conclusion

Since the Second World War a new francophone bourgeoisie has come to life, primarily but not exclusively in Quebec. It is active in the provision of financial services (insurance, trust services, mutual funds), the commercial sector, transportation, real estate, and the manufacturing sector, in which, with the exception of Bombardier Ltd., it is concentrated in traditional industries. It has thus gained entry into sectors in which technology does not play a major role, and where new competitors are not blocked by technological barriers.

The growth of this bourgeoisie has been determined by the development of new sectors such as real estate that are not controlled by the English-speaking establishment. In other cases, the belated concentration of sectors in which there was already a French Canadian petty bourgeoisie, such as retailing, has allowed a number of small businessmen to grow through the absorption of competitors. The rapid increase in the incomes of French Canadians since 1940-45 and their entry as consumers into new markets that had previously been inaccessible to them (financial services, insurance, urban real estate and retail markets) have provided indigenous small capitalists with a steadily growing demand. Finally, the creation of a provincial state apparatus in Quebec endowed with institutions that are willing and able to stimulate the development of a French Canadian bourgeoisie has helped French Canadian capitalism in numerous cases. This has been the central policy of the Quebec Liberal Party, as manifested especially in the Quiet Revolution.

This new bourgeoisie has interests across Canada. It invests its money and sells its products from coast to coast, and for that reason it is opposed to the independence of Quebec. The Parti Québécois cannot represent the interests of this rising class; rather, it represents the liberal professions (especially lawyers and notaries), civil servants, teachers, artists, writers, publishers; in sum, wage-earners and independent producers of services who live by the word. A party whose central policies are based upon the separation of Quebec and cultural nationalism cannot attract businessmen who hope to conquer the Canadian market.

With no independent capacity for research and development, the French Canadian bourgeoisie cannot compete in dynamic industrial sectors. Like the cooperative movement, it is limited to expansion within the traditional sectors, except for the occasional instance in which, following the example of Paul Desmarais, it wrests control of an already established company involving a certain amount of technological complexity from the English-speaking bourgeoisie. If its strategy succeeds, the new francophone bourgeoisie will develop along the same lines and through the same sectors (commerce, finance, transportation and services, real estate) as the English-speaking capitalist class.

The analysis outlined here directly contradicts Marcel Rioux's "ethnic class" conception of the Quebec nation. It also contradicts the analysis of those who see the new French Canadian bourgeoisie as a developing "national" bourgeoisie. The francophone bourgeoisie is, in fact, only the French Canadian section of the Canadian capitalist class. Its markets, its investments, its ambitions are all Canada-wide. While it has helped build up the Quebec government apparatus and depends on it for support, it is not at all interested in the separation of Quebec. On the other hand, the program and practice of the PQ government encourages the petty bourgeoisie, with its institutional base in the co-operative movement, in its dreams of being able to defend itself against the incursions of large-scale capital. The petty bourgeoisie and public-sector workers who live "by the word"[36] are the main producers and transmitters of pro-independence ideology in Quebec today.

CHAPTER 4

Who Controls
State Capitalism?

The question of state-owned corporations in the present monopoly phase of capitalism has been a popular subject for Marxist economists. The extensive literature they have produced has succeeded in clarifying some aspects of the role of publicly-owned corporations in advanced capitalism. It is, however, unsatisfying in other respects. One of the least examined aspects of government-owned corporations under monopoly capitalism is the manner in which they are controlled. Marx showed that capital is a social relationship between those who are in the objective position of producers (in this case, the workers employed by government-owned corporations) and those who control the means of production and can dispose of the product and surplus-value. The question that arises is: who controls government-owned corporations? The capitalist relationship exists between government employees and another group, whose identity is not entirely clear. Is it the private-sector bourgeoisie, a state bourgeoisie, an economic elite or simply a group of government officials? A first step towards answering this question is a review of the Marxist literature on the control of government-owned corporations, and identification of appropriate concepts and working hypotheses for this study. This is followed by an analysis of the Canadian situation.

The Control of Government-owned
Corporations in Marxist Theory

Marx did not produce significant work on government-owned corporations or their control. This is not true, however, of Engels, whose *Socialism: Utopian and Scientific* includes some well-known passages on publicly-owned enterprises:

> In any case, with trusts or without, the official representatives of capitalist society — the state — will ultimately have to undertake

the direction of production. This necessity of conversion into state property is felt first in the great institutions for intercourse and communication — the post-office, the telegraphs, the railways .... The transformation of the great establishments for production and distribution into joint-stock companies, trusts and state property, show how unnecessary the bourgeoisie are for that purpose. All the social functions of the capitalist are now performed by salaried employees .... But the transformation, either into joint-stock companies and trusts, or into state ownership, does not do away with the capitalistic nature of the productive forces .... The modern state, no matter what its form, is essentially a capitalist machine, the state of the capitalists, the ideal personification of the total national capital .... The workers remain wage workers — proletarians. The capitalist relation is not done away with. It is rather brought to a head.[1]

Engels only states the problem; he does not resolve it. He says that "the capitalist relation is not done away with" and workers who work for the state remain proletarians, but his answer to the question of whom they enter into this relation with is ambiguous. On the one hand, he says that "all the social functions of the capitalist are now performed by salaried employees," which implies that one might look in the direction of salaried government officials for an answer. On the other hand, he also says that the modern state is still "the state of the capitalists" (adding, in a phrase clearly inspired by Hegel, that it is "the ideal personification of the total national capital"). Engels looks for the causes of nationalization in the size of investments and the companies that make them: "For only when the means of production and distribution have *actually* outgrown the form of management by joint-stock companies, and when, therefore, the taking them over by the state has become *economically* inevitable, only then — even if it is the state of today that effects this — is there an economic advance."[2]

The founders of historical materialism neither developed the concept of "state monopoly capitalism" nor explained it, and they had no precise idea of who controls publicly-owned corporations. Their only contribution to explaining the appearance of state-owned enterprises is in terms of the scale and natural monopoly of certain large-scale investments (railways, postal service, telecommunications).

Lenin: the Idea of State Capitalism

The term "state monopoly capitalism" is owed to Lenin. Prior to 1917, he did not use the term, and he appears to have had little awareness of the economic instruments of the state. His definition of the state was based solely on its repressive instruments (army, police, prisons, etc.) and not on its economic agencies as such. It was just before the Bolsheviks took power that Lenin formulated his idea of state capitalism. In *The State and Revolution, Imperialism* and *The Impending Catastrophe and How to Combat It,* he used the expression without defining it and without venturing an overall theoretical explanation of the phenomenon.[3]

It should be emphasized that Lenin linked state monopoly capitalism directly to the Great War, which he believed was the antechamber of the socialist revolution. After October 1917, Lenin spoke of "state capitalism" to refer to one of the five social-economic forms existing in Russia in 1918.[4] In texts written at this time, he argued that German "state capitalism" provided a valid example. He further stated that Soviet power turned the management of state enterprises over to former capitalists only temporarily, and not as capitalists but as technicians with special skills or highly-paid organizers. These works do not refer to the control of government-owned corporations under capitalism, and do not explain capitalist nationalization of large companies.

The concept underwent little new development after Lenin. Gramsci, though a sensitive observer of Italian capitalism, paid no attention to the development of publicly-owned corporations under fascism. It was in 1933, while Gramsci was in prison, that the Mussolini regime set up a giant state conglomerate, the *Istituto per la ricostruzione industriale* (IRI) to reorganize the Italian economy, but Gramsci made no mention of it in his writings.

The Theory of State Monopoly Capitalism

Eugene Varga, one of the best known economists of the Stalin era, wrote in 1935 of state capitalism in capitalist countries as a form of organization designed to ease the economic crisis.[5] Along with successive editions of the Soviet textbook *Politicheskaya ekonomiya* ("Political Economy"), Varga's writings between 1930 and 1950 are the most important forerunners of the current theory of state monopoly capitalism. In a more recent work, published in 1967, Varga criticized Stalin's conception of state capitalism as the subordination of the state to monopolies, an idea which appears in *Politicheskaya ekonomiya* and which Varga himself had entertained. In his new book, Varga argued that "there is no one-sided 'subordination' but a joining of forces, which, in spite of this merger, still maintain a certain autonomy."[6] On the question of the control of publicly-owned enterprises, Varga clearly leaned towards an explanation in terms of salaried government officials:

> There is a great difference in the conditions under which the workers struggle for wage increases in private monopoly-owned

enterprises, and in state-owned enterprises. The struggle for wage increases threatens to cut the monopoly bourgeoisie's profits. The management of every enterprise is directly and materially concerned with the outcome of the struggle. In state-owned enterprises, the workers are opposed by directors, ministers, etc., who have no direct material interest in the outcome of the struggle. Therefore, their resistance to the workers' demands is usually less stiff than that of the monopoly bourgeoisie.[7]

During the 1960s, political economists in the Soviet bloc and the pro-Soviet Communist parties of western Europe gradually developed a theory of state monopoly capitalism. While previously, as has been seen, state monopoly capitalism had been explained only in embryonic fashion after 1960 this school redefined and interpreted the phenomenon.

According to the Eurocommunist theory, state capitalism is not the publicly-owned *sector* of advanced capitalist economies. Rather, state monopoly capitalism is a *phase*, the final phase, of monopoly capitalism. Paul Boccara, for example, writes that "state monopoly capitalism is the final phase of imperialism."[8]:

> State activity in the public sector proper is sometimes treated as being essentially different from state intervention in the private sector; the first is defined as "state capitalism" while the second is public intervention on behalf of monopolies within capitalism itself. In the context of state monopoly capitalism, this distinction cannot be justified . . . . State capitalism, consisting of public enterprise, is not fundamentally opposed to other public forms of capitalism, but all these forms together constitute public intervention within state monopoly capitalism . . . . However, publicly-owned enterprises are the highest development of this fundamental process.[9]

Defined as a *phase* of monopoly capitalism, state monopoly capitalism thus includes both publicly-owned enterprises and the whole complex of government economic activities "on behalf of monopolies." There is a wide variety of such activities, including public financing of private production through grants, loans, government purchasing, etc.; the setting of guidelines; the export of public capital to assist the export of private capital, etc.

Eurocommunists explain government intervention under state monopoly capitalism on the basis of the falling rate of profit, as a result of which some enterprises become uneconomic and have to be either taken over or else set on their feet again by the state.

This theory contains only the bare outlines of a description of the control of publicly-owned corporations. The clearest and most explicit treatment of this question appears in a work by the Russian economist Victor Cheprakov, *State Monopoly Capitalism.* Cheprakov takes the view that state monopoly capitalism is the final phase of imperialism, but he also devotes long passages to an analysis of how publicly-owned corporations in advanced capitalist countries are controlled and run. Citing Lenin's theory of the "personal union of the state and private monopolies," Cheprakov concludes that "nationalized corporations are run by representatives of monopoly capital."[10]

Cheprakov's interpretation is thus in direct contradiction with Varga's, which states that publicly-owned corporations are run by civil servants. However, it includes a healthy dose of empirical analysis and provides the only coherent response in this whole theoretical current to the question of who runs publicly-owned enterprises. According to Cheprakov, the boards of directors of government-owned corporations in advanced capitalist countries are composed of the private-sector bourgeoisie.

There has been an economic critique of the theory of state monopoly capitalism that gets to the heart of the matter. The central idea of the theory of state monopoly capitalism is the "pillage" to which the monopoly capitalist class subjects the people through the state. According to the theory, this pillage is due to capitalism's overripe state, in which the falling rate of profit demands a devaluation of social capital. Using the state, monopolies extort the profits of non-monopoly capital and some of the income of the middle strata of the working class through fiscal policy, inflation, grants to monopolies, etc. The theory also maintains that all public financing and public expenditures, including consumption by the state, constitute a devaluation of public capital. However, B. Théret and M. Wieviorka offer a clear refutation of this theory:

> *For the most part, public funds do not function as capital.* Most government expenditures go toward paying salaries to the employees of government agencies, buying goods from capitalists ..., making income allocations to households ..., paying interest on the public debt, and making grants and loans to public and private companies. Contrary to the thesis of state monopoly capitalism, we maintain that with respect to these activities it is impossible to speak of capital or of (lessening of or dis-) investment ... What occurs is an expenditure of government revenues, pure and simple, and not a transformation of revenues into capital.[11]

On the other hand, when the state itself invests its revenues to produce goods and services that will be sold in the marketplace, it transforms these revenues into capital: this is the sector consisting of government-owned enterprises. Exploitation, creation of surplus-value and profits exist therein. A state proletariat exists and another group (not identified by Théret and Wieviorka) plays the role of capitalist. The basic task of the public banking, industrial and commercial sector — government-owned enterprises that carry out manufacturing, mining, public service, commercial, financial and other operations — is to ensure its own accumulation through undistributed profits and/or loans floated on the bond market. Most of these are profitable companies, in which capital is enhanced rather than devalued. And these state-owned corporations ensure the reproduction of *all* of private capital, and not just its monopoly sector as the theory of state monopoly capitalism asserts.

Hence, the "massive devaluation of social capital" described by the state monopoly capitalism school disappears. The majority of public funds are not capital but government revenues spent to maintain the state itself (army, police, judicial system) or to ensure the reproduction of the work force (health system, schools, welfare, unemployment insurance, etc.). And the part that does become capital through investment in government-owned corporations must meet profitability criteria.

There is no need here to deal with the *political* conclusions that the Eurocommunists draw from their analysis, aspects of which have been criticized by other writers.[12] These conclusions are implicit in the term "monopoly" that the school tacks on to the phrase "state capitalism." When Lenin spoke of state monopoly capitalism, he was referring to a situation in which a government-owned enterprise was the sole producer in a given sector. Eurocommunists, on the other hand, are trying to show that the public sector serves monopoly capital exclusively, and they deduce from this that the workers should form alliances with non-monopoly sectors of the bourgeoisie. The distinction between "state capitalism" and "state monopoly capitalism" is discussed later in this chapter.

Baran and Sweezy: the Idea of State Capitalism Rejected

Baran and Sweezy take a fundamentally different position from other Marxists on the question of state capitalism. They reject the terms "state capitalism" and "state monopoly capitalism," preferring "monopoly capital" instead. They cite two reasons for this:

In the first place, the state has always played a crucial role in the development of capitalism, and while this role has certainly increased quantitatively we find the evidence of a qualitative change in recent decades unconvincing. Under the circumstances, to lay special emphasis on the role of the state in the present stage of monopoly capitalism may only mislead people into assuming that it was of negligible importance in the earlier history of capitalism.

Even more important is the fact that terms like "state capitalism" and "state monopoly capitalism" almost inevitably carry the connotation that the state is somehow an *independent* social force, coordinate with private business.[13]

Baran and Sweezy's rejection of the term "state capitalism" is, of course, not wholly unrelated to the fact that government-owned corporations have played and continue to play a less significant role in the United States than in any other capitalist industrial country. Frédéric François-Marsal has estimated that between 1965 and 1970 government-owned enterprises accounted for 6 per cent of all business investment in the United States, compared to 15 per cent in Canada (François-Marsal estimated 10 per cent, but that is too low), 25 per cent in Sweden, 30 per cent in Italy and 33 per cent in France.[14] It would be surprising to find a highly developed theory of state capitalism in the country where that form of capitalism has been slowest in developing. Conversely, it is not surprising that the theory of state monopoly capitalism — and theoretical consideration of the economic role of the state in general — is most highly developed in those countries where the government-owned sector has assumed the largest proportions, notably in France, Italy and Brazil.

In replacing "state capitalism" and "state monopoly capitalism" with the unqualified term "monopoly capitalism," Baran and Sweezy appear to neglect the central role of the state in most capitalist economies — a role that is larger in all other capitalist economies than in the United States. It should be noted that the concept of state capitalism allows the state a degree of independence from the economic interests of private capital. Far from being a defect, this attribution of relative independence to the state is, in this writer's view, one of the concept's strengths. The terms "monopoly capitalism" and "state capitalism" are examined further in the conclusion to this theoretical discussion.

State Capitalism and State Bourgeoisie

In the last few years, Marxist economists and sociologists have been using the term "state bourgeoisie" to refer to the social group that has effective control of nationalized companies. This term has been used in very different contexts: Charles Bettelheim, for instance, employed it in his analysis of Soviet society to designate the people who run publicly-owned corporations:

> We cannot develop the idea of a "state bourgeoisie" (or bureaucratic state bourgeoisie) here. Let us simply say that it refers to agents of social reproduction who are not direct producers and who — as a result of existing social relationships and dominant social practices — are *effectively able to dispose of means of production and products that belong formally to the state.*[15]

While Bettelheim has applied the concept of state bourgeoisie to his analysis of the social structure in the USSR, Fernando H. Cardoso has been using it since 1973 to explain the accumulation of public capital in Brazil. According to Cardoso, in the last fifteen years there has been a process of "dependent-associate" capitalist development run by three sectors: foreign multinationals, Brazilian government-owned corporations and the largest companies in the domestic private sector. In this alliance of dominant sectors, government-owned corporations play a relatively autonomous, hegemonic and expanding role. On the one hand, almost a third of the money invested in Brazil in the 1970s has been invested by government-owned corporations, and this proportion is steadily growing. On the other hand, government-owned corporations are able to take the initiative in economic development and set the rules of the game for the other two partners. The government-owned sector has given birth to a social group that effectively controls it: this group arises in part from the top management of publicly-owned corporations and is closely linked to the higher ranks of the armed forces:

> In part, the state in dependent capitalism is in charge of its own social base, to the extent that its productive function — ensuring the accomplishment and growth of accumulation — has created a group of public-sector businessmen. We call this group the "state bourgeoisie" to emphasize that, while they do not own the means of production, these social agents are more than simple bureaucrats.[16]

Cardoso is using the concept of state bourgeoisie in a somewhat different sense from Bettelheim, in that here it designates the top professional management of government-owned corporations *in a country where private-sector capitalism is numerically predominant.* The state bourgeoisie is recruited among the "higher levels of the bureaucracy, both civil and military, among technicians and members of the liberal professions, and sometimes among local businessmen who have lost their positions in the private sector." It is not a bureaucracy because it has access to real spheres of control and appropriation; in other words, because it does not simply carry out orders.[17]

Other analysts of the Brazilian case have worked within the perspective established by Cardoso and have helped establish a certain credibility for the notion of a "state bourgeoisie." One of the more convincing aspects of their work has been their comparison of Brazil with other countries, such as Spain and Italy, where publicly-owned corporations seem to be under the control of private capital in alliance with civil servants. In these cases, no specific social group with internal recruitment, ideological homogeneity and a degree of autonomy from private capital appears to have arisen. Scholars in other countries have not done studies in the same perspective, but it does seem that Brazil is something of a special case. The remarkable autonomy of Brazilian state capitalism could be related to the specific period of development Brazil is experiencing. Heavy industry, for example, is only now being developed.

In the early twentieth century, overcoming the obstacles to industrialization required close cooperation between the banking sector and the private industrial sector (leading to bank-industry coalitions and control of industry by the banks in various forms). Countries that were not industrialized by mid-century, however, had fallen so far behind that today only the state can act as the driving force of capitalist industrialization. In dependent countries that are belatedly trying to industrialize (Brazil is the most striking case, but not the only one, India being another example), the state has to impose discipline on indigenous capital and the multinationals. The result is a dependent-associate form of development, in which publicly-owned corporations take the lead, make risky investments in sectors that will only become profitable after a number of years, install advanced technology and use massive amounts of public funds during the phase of capital-goods import substitution. During this period, which may last several decades, it seems that the formation of a "state bourgeoisie" is possible under private capitalism. It is impossible to guess how well this group will maintain its cohesion and social resistance in the future, but the examples of Italy and Spain would seem to indicate that it is destined to disappear after the modern industrial sector becomes consolidated, to be replaced by managers from private companies.

A New Conceptual Framework

As seen previously, Lenin was the first to use the expressions "state capitalism" and "state monopoly capitalism," and he neither defined them nor offered any explanation for the reality they refer to. Marx,

Engels, Lenin and Gramsci barely touched on the question of the control of government-owned corporations; and it would be pointless to look to them for the foundation of a new theoretical framework for this study.

The control of government-owned corporations under monopoly capitalism is a controversial subject. Some writers, such as Eugene Varga, take it for granted that these corporations are directed by civil servants; Victor Cheprakov maintains that they are run by the private sector bourgeoisie; and F.H. Cardoso uses the term "state bourgeoisie" to denote the people who administer publicly-owned companies. Other writers, such as François Morin, use these explanations in combination — they see government-owned corporations as being jointly controlled by government officials and the private sector bourgeoisie.[18]

Empirical analysis conducted from a Marxist perspective tends to support Cheprakov's explanation, at least in the case of advanced capitalist countries. This explanation is also the easiest to test against the evidence while the distinction between a state bourgeoisie and a group of career civil servants is a subtler one. What degree of stability is necessary for the managers of government-owned corporations to constitute a class or at least a segment of the ruling class? What kind of recruitment? What social origins? What career patterns? The concept of "state bourgeoisie" offers no answers to these questions, at least at the present state of research.

In what follows, the group of public officials who sit on the boards of directors of government-owned corporations after long careers in those same corporations will be called the "state bourgeoisie." These officials are almost always the *inside* directors of publicly-owned corporations (chairman of the board, president, vice-president, governor, commissioner), and this function constitutes their main activity. They are thus clearly distinct from the *outside* directors, who only sit on the boards of directors and who may be government officials (ministers, deputy ministers, etc.), private-sector capitalists, or legal, financial or other advisers. In other words, the state bourgeoisie consists of the full-time managers of publicly-owned corporations, who participate actively in the control of these corporations and receive salaries that are comparable to those of managers in the private sector.[19] The analysis that follows will try to delineate the respective positions of the state bourgeoisie, the private-sector bourgeoisie, and government officials on the boards of directors of publicly-owned corporations in Canada.

As for the more fundamental question of whether or not to use the expressions "state capitalism" and "state monopoly capitalism" and whether to define them in terms of a phase of capitalism or in terms of a sector, it should be remembered that often without realizing it, writers are strongly influenced by specific economic and political conditions in the countries where they live. If Baran and Sweezy reject the concepts of "state capitalism" and "state monopoly capitalism," it is because at present publicly-owned corporations play a much less significant role in the United States than in any other advanced capitalist country. Similarly, Lenin defined the state as a repressive instrument because repression was the main characteristic of the Tsarist state that he opposed as a revolutionary. It is no coincidence that he became aware of the state's vast economic machinery just before the Bolsheviks seized power, when the problems of economic management and regulation confronted him for the first time. But Lenin never had time to reformulate his concept of the state to make room for its economic machinery.

Gramsci was faced with yet another situation. The problem of the social order in Italy was not one that could be dealt with through the repressive machinery of the state. Gramsci therefore explained the persistence of the capitalist order through the concepts of the ideological machinery of the state, consensus and hegemony. But the possibility of an eventual seizure of power never occurred to him, and so he never dealt with the problems of managing the state's economic machinery.

State power has appeared to be within the grasp of French and Italian Communists ever since the Second World War. It is therefore no coincidence that they have given the question of state capitalism the most extensive consideration and produced the bulk of the literature on it. However, it is possible to identify some serious problems with their conception of the state's economic machinery. First of all, they explain its current development in terms of the law of the falling rate of profit, a law that many Marxist economists today question both empirically and theoretically.[20] Second, the theory of state monopoly capitalism does not offer a convincing explanation (except for Cheprakov's) of the control of state-owned corporations. Third, it neglects political factors (such as the relative influence of left-wing parties or an emerging bourgeoisie) in the creation of a sector of government-owned enterprises. Finally, the theory is too closely tied to the changing requirements of tactical politics and is influenced by sectarian considerations. Other writers have dealt with this last point and there is no need to elaborate here.

On the other hand, Marxists in Anglo-Saxon countries (the U.S., United Kingdom and Canada) have not had to worry about coming to power. As a result, with a few exceptions, they have given only embryonic consideration to the administrative and economic machinery of the state.[21]

The term "state capitalism" is used to denote government-owned corporations in Canada. The use of the term here is similar to that of James O'Connor. In not using the term "monopoly," a deliberate distance is being kept from the Eurocommunist state monopoly capitalism school, for a number of reasons. First of all, with some exceptions, government-owned corporations in Canada are not monopolies in that they participate in oligopoly or competitive markets. Second, in this study's perspective, state capitalism is not seen as a *phase* of capitalism (specifically, the last phase before the coming of socialism) but as a *sector* or a *mode of production*.[22] Third, this writer believes that government-owned corporations, in Canada and elsewhere, do not serve the interests of the monopoly sector alone: on the contrary, in Canada they have often helped regional petty and middle bourgeoisies get off the ground and supported them against large-scale Canadian capital. Finally, in rejecting the concept of state monopoly capitalism, a distance is kept from its political connotations and theoretical foundations (the law of the falling rate of profit, the confusion of revenues with public capital, etc.).

Government-owned Corporations in Canada

An empirical study of government-owned corporations in Canada and how they are run raises a number of serious problems. The first of these, and not the least, is that some publicly-owned corporations are under federal jurisdiction while others are under provincial jurisdiction. Consequently, adequate data for a concrete analysis can be obtained only by going to a variety of sources. Second, the legal basis for publicly-owned corporations at both levels is various and complex. What is more, even when publicly-owned corporations are under the jurisdiction of the same level of government and the same legal authority, how they are actually administered can vary enormously from corporation to corporation. And finally, official sources differ as to how many government-owned corporations exist.

In order to deal with these problems, it was necessary to make some methodological choices. First of all, both federal and provincial corporations were analysed, because as will be seen, they are of comparable size and importance. For corporations at both levels of jurisdiction, a threshold was established of total assets of $100 million at the end of 1975, so that the list would include only large-scale corporations and so that the results would be comparable with those of *The Economy of Canada's* study of large Canadian corporations in the private sector. Second, it was necessary to eliminate at the outset all crown corporations that hold no assets in their own name, and as a result do not publish a financial statement. These are the so-called "departmental" corporations under federal jurisdiction, one of three categories of crown corporations established by the Financial Administration Act.[23]

This act, passed in 1951 and amended in 1958, defines crown corporations as corporations that must account to Parliament through a minister for the conduct of their affairs, and divides them into departmental, agency and proprietary corporations. (There are also two categories of corporations not classified under the act: corporations that are governed by their own acts of incorporation and independent government-owned corporations that are not subject to the Financial Administration Act and not accountable to Parliament.) The departmental corporations include the Unemployment Insurance Commission, the Economic Council of Canada and the National Research Council.[24] They are classified as departments of the civil service and do not hold assets under their own name, and are thus excluded from this study. This leaves one with the agency, proprietary and unclassified crown corporations that are subject to the Financial Administration Act.[25] Financial statements of forty-three of these corporations were published in the 1975-76 edition of the *Public Accounts of Canada,* while the 1976-77 *Canada Year Book* contains a list of forty-five such corporations.[26] Of these, seventeen had assets of more than $100 million in 1975. There is also one "independent" federally-controlled corporation with assets of more than $100 million, the Canada Development Corporation, and it was added to the list. This provides eighteen federally-chartered, publicly-owned corporations, comprising all the corporations under federal jurisdiction with assets over the minimum. This list is highly representative, and the assets of the corporations on it amount to more than 99 per cent of all the assets of the forty-three crown corporations whose financial statements were published in the 1975-76 edition of the *Public Accounts of Canada.*

Also chosen for study were eighteen provincial crown corporations with assets of more than $100 million. This list, however, is not exhaustive. There is a fairly large number (at least thirty-one) of provincial crown corporations with assets which surpass the threshold and this was one reason for limiting the list. More significantly, provincial crown corporations are also subject to a plethora of legal regimes and regulations, varying from province to province and corporation to corporation. Thus, only the largest publicly-owned corporations in each province were chosen. Appendix 4 is a complete list of federal and provincial crown corporations included in the study, with their assets at the end of 1975, while the distribution of these corporations by jurisdiction is summarized in table 4-1.

An examination of the main characteristics of the sample is in order. To begin with, nineteen of the corporations, more than half the sample, are utilities: nine large electrical utilities (all provincial), three provincial telephone and telecommunications companies, two railways (one

TABLE 4-1
Federally- and Provincially-owned Corporations
Studied, by Jurisdiction, 1975

Jurisdiction	Number of Corporations	Average Assets ($ million)
Federal	18	$2,034
agency	3	
proprietary	12	
unclassified	2	
"independent"	1	
Provincial	18	$1,991
Quebec	4	
Alberta	2	
British Columbia	2	
Manitoba	2	
Saskatchewan	2	
Newfoundland	2	
Nova Scotia	2	
New Brunswick	1	
Ontario	1	
Total	36	$2,013

federal, one provincial), an airline (Air Canada), etc. As a result of the distribution of powers between the federal government and the provinces, no less than two thirds of these utilities are under provincial jurisdiction. By contrast, only three of the ten large corporations in the financial sector are provincial. Both the industrial sector (four companies) and the commercial sector (two companies) are poorly represented.

The largest provincial corporations are electrical utilities, with Hydro-Quebec and Ontario Hydro heading the list, while the largest federally-owned corporations are financial institutions: the Bank of Canada and the Central Mortgage and Housing Corporation. The federal corporations on the list are a little larger than their provincial counterparts, with average assets of $2.034 billion as compared to $1.991 billion. The gap would be wider if the list included *all* provincially-owned corporations with assets of more than $100 million instead of just the largest ones.

Appendix 5 and table 4-2 show that all the currently existing large publicly-owned corporations in Canada are products of the twentieth century. Sizeable publicly-owned corporations were established by the federal government in the nineteenth century, notably in the railway field, but some of these were turned over to private interests as the three great transcontinental railway systems were built up.

It is interesting to note that among the publicly-owned corporations that still exist, the earliest ones were created by the provinces, with the establishment of Ontario Hydro in 1906 and the conversion to public ownership of the telephone systems in Manitoba, Saskatchewan and Alberta in 1908. The first large federal crown corporation, Canadian National Railways, was formed in 1919, and it was not until 1932 that it was followed by a second one, the entity that was to become the Canadian Broadcasting Corporation. The most prolific period for the establishment of publicly-owned corporations was the Second World War, when dozens were founded. Many of these were turned over to private interests after the war, but others flourished under public ownership: the Farm Credit Corporation, the Federal Business Development Bank, the Export Development Corporation and Eldorado Nuclear (all founded under other names in 1944) at the federal level, and Hydro-Quebec and British Columbia Hydro at the provincial level.

Almost all publicly-owned corporations in Canada, at both the federal and the provincial level, have been created by Liberal governments. The Conservatives were responsible only for the creation of Ontario Hydro in 1906, the Manitoba Telephone System in 1908, CN in 1919, the CBC in 1932, the Bank of Canada in 1934, the Canadian Wheat Board in

TABLE 4-2
Federally- and Provincially-owned Corporations
Studied, by Year of Incorporation and Jurisdiction

Year	Federal Corporations	Provincial Corporations	Total
1901-1910	—	4	4
1911-1920	1	3	4
1921-1930	—	1	1
1931-1940	5	—	5
1941-1950	6	3	9
1951-1960	2	2	4
1961-1970	3	4	7
1971-	1	1	2
Total	18	18	36

1935, the Sydney Steel Corporation in 1967, and the Churchill Falls (Labrador) Corporation in 1974 (see appendix 5). This is partly explained by the fact that the Conservatives have formed fewer governments than the Liberals, but it also seems evident that the Liberals have had a more favourable attitude towards public enterprise than the Conservatives.

Since the Second World War the provinces have established and developed publicly-owned corporations more aggressively than other levels of government. In 1949, the total amount of money invested by federally-owned corporations was approximately equal to the amount invested by provincial ones, with each group of corporations accounting for about 5 per cent of all money invested in Canada. In the following twenty-nine years, provincial corporations' share of total private and public investment grew almost continuously, reaching 12 per cent in 1978. However, federal crown corporations' share fell to 3 per cent of the total and the share accounted for by municipal corporations declined from 2 to 1 per cent. Overall, the increase in publicly-owned corporations' share of total investment in Canada from 12 to 16 per cent between 1949 and 1978 was attributable solely to the growth of provincial crown corporations (table 4-3).

Privately-owned corporations have accounted for nearly three quarters of total investment in Canada since the Second World War; in that time, the public sector's share of total investment has increased only marginally.

The Control of Publicly-owned Corporations in Canada

In strict legal terms, as outlined in the Financial Administration Act of 1951 (as amended in 1958), federal crown corporations are subject to the ultimate authority of Parliament, exercised through a minister. However, the few writers who deal with the question of how publicly-owned corporations are controlled agree that this legal fiction does not reflect reality. In one of the rare books on federal crown corporations, C.A. Ashley and R.G.H. Smails maintain that only a few publicly-owned companies are tightly controlled by a minister, while others are completely independent and most of them fall between these two extremes. The authors believe that the boards of directors of crown corporations play a key role in their control[27] and, in a general way, they outline some of the characteristics of these boards of directors. They state that the employees of federally-owned corporations and the unions that represent them are not generally invited to sit on the boards of directors of

TABLE 4-3
Percentage Distribution of Public and Private Investment in Canada, 1949-1978

Year	Publicly-owned Corporations			Total Public Investment	Private Investment
	Muni-cipal	Provin-cial	Federal		
1949	2	5	5	26	74
1960	2	5	5	30	70
1961	2	5	4	29	71
1962	2	5	3	29	71
1963	2	6	4	29	71
1964	2	6	3	27	73
1965	2	7	3	29	71
1966	2	7	4	30	70
1967	2	7	4	30	70
1968	1	7	3	29	71
1969	1	7	3	28	72
1970	1	7	4	28	72
1971	1	7	3	28	72
1972	1	7	3	27	73
1973	1	8	3	26	74
1974	1	8	3	27	73
1975	2	11	3	31	69
1976	1	10	3	28	72
1977	1	11	3	28	72
1978	1	12	3	29	71

Source: Statistics Canada, *Private and Public Investment in Canada. Outlook* (catalogue no. 61-205), 1951 and 1962-78.

those corporations; that the crown is represented on some boards by government officials; and that during the Second World War many businessmen sat on the boards of crown corporations.[28] These statements, however, are not supported by data and are wide open to interpretation. The following will try to answer the question of who actually sits on the boards of directors of both federally- and provincially-owned corporations.

The hypothesis of parliamentary control can be eliminated at the outset. Even though the law says that crown corporations are controlled by Parliament no writer or document — public or private — maintains that this actually occurs. A few examples will illustrate this independence. In 1977, the federal government issued an important report prepared by the Privy Council Office, entitled *Crown Corporations — Direction, Control, Accountability — Government of Canada's Proposals*. This document stated:

> The relative independence of proprietary corporations from Parliament and government has been considered necessary to establish an environment which would attract businessmen to the management of an entrepreneurial activity on behalf of the public. Some independence from Parliamentary scrutiny is also considered necessary to protect the commercial secrecy of competitive Crown corporations.[29]

The report does not aim to reduce the central role of boards of directors in administering publicly-owned corporations, but rather to ensure (a) that these corporations are guided by *general objectives* laid down by Parliament, (b) that the corporations listed in Appendix D of the report are profitable and that they are reimbursed for any uneconomic expenditures they undertake at the request of the government, (c) that crown corporations and their subsidiaries publish separate accounts and that the creation or acquisition of any new subsidiary is authorized by the Governor in Council, (d) that the section of the Corporations Act dealing with the duties and responsibilities of boards of directors applies to crown corporations, and (e) that the creation of any new crown corporation is authorized by the Governor in Council.

Theoretically, parliamentary control of government-owned corporations is exercised through standing committees — at the federal level, through the public accounts committee of the House of Commons. However, when the "commissions" paid by Atomic Energy of Canada Ltd. (AECL) to foreign customers led to a scandal, the public accounts committee learned a few things about the corporations it was supposed to be controlling. The information it obtained included a complete list of these corporations — the civil servant who drew up the list described it as provisional and said it was the first time such a list had ever been compiled.[30] There are 366 companies of all kinds on the list, including subsidiaries (Canadian National has sixty-one subsidiaries and the Canada Development Corporation has seventy-eight).

During the storm surrounding Atomic Energy of Canada, the public accounts committee called on members of the board of directors of the company to testify. The testimony was revealing, both of the high degree of independence from Parliament enjoyed by the boards of directors of crown corporations, and of the way in which directors are recruited. In response to criticism from the auditor general of Canada, the AECL board of directors, acting on its own authority, set up a five-member committee in November 1976, which included the corporation's board chairman, Ross Campbell; its president, Harry W.

Macdonnell (a former president of Brinco); and other directors, including David Culver, president of the Aluminum Company of Canada. The committee was mandated to find a vice-president of finance, and it came up with Hardwick, former president of Alcan (Asia) Ltd. In addition, in the summer of 1976 the AECL board of directors undertook an internal reorganization, about which Ross Campbell testified:

> This was no reflection whatsoever on the individuals who had served before but ... we formerly had on the Board three representatives from the principal utilities who were users of our main product, the CANDU reactor.
> This was considered a conflict of interest that perhaps might interfere with their representing fully the generality of the public of Canada and they were advised of the government's intention to reconstitute the Board in a way that would serve two objectives. I think one of them is the one you are speaking of, Mr. Chairman. The first was a business one to acquire four to five new directors of the Corporation with deep business experience to reflect the increasingly commercial orientation of the AECL's activities. We needed people accustomed to doing business and making a profit at it thereby relieving undue burden on the taxpayers of this country.
> But, secondly, the second objective was a better equilibrium between government and business in the affairs of the Corporation. And by government, I mean again representing the interests of the principal shareholder, the minister and, through him, the the public of this country. So we introduced three Deputy Ministers to the Board of Directors. So we got a new crop of businessmen and three Deputy Ministers.[31]

This testimony shows that even during a crisis the board of directors of a crown corporation chooses its own members, and the business community is the principal pool from which it makes its choices. These boards of directors will now be examined more systematically, beginning with their size.

The average number of directors in the thirty-six corporations under study is nine, but there are wide divergences from corporation to corporation. Some — such as the Canadian Dairy Commission, the National Harbours Board and the St. Lawrence Seaway Authority (three members each) — have very small boards, while others, including the Canada Development Corporation (twenty-one members), have boards of directors as large as those of private companies. In general, however, boards of directors of publicly-owned corporations are smaller than those of private companies of comparable size. There is no significant difference between federal and provincial corporations in terms of the size of their boards, and both have the same average number of directors.

Nearly 80 per cent of the directors of the thirty-six corporations are outside directors. That is to say, they are not officers (president, vice-president, general manager) of the corporation on whose board they sit, and are affiliated with it only on a part-time basis, and have a principal occupation outside the corporation. The principal occupations of the outside directors of the thirty-six corporations were surveyed, and the detailed results of this survey are reported in appendix 6. Nearly half the outside directors are either businessmen who run their own businesses, or corporate lawyers, accountants or executives who sit on the boards of private companies. *Canadian capitalists* (non-Canadians are legally excluded from the boards of directors of crown corporations) *and their advisers and managers are the main professional group represented on the boards of directors of publicly-owned corporations.*

Nearly a quarter of the outside directors are government officials. Some corporations stipulate how many outside directors must come from within the government. Thus, the act establishing the Central Mortgage and Housing Corporation specifies that there must be eight outside directors, three of them from the civil service. The act establishing the Alberta Municipal Finance Corporation determines that there can be only one government official on its board. In the case of the Federal Business Development Bank, the board must include fourteen outside directors (out of fifteen members all told); four of these have to come from the civil service and the other ten from outside the civil service. In some instances elected officials are directors of publicly-owned corporations. For example cabinet ministers sit on the boards of a number of provincial corporations, including British Columbia Hydro, British Columbia Railway, Saskatchewan Telecommunications and the Saskatchewan Power Corporation. In general, there are more government officials on the boards of provincial corporations, especially under NDP governments.

Finally, roughly a quarter of the outside directors are from miscellaneous professional backgrounds: university professors, independent lawyers, farmers, managers of cooperatives, accountants, etc. There are even two trade union leaders among the 242 outside directors of the corporations on the list: W.C.Y. McGregor, vice-president of the Canadian Labour Congress, on the board of the Canada Development Corporation, and Louis Laberge, president of the Quebec Federation of Labour, on the board of the Caisse de Dépôt et de Placement du Québec.

These data are roughly consistent with Ashley and Smails' assertion that there are no workers on the boards of publicly-owned corporations in Canada and only a relatively small proportion of government officials. It is also clear that the largest group, the group of Canadian businessmen and their managers and advisers, represents all regions of the country and all varieties of business, and not just "monopoly" enterprises. The Canada Development Corporation is fairly typical in this respect. Six of the twenty-one ordinary directors, or 28.5 per cent, are French Canadian. Sixteen directors come from business, including the chairman of the board (who is also vice-chairman of the board of the Bank of Montreal) and the vice-chairman (Louis R. Desmarais, chairman of the board of Canada Steamship Lines). Among the Quebec capitalists on the board are Laurent Beaudoin (president of Bombardier), Philippe de Gaspé Beaubien (president of Télémédia) and R.B. Casgrain (president of Casgrain & Co.). The English-speaking businessmen include H.H. McCain of New Brunswick (chairman of the board of McCain Foods), F.H. Sherman (chief executive officer of Dofasco) and S. Maislin (executive vice-president of Maislin Transport).

The ten-member board of the Export Development Corporation includes five government officials; the other five directors are businessmen: A.H. Zimmerman, executive vice-president of Noranda Mines, A. K. Stuart, chief executive officer of The Electrolyser Corp., R. Lavoie, chief executive officer of the Crédit Foncier Franco-Canadien, and the presidents of two smaller companies.

There are only nine publicly-owned corporations whose outside directors do not include any businessmen, managers or corporate advisers: the Farm Credit Corporation, the Canada Deposit Insurance Corporation, Hydro-Quebec, Manitoba Hydro, Newfoundland Hydro, the Alberta Government Telephone Commission, Saskatchewan Telecommunications, the Manitoba Telephone System, the St. Lawrence Seaway Authority and the National Harbours Board. These are corporations whose functions consist of providing infrastructure and are essentially technical in nature. They are also the corporations with the smallest boards of directors (an average of five members). At the opposite extreme are corporations in which businessmen and their advisers form an absolute majority of the board of directors: the Bank of Canada, the Federal Business Development Bank, the Canada Development Corporation, Sidbec, Sysco, Canadian National, Air Canada, Eldorado Nuclear, New Brunswick Power and Teleglobe Canada (see appendix 6).

The situation of the 20 per cent of board members who are inside directors is quite different from that of the outside directors. Inside directors are full-time employees and generally hold their positions for a longer, although variable, span. Thus, Louis Rasminsky was governor of the Bank of Canada for twelve years (1961 to 1973), and Jean-Paul Gignac was president of Sidbec from 1966 to 1979. The members of the Canadian Dairy Commission, however, are removable at will.

Inside directors receive substantially higher pay than outside directors, who are paid only an honorarium for attending board meetings. Thus, the nine directors of the Central Mortgage and Housing Corporation received a total of $4,000 in 1975 for their attendance at board meetings, while four officers, two of whom were also on the board, received a total of $176,000.[32] The *Public Accounts of Canada* frequently contain information concerning the remuneration of the officers and directors of the major federal crown corporations. Here are a few examples for the year 1975-76:

- The Federal Business Development Bank: "As at March 31, 1976, the Bank had fourteen directors and nine senior officers. Remuneration of $27,875 was paid to the nine directors selected from outside the public service of Canada. Remuneration of $207,387 was paid to the senior officers. One senior officer is also a director."
- The Export Development Corporation: "In 1975 the aggregate remuneration paid by the Corporation to directors was $16,000 and to officers $316,000."
- Atomic Energy of Canada Ltd.: "The Company had 13 directors during the year, whose aggregate remuneration for the year as directors was $14,400 .... The company had 10 officers during the year, whose aggregate remuneration for the year as officers was $397,000 .... Two of the officers were also directors."
- The Canadian Broadcasting Corporation: "The aggregate remuneration paid by the Corporation during the year to its fifteen directors and three officers of whom one is also a director was $22,300 and $142,853 respectively."[33]

In these examples, the "officers who are also directors" are what have been referred to here as inside directors.

Where do these inside directors come from? An attempt was made to trace the career pattern of the principal officer/director of each of the thirty-six corporations on the list, and it was possible to find information concerning twenty-four of them. Of these twenty-four, nine were businessmen or corporate advisers, nine were career civil servants or elected officials, and six were career employees of the corporations they headed. Jean-Paul Gignac, chief executive officer of Sidbec from May 1966, is an example of the first type. He inherited the Moulin Albert Giguère in Shawinigan and managed it from 1951 to 1968, when it was sold to the Quebec General Investment Corporation. David Barrett, premier of British Columbia from 1972 to 1975 and also chairman and president of the B.C. Railway Company, is an example of the second type, the elected official. Gerald K. Bouey, governor of the Bank of Canada since 1973, started with the bank's research department in 1948; he became head of the research department in 1962 and deputy governor of the bank in 1969. He is an example of the officer/director whose career has been within the crown corporation.

Several conclusions can be drawn from the foregoing analysis of the boards of directors of the major publicly-owned corporations in Canada. First, since roughly half the members of these boards are Canadian businessmen or their legal, financial or other advisers, the results of this study are more consistent with Victor Cheprakov's explanation than with Eugene Varga's. *Private-sector capitalists play an essential role both as outside and as inside directors.* A quarter of the outside directors and a third of the inside directors are elected officials or career civil servants; this is the second most important group. Finally, a quarter of the outside directors come from miscellaneous backgrounds, mostly from the petty bourgeoisie.

Businessmen who sit on the boards of crown corporations as either inside or outside directors come from companies of all sizes. The heads of giant corporations sit on these boards alongside the owners of small and middle-sized personal and family businesses. This tends to invalidate the theory of state monopoly capitalism (as does the historical analysis in the next section); crown corporations in Canada, federal and provincial, are in no sense under the control of Canadian "monopoly capital."

Is it possible to speak of a state bourgeoisie? Whatever definition is used for this term, it seems that this is a limited group, closely tied to the private-sector Canadian bourgeoisie. Whether "state bourgeoisie" refers to all the inside directors and officers of publicly-owned corporations or whether the term is restricted to career public executives alone, it refers to only a few hundred people. Furthermore, some of these inside directors come from the Canadian bourgeoisie and all of them, without exception, are in close contact with members of the capitalist class. Through their effective control of publicly-owned corporations and through the remuneration they receive, the officer/directors are full members of the Canadian ruling class, of which they form a specific segment, the segment that administers "public" capital. The autonomy of this segment should not be exaggerated, however, at least not in the Canadian context, where, as will be shown in the next section, "public" capital serves as a crutch for Canadian private capital.

Crown Corporations in Historical Perspective

At the beginning of this chapter, theoretical arguments were provided against the explanations offered by the state monopoly capitalism school. A historical study of the emergence and development of federal and provincial crown corporations in Canada provides further evidence against these explanations, and helps confirm this chapter's hypothesis that crown corporations serve the Canadian private-sector bourgeoisie as a whole.

The theory of state monopoly capitalism explains the formation of publicly-owned corporations through the falling rate of profit, the devaluation of public capital and the pillage of the state by monopolies. It will be valuable to try to see if there are other explanations for the emergence of publicly-owned corporations in Canada.

In an in-depth study of publicly-owned sectors in Britain, Leonard Tivey identified a number of factors that contributed to the development of British government-owned corporations.[34] The economic factors he cited include:

(a) Many new industrial and service sectors had to be organized as monopolies to reach an acceptable level of efficiency. Electricity is a good example. The need for uniformity in rates and technical characteristics of the electrical system, the size of investments, electrification of rural and peripheral areas, and research costs are all reasons why a number of capitalist countries opted for public ownership of this sector.

(b) The ruin of some sectors of economic activity during the Depression forced governments to acknowledge the need for such agencies as central banks (many of which were founded during the 1930s) and agricultural marketing boards. In Canada, the Bank of Canada (founded in 1934) and the Canadian Wheat Board (1935) conform to this model.

Other writers have emphasized the fact that crown corporations in Canada tend to be concentrated in sectors of two kinds:

(a) High-risk sectors: Air Canada, for example, was established in 1937 after private transportation companies refused to set up a trans-Canada airline either by themselves or in partnership with the federal government. The private companies considered this a very risky investment.

(b) Low-return sectors: Canadian National was established in 1919 to manage railways that had gone bankrupt under private ownership.[35]

But when all these factors are accounted for, there is still much about the Canadian case that remains unexplained. In sectors such as the production of electricity, telephone service and regional transportation, public monopoly seems to be the most appropriate mode of exploitation, and yet the proportion of public ownership in these sectors varies widely from province to province. Thus, only Alberta, Saskatchewan and Manitoba have publicly-owned telephone systems. All provinces have publicly-owned electrical utilities, but there is a wide variation in the proportion of the market covered by the public sector.

The Depression affected all aspects of the economy of the western world. Why did public authorities concentrate on agricultural marketing and the monetary system in their regulatory activities? A number of low-return sectors, such as textiles, clothing and footwear, and high-risk ones, such as mining exploration, have remained in private hands. Finally, many publicly-owned corporations don't fall into any of the categories mentioned by the economists cited thus far, including the state monopoly capitalism school. For example, how should government-owned corporations whose purpose is to provide credit to small and middle-sized business (such as the Federal Business Development Bank) or farmers (the Farm Credit Corporation) be classified? And what of corporations whose purpose is to encourage entrepreneurship in Quebec (the General Investment Corporation) or in Canada (the Canada Development Corporation)? What about the many corporations that provide credit for housing purchase and construction (the Central Mortgage and Housing Corporation at the federal level, the Ontario Housing Corporation, the Manitoba Housing and Renewal Corporation, the Alberta Housing Corporation, and the Société d'Habitation du Québec)? How should the entry of both federal and provincial governments into *very highly profitable* sectors — the creation of Petro-Canada in 1975, Petro-Canada's purchase of Pacific Petroleum in 1978 or the purchase of Texasgulf by the CDC in 1973 — be explained? And the existence of provincially-owned industrial corporations such as Sidbec and Sysco still requires an explanation.

It would appear that the strictly economic explanations put forward by the state monopoly capitalism school and by academic economists seriously underestimate social and political factors. A large proportion of the government-owned corporations in Britain, France, Italy, Austria, the Scandinavian countries and elsewhere were created by labour, socialist or social-democratic governments, or by governments that included socialists and communists. The nationalization of the steel industry by a Labour government in Britain in 1951 or the deposit banks and Renault factories in France following the Liberation cannot be explained without taking social and political factors into account. In Canada, the NDP (ideologically similar to the British Labour Party) has set up a number of publicly-owned corporations in the three provinces where it has formed the government: Saskatchewan, Manitoba and British Columbia.

The remarkable thing about the Canadian case is the number of transitions to public ownership carried out by governments that were the political representatives of business — most often Liberal governments, but sometimes Conservative and even Social Credit administrations. If the development of state capitalism is to be explained "politically," there has to be more to the explanation than the influence of parties directly or indirectly representing the labouring classes.

It is the writer's view that there are three basic elements underlying the emergence and development of state capitalism in Canada. The first is class structure — the level of development, consciousness and organization of each class and each segment within each class, in Canada as a whole and within each province. Thus, no strictly economic explanation can satisfactorily account for the blossoming of government-owned corporations in Quebec in the 1960s: the Caisse de Dépôt et de Placement, General Investment Corporation, Société Québécoise d'Exploration Minière (SOQUEM), Société Québécoise d'Initiatives Pétrolières (SOQUIP), the growth of Hydro-Quebec, etc. The basic reason for this proliferation was the postwar formation of a francophone bourgeoisie and its accession to power in 1960 through the Liberal Party and the Quiet Revolution. The growth of this new class was examined in chapter 3.

In this case, state capitalism does not "serve the monopolies" as the state monopoly capitalism school would predict, but rather an emerging regional petty and middle bourgeoisie. Larry Pratt has vividly described a similar situation in Alberta. The provincial bourgeoisie that developed as a result of the postwar oil boom took control of the government with the accession of the Conservatives under Peter Lougheed in 1971, and it uses provincial crown corporations for its own extended reproduction. This regional bourgeoisie (and not a "state bourgeoisie") runs Alberta's government-owned corporations.[36]

Situations in which crown corporations are an instrument of a regional bourgeoisie are fairly common and extend beyond Quebec and Alberta, as is seen further on. But there are also other ways in which crown corporations are related to class structure. Some government-owned corporations assist small and middle-sized business. Under monopoly capitalism, farmers and small and middle-sized companies in the industrial sector are at a clear disadvantage, being unable to match the monopoly power of the commercial, industrial, financial and transportation giants. The farmers of western Canada struggled hard against Canadian Pacific with its monopoly of grain storage and transportation, the large Canadian chartered banks with their restrictive farm credit monopoly, and the farm machinery cartel.[37] These struggles resulted in the formation of farmers' unions such as the United Farmers of Alberta (1908), the Saskatchewan Grain Growers' Association (1907) and the United Farmers of Manitoba (1920). The movement also gave rise to periodicals such as the *Grain Growers' Guide* (1908), cooperative grain elevators, and, ultimately, political parties, including the Cooperative Commonwealth Federation (1932), the predecessor of the NDP.

The radicalization of Canada's farmers' movements during the Depression and their alliance with urban socialist parties was a significant factor leading to the creation in 1935 of the Canadian Wheat Board, which was intended to maintain social order in the countryside by paying western farmers a minimum price for their wheat. In 1944 a second crown corporation, the Farm Credit Corporation, was founded with the same goal. Today, an impressive number of federal and provincial corporations exist to compensate farmers for their limited market power in the face of monopoly capital. These include the Canadian Dairy Commission (1966), the Canadian Grain Commission and roughly eighty provincial agricultural marketing boards.[38] Here public funds are used to maintain social and political legitimacy and a certain level of economic activity and employment.

A second central element that must be taken into account in explaining publicly-owned corporations in Canada is regional disparity, or unequal development as it is sometimes called. The financial and geographic concentration of economic activity tends to benefit Ontario. With 36 per cent of Canada's population in 1976, Ontario realized 51 per cent of the country's sales in manufacturing,[39] and the process of concentration has been intensifying steadily for three quarters of a century. Head offices follow economic activity, and relocate to the favoured province.

Not surprisingly under these conditions, other provinces ask questions about their place in Confederation, and create crown corporations to stem the flow of savings, processing activities and centres of control towards Ontario. This is why Sidbec (1964) and Sysco (1967) were set up as provincial crown corporations to manufacture steel in Quebec and Nova Scotia respectively and thus break Ontario's near-monopoly in this vital industry. The topic of the steel industry is returned to later in this chapter. A similar process was at work in the thinly-veiled threat by William Bennett's Social Credit government in British Columbia to buy out MacMillan Bloedel in the face of takeover bids by Domtar and Canadian Pacific in 1978. "Provincialism" is not the effect of multinational corporations on the Canadian political system, as Kari Levitt and Garth Stevenson maintain,[40] but the reaction of the provinces against the process of geographic concentration of economic activity and control in Ontario. The development of provincial crown corporations has been part of this postwar attempt at self-defence.

The third and final element in the explanation of state capitalism in Canada is the belated and dependent nature of its industrial development. The creation of holding companies such as the Quebec General Investment Corporation and the Canada Development Corporation can only be explained by the high degree of foreign control of Canadian industry. The objective of increasing Canadian control is explicitly stated in Bill C-219, the legislation that established the CDC: "... a corporation that will help develop and maintain strong Canadian controlled and managed corporations in the private sector of the economy and will give Canadians greater opportunities to invest and participate in the economic development of Canada."[41]

It makes sense to create corporations to support entrepreneurship in Canada or in Quebec only if the bourgeoisie in question needs to be helped, in a situation where industrialization has been delayed and dependent. It is worth noting in passing that a number of government-owned corporations are, in contrast, concrete expressions of the dependency relationship between Canada and the United States. The St. Lawrence Seaway Authority, for example, is responsible for "constructing, maintaining and operating all such works as may be necessary to provide and maintain, either wholly in Canada or in conjunction with works undertaken by an appropriate authority in the United States, a deep waterway between the Port of Montreal and Lake Erie."[42] In other words, the authority is charged with providing the infrastructure required by north-south trade. Dependency also played an important role in the decision to nationalize the Canadian Northern and Grand Trunk, thus creating Canadian National; as a large borrower on the London market, Canada could not let the two railways, whose bonds had been sold in England, go bankrupt without affecting its own ability to obtain credit.

These three factors (class structure, unequal development, dependent-associate nature of the Canadian economy) cannot be considered in isolation, since they become intertwined in causal networks in which one or another of them assumes a dominant role. It will be useful to examine in more detail the role of regional bourgeoisies in the creation of the two largest provincial hydroelectric utilities: Ontario Hydro and Hydro-Quebec; the role of regional disparities in the creation of government-owned steel companies in Quebec (Sidbec) and Nova Scotia (Sysco); and the relationship between Canada's dependent economy and the strengthening of the Canadian bourgeoisie (Canada Development Corporation) and its French Canadian segment (Quebec General Investment Corporation). In each case, evidence will be presented that is unfavourable to the existence of a state bourgeoisie as an autonomous segment of the Canadian bourgeoisie. The crucial role of the private-sector bourgeoisie in conceiving, creating and running government-owned corporations at both the federal and the provincial levels will also be observed.

Hydroelectricity: The Consolidation of Regional Bourgeoisies

The Canadian constitution attributes jurisdiction over natural resources on crown lands (including waterfalls) to the provinces. As a consequence, companies producing electricity from hydraulic energy were provincially incorporated, and the crown corporations that dominate this sector today are provincially owned. The immensity of Canada's hydraulic resources places these provincial electrical utilities among the largest crown corporations in the country. On the list of the thirty-six largest publicly-owned enterprises in Canada, there are nine provincial hydroelectric utilities, led by Ontario Hydro and Hydro-Quebec. A look at the history of these two utilities shows that their origins were tied to the growth of regional bourgeoisies in Ontario and Quebec, in opposition to large-scale Canadian and American capital.

The first hydroelectric companies in Ontario made their appearance at the end of the nineteenth century. By 1906 there were four companies: (a) the Canadian Niagara Power Co., a subsidiary of an American company, the Niagara Falls Power Co.; it had a capacity of 50,000 horsepower (hp) and exported some of the energy it produced to the United States; (b) the Ontario Power Co., controlled by a group of Buffalo manufacturers, with a capacity of 30,000 hp; (c) the Electrical Development Company, founded in 1902 by a Canadian syndicate headed by Sir William Mackenzie (of the Canadian Northern), Sir Henry Pellatt and Frederick Nichols of Toronto, with a capacity of 37,000 hp in 1906; (d) the Hamilton Cataract Power Light & Traction Co., with a capacity of 16,000 hp.

In response to pressure from a movement that had grown up in a number of Ontario cities since 1902, the provincial government formed a crown corporation called the Hydro Electric Power Commission of Ontario (Ontario Hydro). The movement was headed by manufacturers in Toronto, London, Brantford, Stratford, Woodstock, Ingersoll, and Guelph, all centres where there was dissatisfaction with the growing monopolization of hydroelectric energy by the private companies. The movement's chief demand was that municipalities be enabled to form a pool of energy purchasers under the wing of the provincial government. Ontario Hydro was given a budget by the province, but it was also allowed to receive funds from municipalities. The new corporation was given the authority to acquire, exploit and manage electric companies and sources of electricity, and to transmit and distribute energy. The Conservative provincial government of the time named Adam Beck, a small manufacturer from London, to head Ontario Hydro, and Beck remained in charge of Hydro until his death in 1925. As a local manufacturer who advocated the decentralization of industry and whose interests were opposed to those of large-scale international capital, Beck was representative of the people who had pressed for the creation of Ontario Hydro.

The two major studies of the formation of Ontario Hydro leave little doubt about the class origins of the movement that created and ran the largest hydroelectric company in Canada. According to W.R. Plewman, small manufacturers in southern Ontario were the heart of the movement advocating public ownership of the electrical industry, which until then had been controlled by large Canadian and American companies.[43]

In his classic study, H.V. Nelles writes:

> Hydro made its deepest impression upon the businessmen and small manufacturers in the provincial towns. The thought of boundless cheap hydro-electricity inspired these men of property and industry with evangelical zeal .... From the outset the crusade for public power was a businessmen's movement; they initiated it, formed its devoted, hard-core membership and, most importantly, they provided it with brilliant leadership.[44]

During its first decade of existence, Ontario Hydro purchased electricity from private companies and transmitted it over its own lines for distribution to cities in southern Ontario. But it soon became clear that as Hydro grew it would have to take over producing companies and build new stations. It could no longer buy energy from companies that exported much of their production and had no more electricity to sell. Thus, Ontario Hydro purchased the share capital of the Ontario Power Co. for $22.7 million in August 1917 and increased Ontario Power's capacity from 180,000 to 220,000 hp in 1919. In 1920, it bought out the hydroelectric interests of William Mackenzie and his partners for $32.7 million.

Work on the Queenston-Chippewa hydroelectric plant was begun in 1917, and early in 1922 Hydro brought the new facility into production. With a capacity of 650,000 hp, it was the largest hydroelectric station in the world. Queenston-Chippewa also made Ontario Hydro the world's largest electrical utility and gave it a virtual monopoly of hydroelectric production in Ontario.

Meanwhile, Ontario Hydro had also bought some smaller stations and moved ahead with rural electrification, which assured it of support from the farmers' movement. By 1930 it was considered a profitable, solid enterprise and its continued existence was no longer an issue. Since then, its history has been marked by diversification and the construction and acquisition of new plants.

Support for public ownership was limited to the hydroelectric sector and a few other utilities. It is not surprising that this was as far as a movement led by local manufacturers and merchants went in favouring public ownership. The movement's success can be seen in Ontario's industrial growth, the geographical decentralization of its industry and the consolidation of the regional bourgeoisie.

In Quebec, the initiative for the conversion of hydroelectricity to public ownership came from the provincial government. The change was accomplished in two stages. The first occurred in 1944 when the government created Hydro-Quebec by purchasing Montreal Light, Heat & Power Consolidated, which produced and distributed electricity in the Montreal region. This stage was the work of the Liberal provincial government of Adélard Godbout (1939-44). However, in 1944 the Union Nationale was returned to office and it put a stop to the development of the publicly-owned sector for the next sixteen years. At best, Hydro-Quebec succeeded in maintaining its share of electrical production in the province.

But the return of the Quebec Liberals to power in 1960 set off the Quiet Revolution, and meanwhile, in British Columbia, Premier W.A. C. Bennett announced in August 1961 that the largest electrical production company in the province, the B.C. Electric Co., would become publicly owned. A debate began in Quebec over whether it was an opportune time to buy out the province's electrical production and distribution facilities. The Quebec Federation of Labour, the Confederation of National Trade Unions, and most of Quebec's regional chambers of commerce and municipalities quickly came out in favour of public ownership. But the provincial and Montreal district chambers, representing the largest capitalists in the province, came out against it.[45] The president of the provincial chamber was Claude P. Beaubien, vice-president of Alcan, the second largest producer of electricity in Quebec. While the impetus for public ownership did not come from the same quarters as in Ontario, the scenario and the players were the same — the regional petty and middle bourgeoisie with trade union support on one side, and Canadian and foreign big business on the other.

Four companies accounted for 85 per cent of Quebec's 1961 capacity of 13 million hp; Hydro-Quebec had 35 per cent, the Alcan group 27.5 per cent, the Shawinigan Water & Power group 16.5 per cent and Gatineau Power 5.6 per cent.[46] The provincial government's arguments for public ownership were primarily technical: that private companies failed to coordinate their investments, wasted water power, duplicated fixed costs, charged different rates in different regions, etc. The government called an election for November 1962 on the issue of public ownership and it won an absolute majority of the popular vote. By April 1963, it had acquired more than 50 per cent of Shawinigan, Gatineau Power and five other Canadian-controlled power companies.

In one of the most detailed studies of the public takeover of electricity in Quebec, Carol Jobin analyses the structure of the hydroelectric industry, the takeover of 1962-63 and its class content.[47] Unfortunately, he works within the conceptual framework of state monopoly capitalism, and as a result concludes that the transition to public ownership "objectively served the interest of the monopolies — especially the

American industrial monopolies" that were left untouched in the transition.[48] Jobin is aware of the artificial relationship between his theoretical framework and his data:

> The theoretical framework we have used — what there is of it — is the theory of "state monopoly capitalism." The reader of this work will realize that the theory is not really integrated into it but rather "plastered" onto certain key points in the argument .... The applicability of the model to the case of Quebec can be questioned, and with some justice. Nevertheless, it was established to our satisfaction that the model systematizes the available information on public ownership in such a way that its theoretical advances can be proved. In other words, the body did not reject the graft.[49]

Jobin's error consists in analysing the public takeover of electricity in isolation, without relating it to the whole context of the Quiet Revolution, in which other companies were taken over by the government and new government-owned corporations were created. Had he done so, he might have concluded that the purpose of restructuring the government apparatus was to consolidate and strengthen the emerging regional francophone bourgeoisie. If American interests were not bought out, it is because this class was still too weak to attack American multinationals and preferred to make its economic gains at the expense of its English Canadian rival, whose interests were, in fact, taken over.

The deeper meaning of the public takeover of electricity was understood by the new president of Hydro-Quebec appointed by the Liberal government, Jean-Claude Lessard. Speaking of the "peaceful revolution taking place in Quebec," he told *La Presse* that "signs of the revolution are visible in the expansion of the hydroelectric sector, in the financial aid being provided for the development of French Canadian industries and in the educational reforms taking place at all levels, and especially in technical education."[50]

Both in Ontario and in Quebec, the move to public ownership of electricity was part of the rise and consolidation of a regional bourgeoisie, in opposition to large-scale Canadian and/or American capital. In the case of Quebec, it was the government that took the initiative in the context of a whole series of significant reforms and public takeovers. The Quebec bourgeoisie developed later than its Ontario counterpart, and therefore had a greater need for government support. It is also much more accommodating towards foreign capital; having challenged the indigenous Canadian bourgeoisie, it is careful not to antagonize the comprador bourgeoisie at the same time.

Unequal Development: Sidbec and Sysco

When John A Macdonald introduced the National Policy in 1879, the primary iron and steel industry was in its infancy in Canada. The only company of any size was located in Londonderry, Nova Scotia. A number of factors contributed to the industry's late development: trade policy (oriented towards supplying Britain before 1846 and towards the United States under the Reciprocity Treaty between 1854 and 1864), technical obstacles (the Canadian subsoil had not been explored, and the country had little experience in mining), the lack of adequate means of transporting coal, iron ore and limestone, the scarcity of manpower and capital, a limited domestic market and formidable foreign competition.

During the nineteenth century, Nova Scotia cornered almost the entire Canadian primary steel industry. It had abundant supplies of the three key raw materials needed to produce pig iron and steel: iron ore, coal and limestone. Ontario at that time had the best iron ore deposits in Canada but, like Quebec, it lacked coal and had to import it. The West had all the necessary resources but not the markets. Moreover, its resources were controlled by central Canadian companies.[51]

Between 1897 and 1917, the face of the Canadian steel industry changed completely. In the first place, the industry's growth was explosive. Production of pig iron increased from 97,000 short tons in 1900 to 1.2 million short tons in 1918; steel production increased from 26,000 to 1.8 million short tons in the same period.[52] Second, the industry relocated to Ontario. By 1911, after fifteen years of growth, Ontario had 58 per cent of Canada's pig iron production capacity; Nova Scotia was in second place with 40 per cent and Quebec's capacity was insignificant. Third, there was a movement towards economic concentration between 1899 and 1911.

In 1898 the Dominion Coal Co., which was controlled by Boston financiers (including Henry Whitney, the American steel baron), formed an iron and steel producing subsidiary, the Dominion Iron & Steel Co. The idea was to absorb Dominion Coal's production of coke, which could no longer penetrate the American market because of new tariffs established in 1897. With the help of an $8 million federal subsidy, the company built its mills at Sydney. In 1902 the two companies were sold to Montreal interests, and in 1910 they were merged to form the first Canadian steel giant, the Dominion Steel Co. (Dosco).

Algoma Steel was a result of the growth of an Ontario conglomerate run by an American notary, Francis H. Clergue, who had the support of the provincial government. Algoma was established in 1902 and came under Canadian control in 1909; it immediately became the second largest Canadian iron and steel producer.

Max Aitken, later Lord Beaverbrook, merged five Montreal and Hamilton companies in 1910 to form Stelco. The new company remained under Canadian control.

The newest of the major Canadian iron and steel companies operating today is Dofasco (Dominion Foundries and Steel Co.). Founded in 1917, it was also the result of a merger and was controlled by an American family, the Shermans. Since the First World War, the Canadian steel industry has been an oligopoly of three firms. In 1925, the three dominant companies were Besco (the British Empire Steel Corp., the result of a merger between Dosco and other Nova Scotia firms), Algoma and Stelco. That year Besco had 49 per cent of the daily pig iron production capacity in Canada, Algoma had 30 per cent and Stelco, 14 per cent. In 1940 the proportions were 40 per cent for Algoma, 30 per cent for Dosco and 21 per cent for Stelco.[53] Steel production shows a similar concentration: in 1955 Stelco had 44 per cent of Canada's steel production capacity, Algoma 25 per cent, Dofasco 15 per cent and Dosco (continuing its decline) 14 per cent.[54] In 1974 the proportions were 39 per cent for Stelco, 20 per cent for Dofasco and 18 per cent for Algoma.[55]

Geographical concentration has also remained more or less constant. In 1925, 66 per cent of Canada's pig iron was produced in Ontario and the rest in Nova Scotia. These proportions were the same for 1940. In 1965, just after Sidbec was established, Ontario accounted for 77 per cent of the jobs in the industry and 85 per cent of the value-added.

Quebec entered the postwar era almost completely without a steel industry. As a result of two important developments, however, it became possible to establish a publicly-owned, integrated iron and steel company. The first development was the discovery of large iron ore deposits in Quebec and Labrador during the Second World War. Exploitation of these reserves by a number of American companies — Iron Ore Co. of Canada, Quebec Cartier Mining, Wabush Mines and Hilton Mines — began during the early 1950s. Quebec became the leading province in iron ore production, but it still didn't have a steel industry.[56] The second development was the growing use of electric and oxygen furnaces in steel production. In 1963, these new methods accounted for 10 and 8 per cent of American steel production respectively, and the percentages were increasing rapidly. Quebec's lack of coal was no longer an obstacle to the establishment of a steel industry.

The Quebec market had been identified and was expanding rapidly. As early as 1958, Belgian financiers had looked into the possibility of setting up a steel mill in Quebec. However, the economic dislocation that followed the independence of Belgium's African colonies in 1960 led to the postponement of the project. In 1961, the Quebec government took up the idea, and asked the Conseil d'Orientation Economique du Québec (COEQ) to investigate the province's industrial demand for steel. The findings of the investigation were conclusive: there was a steel shortage, and industrial consumers were forced to pay high transportation costs and customs duties for imported steel. In addition, neither Canadian nor foreign suppliers could meet the demand and there were long waiting lists — often customers were obliged to wait several months. The construction industry, the largest consumer of steel, was particularly interested in seeing a steel industry developed in Quebec.[57]

COEQ was created in February 1961 by the government, and was administered by members of the Chambre de Commerce de la Province de Québec. René Paré, president of the Chambre de Commerce, was also chairman of COEQ. The premier of Quebec responded to COEQ's report on the steel industry on September 1, 1961, by announcing the formation of an investment corporation, among whose objectives would be to create an integrated steel industry in Quebec. The investment corporation was to be under joint public-private ownership, with the government subscribing a minority of its share capital, the remainder to be held by the public, Canadian financial institutions and foreign investors.[58]

It was 1964 before a start was made on setting up the steel company itself. The government formed a committee on the steel industry early in 1962. The committee repeated the COEQ study, drew up plans and submitted its report two and a half years later. The report reached the same conclusion as the COEQ study — the absence of this key economic sector had to be remedied by establishing an integrated steel industry in Quebec.

The Sidbec Charter was drawn up in November 1964 and Sidbec was incorporated under part one of the Companies Act. *It was not a government-owned corporation;* rather, it was intended to be owned jointly by the government and private interests, with the government's share being sold to private investors once it became profitable. Its first board of directors was composed exclusively of Quebec businessmen: René Paré (by now president of the Quebec General Investment Corporation), Gérard Plourde (chief executive officer of UAP Inc.), Pierre Gendron (president of Dow Breweries), Peter N. Thomson (Power Corp.'s president and largest shareholder), and Gérard Filion (general manager of the GIC). Filion was president for the first two years, and there was close coordination with the GIC, which was to be the government's vehicle for investing in Sidbec. Meanwhile, a number of projects were studied, but none of them took shape. In May 1966 Jean-Paul Gignac replaced Filion as president of Sidbec. It is noteworthy that in a letter to

Premier Jean Lesage, Filion reiterated his belief that Sidbec should be a joint public-private corporation:

> After a year of studies, work, visits and consultations, I am convinced that Sidbec cannot succeed without the full support of the government and without the financial, technical and commercial backing of the private sector. Even with both of these, a double measure of work and energy will be needed. A wholly publicly-owned steel industry makes no sense in North America, unless Quebec is moving towards becoming a separate state with its own borders and customs duties. A wholly privately-owned steel industry will not be possible for a generation of more — Dosco's attempt bears witness to that. Only a joint effort by the government and private capital can lead to the project's success . . . . I might also mention Mr. Kierans' most recent sally, threatening public ownership if the Americans don't lend us the money we need. In a psychological and political climate such as this, in the face of the hostility of one part of the government, the indifference of the other part and the suspicion of private capital, building Sidbec is becoming impossible.[59]

Sidbec would probably never have seen the light of day if it had not been saved by an external circumstance. In 1965, Dominion Steel & Coal (Dosco) began building a rolling mill at Contrecoeur to process the steel produced at its Sydney, Nova Scotia mill. Dosco also began losing money in 1965, and its British parent, Hawker Siddeley, wanted to dispose of it. In 1966 Dosco sold its iron mines in Newfoundland to the government of that province and a hydroelectric subsidiary to the Nova Scotia Power Commission. In 1967 it sold all its steel interests in Nova Scotia to the province's government, which in turn created the Sydney Steel Corp. (Sysco). In March 1968, its Cape Breton coal mines were turned over to the federal government, which established the Cape Breton Development Corporation.

Negotiations with Sidbec for the eventual purchase of its Quebec assets began in December 1966 and continued until December 1967. Dosco offered Sidbec its mills at Contrecoeur (sheet and bar rolling mills), Montreal (finished products and two small rolling mills), La Salle (finished products) and Toronto (wire). Quebec was not buying an integrated steel mill, but it was getting the most profitable components of a steel mill, and the parts most likely to bring Quebec the secondary industry it wanted. Sidbec's president Gignac saw enormous advantages in the purchase of Dosco: Sidbec would be getting a market, a long-term debt at advantageous rates, a financial structure and a skilled labour force; an eventual competitor would disappear; and the price was reasonable.[60]

During the debate on the subject in the Quebec Legislative Assembly, Premier Daniel Johnson confirmed that the government still wanted to keep its options open as far as Sidbec's corporate structure was concerned, and didn't exclude the possibility of participation by Canadian steel companies in its share capital. It was the board of directors under Gignac's leadership that finally brought matters to a head in 1968 by coming out in favour of public ownership.[61] The legislature voted to grant Sidbec the money it requested and Sidbec's charter was amended in July 1968. In November and December of the same year Sidbec became an operating company by taking control of Dosco, to which it sold back the assets it didn't want. In its corporate structure, Sidbec was made a corporation wholly owned by the government, but not a crown corporation.

Sidbec launched phase one of its expansion in 1969 with the help of the financing obtained from the government the previous year. During this phase it built an electric steel mill at Contrecoeur and installed a small electric furnace in its Montreal plant. In 1974, Sidbec's chief executive officer again appeared before the legislature to obtain the funds needed for phase two of its expansion. During this second phase, Sidbec aimed to improve its financial structure by reducing the share of its capitalization accounted for by long-term debt and to exploit the iron ore deposits of northern Quebec by opening a mine and building ore concentration plants at Gagnon and Port Cartier.[62]

This upstream integration was completed with the opening of the Fire Lake mines in 1977, and in November 1978 Sidbec submitted plans for phase three to the cabinet in Quebec City.[63] The goal of this phase was to overhaul the company's installations so as to make it more competitive.

A number of conclusions can be drawn about Sidbec. It was first conceived by the businessmen who made up the Conseil d'Orientation Economique du Québec and was established to combat the geographical concentration of the steel industry in Ontario. It was run from the start by Quebec businessmen, and its initial charter and capitalization reflected its intention to be a joint public-private company. It was only when private capital's lack of interest in the project became clear and deficits began to accumulate that the government had to take full responsibility for it, although its management was still left to Quebec businessmen. Successive premiers repeated their intention to involve private companies in Sidbec, while Jean-Paul Gignac said that it would be turned over to private interests as soon as it became profitable.[64] Meanwhile, Sidbec has been slow in gaining control of the Quebec market. While in 1974 its market share was 30 per cent, in 1976 it was only 18 per cent. By Canadian standards it is a marginal company, well behind the three steel giants; its share of Canadian raw steel production capacity in 1974 was only 6 per cent.[65] In 1975, a majority of its board of directors continued to be businessmen. They included René Paré, A.C. de Léry, H. Marceau, J.H. Stevens and C.F. Carsley.

In terms of the original question posed, it can be said that Sidbec does not serve Canadian monopoly capital and is not run by a state bourgeoisie. It is rather one of the instruments of the Quebec bourgeoisie, which conceived it and runs it for its own benefit. It has been developed under public ownership mainly because Canada's regional disparities prevent a primary steel industry in Quebec from being very profitable or very attractive to private capital.

Sydney Steel Corp. (Sysco) was created in late 1967 by the Nova Scotia government to take over the Dosco steel mill in the province. At the same time, the federal government took over Dominion Coal, Dosco's Cape Breton coal-mining subsidiary, and created another publicly-owned corporation, the Cape Breton Development Corp. (Devco). For Hawker Siddeley, the British parent company, it meant divesting itself of two money-losing subsidiaries; Dosco lost $1,923,333 in 1966, not counting the losses posted by Dominion Coal. The Sydney mills dated from the late nineteenth century, and were the oldest in Canada. They used Cape Breton coal to produce roughly a million tons of steel in the form of rails (25 per cent of production), ingots, bars, nails, bolts, etc. Some of the ingots were sent to Quebec for further processing closer to consumer markets. Dosco had a more serious problem than its aged mills. The main difficulty affecting the Sydney plant was its distance from its markets, Toronto and Montreal in particular. In October 1967, at the time Dosco announced the closure of its Sydney mill, a special study of the mill by Nova Scotia's Voluntary Planning Board in conjunction with the Atlantic Development Board concluded that the location of its blast furnaces was a fatal handicap for the company.[66]

The study recommended against modernization of the mills for the same reason — the markets for steel had moved west. But Premier G.I. Smith's Conservative government, aware that the very existence of the town of Sydney depended on the steel mill and its payroll of 3,200 employees, bought the mill in late 1967 for $14.3 million. The government appointed a Nova Scotia businessman, Robert B. Cameron, president of Maritime Steel & Foundries, to head Sysco. The government promised to keep the mill open at least until April 30, 1969, a year after Dosco's closing date. The cost of modernization was estimated at $60 million spread over five years.

In the first three years the company achieved remarkable results.

Output increased from 671,000 tons in 1967 to 1,000,000 in 1970, and the company even showed a profit. The steel market was expanding and Sysco was able to export part of its output. In addition, Sidbec had not yet completed its mill and was still buying ingots from Sysco. But even in this period of expansion, experts continued to express doubts about the mill's profitability.[67]

Because of the mill's handicap with respect to central Canadian steel producers, Sysco's management tried to redirect its sales efforts towards export markets. The chairman of the board said in July 1970 that in three or four years Sysco would export 70 per cent of its output, compared with 15 per cent in 1969. The modernization plan included increasing specialization in rails and semi-finished products but no growth in production capacity.[68]

But the Sysco miracle ended in 1971. That year Devco, the federal coal-mining corporation that supplied Sysco with 80 per cent of its coke, was unable to provide the amount of coke contracted for. Sysco had to buy more expensive European coal, and this adversely affected its profitability. Output fell from one million tons in 1971 to 850,000 in 1972. Sidbec drastically cut back its purchases of steel from Sysco and exports didn't grow as forecast. With the world steel industry in crisis, Sysco's situation deteriorated. The mill continued to operate at 70 per cent of capacity, and losses increased from $11 million for the fiscal year ending in March 1975 to $46 million for 1976.[69]

In conclusion, Sysco has been unprofitable not because of the falling rate of profit, as the theory of state monopoly capitalism would predict, but because of its unfavourable geographical situation, which makes any attempt at modernization risky. The government bought the mill from Hawker Siddeley not "to play monopoly capital's game," but to save 3,200 jobs in Sydney when the company was prepared to close the mill and abandon it. It is hard to say what role strictly political considerations (jobs are a highly political question in the Canadian hinterland) or economic interests in the province (since local industries bought steel from Dosco) played in the government's purchase of the mill. It is clear however, that local businessmen were entrusted with the management of Sysco, and since 1967 they have formed an absolute majority of the board of directors. There are also a few senior government officials on the board.

Sidbec and Sysco have characteristics in common. Both steel mills are at a geographical disadvantage. Sidbec has new installations and Sysco has very old ones, but both companies are publicly-owned because private capital won't take the risk of investing in peripheral steel mills. Both are managed by regional private-sector bourgeoisies that were prepared to take them over if they ever became profitable. Here, as elsewhere, public capital serves private capital.

Serving a Weak Bourgeoisie: the GIC and the CDC

For late-blooming bourgeoisies, government-owned corporations have
served as an instrument of domestic capital accumulation, allowing
them to compete with companies in other countries. One example is the
Istituto per la Ricostruzione Industriale (IRI), set up in Italy in 1933 as a holding
company to take control of two of the country's three major private
banks, half its iron and steel production, two thirds of its telephone
service, four fifths of its naval construction, one sixth of its engineering
industries, etc.[70] S. Abranches has written: "The double role of the IRI
was consolidated in the contact between executives of the Italian state-
owned enterprise and private businessmen on the boards of directors of
large corporations; on the one hand, the IRI was an instrument of state
intervention, and on the other hand, it was an access channel for large
industrial and financial groups to the decision-making centres of the
government."[71]

Through such public holding companies, government revenues become public capital under private control and eventually fall under
private ownership. These public holding companies have a number of
advantages over their private counterparts — easier access to a vast
reservoir of funds (the state treasury) which they can use even to
sustain a loss, the authority that government participation confers, and
the possibility of integrating their projects with those of other government-owned corporations and the public sector as a whole.

In Quebec, the idea of launching a business development bank with
provincial government participation was first suggested at the 1955
annual convention of the provincial Chamber of Commerce. After the
convention, the chamber's economic orientation commission set up a
subcommittee whose members included chamber president Fridolin
Simard, Jacques Melançon and François-Albert Angers.[72] Premier
Duplessis rejected the idea, but the chamber revived it after the Lesage
Liberal government took office. In February 1961 the Conseil
d'Orientation Economique du Québec was created as a public body with
essentially the same membership as the chamber's economic orientation
commission. A few months later COEQ proposed that a business
development bank be set up with government participation.[73] Premier
Lesage announced its creation on September 1, 1961, and on July 6,
1962, a provincial act established the General Investment Corporation
(Société Générale de Financement).

The new institution differed both from existing holding companies
and from banks (such as the Industrial Development Bank) devoted to
providing credit to small and middle-sized business. The GIC was
authorized to take over existing companies, to participate in companies'
share capital without taking control, and to buy corporate bonds or

debentures. This set it apart from holding companies, which do not make industrial loans or participate in the share capital of corporations they don't control. It is also set apart from the Industrial Development Bank, which at the time did not participate in the share capital of companies. The GIC could also start new companies from scratch, and was geared not towards small business but towards middle-sized companies that had already issued securities.

The GIC's capital structure not only ensured that private businessmen would control it but also made it inevitable that the government would not realize a profit on its investment of public funds. From 1962 to 1972 the GIC was a joint private-public corporation, but the government could appoint only a quarter of its directors, regardless of the percentage of GIC shares it owned. A quarter were to come from the cooperative sector and half from the business community. As it turned out, the directors appointed by the provincial government were also businessmen so that private enterprise had a majority on the board. In addition, the shares the government took for itself carried a deferred dividend, which was never paid; meanwhile, the other common shares of the GIC paid dividends between 1965 and 1970.

The provincial government was initially a minority stockholder in the GIC and later became the majority stockholder, although until 1972 there was still private participation in its ownership. The size of the board was increased from twelve to sixteen directors in 1966, but the government still only appointed a quarter of them. René Paré was president of the GIC, and he surrounded himself with a number of businessmen, including Anson McKim, A. Ludger Simard and R. Lavoie and Gérard Filion, who was vice-president and general manager. In 1972, after ten years of operation as a joint private-public corporation, the GIC had acquired an interest in the following Quebec companies:

1963: Forano
      Volcano
1964: Compagnie de Fabrication
      de Meubles
      David Lord Ltée
      LaSalle Tricot Ltée
      Montel (electrical
      equipment factory)
1965: Marine Industries

1966: Maki Corporation
      Valcartier Industries Ltd.
1967: Donohue Ltée
1968: Bonnex Inc.
      Albert Gigaire Ltée
1969: Stuart Biscuits Ltd.
1971: Centre Educatif et
      Culturel Cégélec[74]

A number of these companies were sold when the GIC was transformed into a wholly government-owned corporation in late 1972. The GIC also set up four new companies: the Société de Montage Automobile (SOMA), which assembled Renaults and Peugeots between 1965 and 1972, CEGEDEC (a porcelain insulator manufacturer), Sogefor (a fibreboard manufacturer), and Les Engrais du St-Laurent (fertilizer).

As of the end of its 1971 financial year, the GIC's policy had clearly been to invest most of its money in corporate shares; 74 per cent of its assets were in the form of long-term investments in its nineteen subsidiaries. Only 14 per cent of its assets were in other forms of industrial finance, and all of these investments were in the bonds or debentures of its subsidiaries. This investment policy made the GIC look more like a holding company than a business development bank. But while the GIC *participated in the control* of its subsidiaries, it didn't hold effective control of them. Only two or three GIC directors were on the boards of its subsidiaries, and they didn't hold the key positions. Nor did the GIC dictate the development policies of the companies in which it held stock.

The poor profit performance of GIC-controlled companies led to public ownership of the GIC in 1972. As a result of the losses sustained by a number of subsidiaries and the halt in dividend payments in 1970, the provincial Department of Industry and Commerce formed a committee headed by Robert DeCoster that same year. The committee's report was submitted in 1972 and was not made public, but essentially it recommended that the GIC should be made publicly-owned, its investments concentrated in a smaller number of companies (which would still be of intermediate size) and its board reduced from sixteen directors to seven.[75] In December 1972, the GIC's charter was amended to put these recommendations into effect. Yvon Simard, president of Gold Star Sales, was named president of the GIC in November 1972. René Paré, R. Lavoie (of the Crédit Foncier), M. Latraverse (president of Corpex), Y. Graton (president of UAP Inc.), G. Godbout (president of Valcartier Industries), P. Pariseau (general manager of the Coopérative Agricole de Granby) and J.H. Dinsmore (assistant deputy minister of industry and commerce) filled out the new board.

As a government-owned corporation, the GIC divested itself of a number of its subsidiaries. It lost money in 1973, made profits for three successive years between 1974 and 1976, and then sustained losses again in 1977 and 1978. In 1978 it underwent the most serious crisis in its history. Marine Industries had built six multipurpose vessels for a Greek shipowner who had ordered them in 1973 and withdrew the order in 1977. The ships had cost $135 million and the collapse of the world shipbuilding market made it impossible for Marine to find another buyer. In December 1978 the National Assembly increased the GIC's share capital from $140.9 million to $200 million to save Marine from bankruptcy and convert it exclusively into a builder of railway cars and hydroelectric equipment. Marine was already active in these areas and was making a profit in them, while its shipbuilding division had been losing money for ten years.[76]

This new crisis is a good illustration of how the Quebec bourgeoisie uses the GIC. On the one hand, some of the companies it has sold to the government have been "money-losers" that even public funds have not been able to turn around. Marine Industries (Simard family) and Albert Gigaire Ltée (Jean-Paul Gignac and family) are cases in point. On the other hand, control of these companies has remained essentially in the hands of their former owners. The Simards still ran Marine Industries even after the majority block of shares had been sold to the government, and P.M. Forand remained president of Forano after the government acquired its share capital. Under these circumstances, the GIC — which is also managed by private-sector businessmen — looks more like a salvage operation for companies in trouble than a public economic development agency. It has served not "monopoly capital," but the middle sectors of Quebec business. It has not created a group of public-sector executives, a state bourgeoisie; Quebec businessmen have taken turns serving on its board of directors.

The Canada Development Corporation appeared on the scene in 1971, nine years after its Quebec counterpart, but Canadian business-men had been advocating its creation for a long time. In 1956 Gordon R. Ball, then president of the Bank of Montreal, proposed the creation of a financial institution to reduce Canada's dependence on foreign capital in a statement before the Royal Commission on Canada's Economic Pros-pects.[77] The Commission, headed by Walter Gordon, adopted the idea. Gordon, a Toronto businessman and nationalist spokesman within the Canadian bourgeoisie, is himself the major stockholder and chairman of a holding company he founded after the Second World War, Canadian Corporate Management.

In 1963, when Gordon became minister of finance in the Pearson government, he revived Ball's idea. He promoted it within the cabinet between 1963 and 1965, but without success.[78] The next initiative was taken by the Watkins task force on foreign ownership and the structure of Canadian industry, which recommended the creation of the Canada Development Corporation to strengthen Canadian business in the face of increasing foreign control of the Canadian economy.[79] Watkins pointed to similar corporations established in other countries, especially the Industrial Reorganization Corporation in Britain, set up by the Labour government in 1966 (and dismantled by the Conservatives in 1971).

In the spring of 1970, the proposal to set up the CDC reappeared with renewed vigour. According to the *Financial Post*, the revival of the project by the Trudeau cabinet was not unrelated to the attempt by foreign interests to take over Denison Mines (an attempt that was blocked by the federal government). At the same time a cabinet minister, Herb Gray, was given the responsibility of studying foreign direct investment in Canada and making recommendations to the government. Like the GIC, the CDC would be entrusted to Canadian capitalists and would be free from government intervention (although it would have access to public funds). The *Financial Post* reported:

> Finance Minister Edgar Benson is confident he can enlist a blue-ribbon board from the financial community that will be completely free from federal persuasion and, as important, will be able to convince shareholders of this.... Although the federal government will put up most of the money to get the corporation going ... it is unlikely there will be more than one or two government representatives on the board of directors.[80]

The Canada Development Corporation was created in 1971 by a special act of Parliament. It is not a crown corporation and thus is not responsible to the government. The government holds a majority of its shares, but they are to be gradually transferred to "the public." There are only two government officials on its twenty-two-member board of directors (at the end of 1975 they were the deputy ministers of finance and industry, trade and commerce); the other twenty directors are businessmen representing all regions of Canada. These include Louis R. Desmarais of Canada Steamship Lines (vice-chairman of the board of the CDC), Laurent Beaudoin of Bombardier, R.B. Casgrain of Casgrain & Co., H.H. McCain of McCain Foods, F.H. Sherman of Dofasco, J.E.P. Gallagher of Dome Petroleum and S. Maislin of Maislin Transport.

In its first years of existence the CDC acquired some sixty companies. The board of directors identified six priority sectors in which Canadian ownership was low: oil and gas, petrochemicals, mining, pharmaceutical products, pipelines and risk capital investment. In the first sector it bought CDC Oil & Gas in 1975; in the second it took over Polysar and its subsidiary Petrosar from the federal government; in the third, it bought Texasgulf from its American owners in 1973; in the fourth it purchased Connlab Holdings; and in the fifth it invested in Canadian Arctic Gas Pipeline.[81]

The CDC is about ten times as large as the General Investment Corporation. If the assets of its subsidiaries were consolidated with those of the parent corporation, the CDC's holdings would amount to about $2 billion for the end of 1975, as compared to $276 million for the GIC. Unlike the GIC, the CDC has entered profitable sectors. Its largest subsidiary is Texasgulf, which has paid dividends to the CDC continuously since 1973. Another difference is that the CDC specialized in a few sectors from the beginning, while the GIC did so only after it became publicly-owned in 1972. Finally, the CDC has repatriated a number of foreign-owned companies, notably Texasgulf, while the GIC has served as an escape hatch for the francophone bourgeoisie of Quebec. But each in its fashion has served to strengthen the Canadian bourgeoisie.

The Liberals, the Conservatives and Federally-owned Corporations

The Liberal Party has been in power in Ottawa with only brief interruptions for the last forty years, but its attitude towards public enterprise has not been constant. Tables 2 and 3 show that the federal government established a substantial number of publicly-owned corporations during the Second World War. Although the Liberals remained in office, these gradually dwindled after the war. In the next chapter it is seen that there was a rebirth of nationalism in the Liberal Party in the late Sixties. Between 1967 and 1978 the Liberals brought in a considerable body of legislation favouring Canadian ownership, and a number of publicly-owned corporations were established or developed in the same period. After 1974, the pace of nationalization seemed to quicken, with the federal government's purchase of De Havilland and Canadair, the establishment of Petro-Canada in 1975 and Petro-Canada's absorption of Atlantic Richfield Canada in 1976 and Pacific Petroleum in 1978.

After the 1979 election, the new Conservative government reversed the Liberals' course, at least to some extent. In September 1979, Treasury Board President Sinclair Stevens confirmed that the government intended to sell at least four of the most profitable companies it owned: Canadair, De Havilland, Eldorado Nuclear and the Northern Transportation Company. The government had bought Canadair, the Montreal aircraft manufacturer, from General Dynamics in 1976, when it was sustaining substantial losses. In three years it had become profitable. Canadair has assets of $247 million and is the largest aircraft manufacturer under Canadian control. De Havilland of Toronto, purchased in 1974 from its British owner, Hawker Siddeley, has assets of $185 million; it too became profitable under federal control. Eldorado Nuclear is a mining company acquired in 1942 for military reasons; it has assets of $320 million and has always been highly profitable. The Northern Transportation Company, a subsidiary of Eldorado Nuclear, was acquired at the same time as its parent. It has holdings of $59 million and sustained a small loss in 1978.

The Conservatives also promised to return Petro-Canada, or at least its profitable components, to private enterprise, following the recommendations of a working group set up by the government. The subsequent defeat of the Conservatives is at least partly attributable to the opposition of the Liberals and New Democrats to this proposal. The Liberals were also supported in their opposition to the dismantling of Petro-Canada by eastern Canadian businessmen and by the Canadian Federation of Independent Business, a newly-formed lobby.

As a group, small and middle-sized business is afraid of rising prices and the oil multinationals' discriminatory tactics against independent retailers and small consumers.[82] Again, a publicly-owned corporation appears to be a bulwark of small business against an oligopoly of large companies in a highly concentrated industry. Again, reality bears little resemblance to the model suggested by the theory of state monopoly capitalism, according to which the state always serves the monopolies and buys up unprofitable sectors. Again, the Liberals appear to represent smaller business which, with the help of a publicly-owned enterprise, wants to break down the barriers in a market where there are high profits but very little competition.

Nor was the sale of crown corporation by the Conservatives going to stop there. Nordair, purchased by the Liberal government through Air Canada in January 1979, was to find a new private owner, and there was even talk of selling the Central Mortgage and Housing Corporation, in whole or in part. One might speculate about whether the Conservative government would have chosen Canadian or international buyers for these corporations, and what forces would have come into play in the process of "privatization." It can be presumed, however, that the Canadian establishment would have received the lion's share, and small and middle-sized companies would have been the fiercest opponents of denationalization.*

---

*The return of the federal Liberals to office in 1980 put an end to the Conservatives' privatization drive. More important, new policies aimed at accelerating the Canadianization of the economy were not long in coming.

The National Energy Policy was introduced in October 1980 to bring about the takeover of foreign subsidiaries by Canadian interests. In March 1981, Petro-Canada purchased Petrofina Canada, the Canadian subsidiary of the Belgian multinational. Dome Petroleum increased its Canadian ownership, and took over Hudson's Bay Oil and Gas from American interests in June 1981. Meanwhile, several smaller oil companies were sold to Canadian interests; most important among these was Candel Oil, bought by Power Corp. in April 1981 for almost $600 million. Other larger oil companies — such as Gulf Canada, Texaco Canada, Amoco Canada and Suncor — seemed likely to sell their holdings to Canadian corporations.

The oil and gas policy of the federal government is thus another element in the nationalist program adopted by the Liberal Party in the 1970s and designed to reduce foreign control of the economy.

Conclusion

From the theoretical discussion at the beginning of this chapter, one can conclude that while Marxist analysis has established the existence of state capitalism, it has not succeeded in pinpointing or defining the phenomenon or in explaining its appearance and development. A definition of state capitalism was adopted according to which it applies only to publicly-owned enterprises, and not to the bureaucratic apparatus of the state as such. A healthy distance was established from both the Eurocommunist school of state monopoly capitalism and Baran and Sweezy's idea that the whole concept of state capitalism should be laid aside.

It was shown early in this chapter that Marxism gives three different answers to the question of who controls state-owned corporations. According to the answer most commonly given — notably by Victor Cheprakov — nationalized corporations are seen as being under the control of the private-sector bourgeoisie. A second interpretation attributes the control of publicly-owned corporations to the bureaucratic apparatus of the state — in other words, to government officials. Eugene Varga is part of this current. And finally, a number of writers, influenced by the Chinese Communist Party's analysis of the Soviet Union, use the concept of "state bourgeoisie" to designate the people who run the nationalized sectors of capitalist economies. Fernando H. Cardoso is one of the more prestigious advocates of this concept. For this study, the idea of a "state bourgeoisie" was adopted to denote the career executives in the state capitalist sector, and the hypothesis that federally- and provincially-owned corporations were run by this group was put to the test.

The results tend to favour the Cheprakov interpretation: the boards of directors of the corporations in the sample used (the major federal and provincial publicly-owned corporations) are composed essentially of private-sector capitalists. In the most important of these corporations (Bank of Canada, Canada Development Corporation, Canadian National, Air Canada, Federal Business Development Bank, etc.) they even form an absolute majority on the board. State managers are a very small minority, occupying barely 10 to 15 per cent of the directorships in the corporations studied. In addition, most of these directors are removable at will. Most directors — even inside directors — are appointed for periods ranging from two to ten years. Most full-time officers of government-owned corporations come from the private sector or the civil service and return to their careers in these domains. Publicly-owned corporations seem most likely to be controlled by government officials, and especially by elected officials, under NDP governments. The Liberals, at both the federal and the provincial level, tend to develop the state capitalist sector and to put Canadian business-men and their advisers in charge of it. The state bourgeoisie is numerically strongest in corporations whose function is to provide infrastructure (harbours, communications, electricity). The more sensitive financial and industrial sectors are under the direct control of the private-sector Canadian bourgeoisie.

Strictly economic explanations of state capitalism were rejected, both Eurocommunist (falling rate of profit, pillage of the state by the mon-opolies) and academic (rationalization of "natural" monopolies, external influence of political factors on economic ones). As an economic instru-ment of domination, the state reflects the interests of *all* the ruling classes. However, conflicts among different segments of these classes and between them and the subordinate classes are also visible in state-owned corporations. The emergence of regional bourgeoisies (Ontario in the early twentieth century, Quebec in the 1960s, Alberta in the 1970s) has given rise at the provincial level to the creation of crown corporations that have largely, but not exclusively, served the interests of these developing power bases. Here too, the hegemony exercised through the state has led to economic policies that take the interests of the lower classes into account, at least to some degree. Developing regional bourgeoisies have sought and obtained mass support of the creation and expansion of publicly-owned enterprises.

Provincial crown corporations (which have grown much more rapidly than their federal counterparts) have often developed within the con-text of the unequal development of Canadian capitalism that has resulted in economic activity being concentrated in Ontario. Faced with the absence or the collapse of a key sector of activity (such as the steel industry), provincial governments often resort to publicly-owned corporations to fill the gap. Unequal development is behind both Canadian provincialism (for which the NDP wrongly blames multi-national corporations) and the proliferation of provincial crown corporations outside Ontario.

Finally, the other great constant in the Canadian economic structure, dependent-associate development, is a source of both cooperation and conflict between the Canadian bourgeoisie and its dominant American partner. As foreign capital increased its hold on the Canadian economy, the Canadian capitalist class established publicly-owned corporations, notably the Canada Development Corporation, in an effort to strength-en itself. The CDC's task is to repatriate foreign-owned companies in Canada, while its Quebec counterpart, the General Investment Corpo-ration, has played a more defensive role, trying to save Quebec companies from going bankrupt or being taken over by English Ca-nadian or foreign capital.

It is impossible to understand crown corporations without referring, as has been done here, to the overall structure of society — to social classes. Other examples could have been chosen: the Federal Business Development Bank, designed to provide credit to small and middle-sized industrial corporations; the Farm Credit Corporation, which gives credit to farmers; or the Export Development Corporation, designed to promote foreign sales by Canadian companies of all sizes. These examples demonstrate that the economic instruments of the state do not serve the "monopoly" sectors of the Canadian bourgeoisie exclusively, but ensure the reproduction of all the dominant classes.

The theory of state monopoly capitalism is not consistent with the data in this study. Publicly-owned corporations have often been established as a result of demands by small and middle-sized business; a corporation created under these conditions has often had the effect of breaking a tight oligopoly of private companies, as in the case of hydroelectricity, the primary steel industry or oil (Petro-Canada). These crown corporations have entered profitable but closed markets and have complemented other publicly-owned enterprises designed either to strengthen Canadian entrepreneurship or to compensate for the limited market power of farmers and other small entrepreneurs. Representatives of big business are not alone on the boards of publicly-owned corporations; small business is also present, especially at the provincial level. The Liberal Party has been the most common political vehicle of smaller business, but the Conservative Party in Ontario, Social Credit in British Columbia and other parties have also at times lent a sympathetic ear to the demands of regional business groups.

CHAPTER 5

The Subsidiaries of Foreign-owned Companies

The preceding chapters analysed the main characteristics of the Canadian bourgeoisie, the emergence of its new French Canadian component after the Second World War and the Canadian capitalist class's control of government-owned corporations. This chapter is devoted to analysing the other major part of Canada's bourgeoisie, the comprador bourgeoisie, which administers the subsidiaries of foreign-owned companies in Canada. There will also be an examination of the links between this part of the bourgeoisie and the indigenous capitalist class.

An appropriate beginning is a review of the Canadian literature on the comprador bourgeoisie, with a view to establishing definitions, methods and working hypotheses. This will be followed by a study of the control of the foreign parent companies themselves. In the third section of the chapter, an attempt is made to understand the links between the comprador bourgeoisie and the intelligentsia that surrounds the Canadian bourgeoisie and sits on the boards of directors of both foreign-owned and domestic corporations (this group of professionals includes corporate lawyers, financial consultants, consulting engineers and others). The final section of the chapter will analyse the links between the indigenous bourgeoisie and the comprador bourgeoisie, examining corporate control, interlocking directorships and recent tendencies relating to foreign control of the Canadian economy. The results should allow one to conclude that the two major segments of Canada's bourgeoisie (indigenous and comprador) are relatively distinct and that the indigenous bourgeoisie is the economically dominant partner in an association that is not free of tensions and conflicts.

Themes, Definitions and Methods

The two major segments of the bourgeoisie (indigenous and comprador) have been fairly clearly identified in Canadian socialist literature. However, writers express different views on the role and relative importance of each of the segments. According to most writers, the comprador bourgeoisie has become both economically and politically dominant since the Second World War. Thus, Cy Gonick writes:

> It is important to distinguish between two segments within Canada's own capitalist class. There is an independent segment, largely the descendants of merchant-finance capital.... There is also a dependent segment composed of leading Canadian executives who have been relegated to the position of managing branch-plants for foreign masters.... The dominant economic force in Canada is clearly the American-based multinational corporation.[1]

Other writers make a similar judgment about the control of the Canadian state. In *(Canada) Ltd.* James Laxer maintains: "In the post-1945 period Canada's financial capitalists were no longer dominant in the running of the Canadian state. They were locked into a junior partnership with American corporations which now securely controlled primary and secondary production in the economy."[2] Elsewhere in the same book, John Hutcheson writes: "The Canadian state is now in the control of the dominant section of the ruling class in Canada — the U.S. corporations."[3]

In the preceding chapter, evidence was presented that suggests the contrary — that the indigenous Canadian bourgeoisie is in exclusive control of at least that half of the state apparatus composed of public corporations. This study does not attempt to demonstrate that the government itself is also dominated by the indigenous bourgeoisie. However, some evidence is presented that would tend to support such an argument in a discussion of the role of the federal and provincial governments in buying back the Canadian economy during the 1970s.

Some writers do depart from the view that the comprador bourgeoisie is the dominant segment. According to one such writer, Wallace Clement, it is necessary to distinguish among three major groups within the elite that controls large Canadian corporations: an "indigenous" section tied to dominant corporations under domestic control, a "comprador" section consisting of the people who run the subsidiaries of foreign-owned corporations, and a "parasite" section which runs the parent corporations of these subsidiaries. These sections do not necessarily conflict with one another. Rather, they maintain a double relationship, consisting of domination of the comprador elite by the parasite elite and partnership between the comprador and indigenous elites.

This partnership is based on a division of labour that developed historically — the indigenous elite controls the major companies in the financial, commercial, transportation and service sectors, while the comprador elite dominates the manufacturing and mining industries.

The partnership is visible in the long-term maintenance of Canadian control in low-technology sectors, and in the persistence — and even the growth — of foreign control in genuinely industrial sectors. It is also evident in the interlocking directorships between Canadian- and foreign-controlled companies. In Clement's view, the partnership does not imply that either segment is economically dominant. Since Clement postulates that the economic and political elites possess a degree of autonomy relative to each other, he does not take a position on the possible control of the state by the Canadian economic elite (or either of its main segments).[4]

Clement's conception of the relationship between the two major sections of the Canadian bourgeoisie is much more complex and subtle than the others cited thus far, but it is not without its deficiencies. In the first place, as shown previously, there is the confusion between the concept of the bourgeoisie and that of the elite, which leads to a degree of imprecision in the semantic content of the two concepts.[5] A second problem is the inclusion of advisers who are not owners in the bourgeoisie, which makes it impossible to carry out a separate analysis of the intelligentsia of the Canadian ruling class, the group of organic intellectuals who are active both on the boards of directors of large corporations and in politics. Third, the evidence presented in the last chapter of the active presence of the indigenous bourgeoisie in the economic apparatus of the state and in the control of crown corporations contradicts both the Hutcheson/Laxer thesis that the state is run by the comprador bourgeoisie and Clement's contention that the economic and political elites are autonomous. A fourth weakness is Clement's underestimation of the conflict between the two leading segments of Canada's bourgeoisie. In the last section of this chapter, evidence is presented that suggests that there is a "partnership with conflict" between the indigenous bourgeoisie and the comprador bourgeoisie, in which the indigenous bourgeoisie uses the state apparatus at both federal and provincial levels to regain ground it lost during the quarter-century following the Second World War.

This chapter is intended as a contribution to the debate that has just been outlined. The *comprador bourgeoisie* is defined as the social group of Canadian inside directors of foreign-owned corporations. Inside directors (members of the board who are also senior executives of the company, such as the president, vice-presidents, etc.) are distinguished from outside directors, who are not employed by the company and only sit on the board. The inside directors receive salaries that often run to six figures, have expense accounts and benefit from preferential stock purchase plans. In contrast, outside directors only receive fees for attending board meetings and have a purely advisory function in the company. The *indigenous bourgeoisie* is composed of the controlling stockholders and inside directors of Canadian-controlled companies. Canada's *foreign bourgeoisie* or parasite bourgeoisie is the group of foreign controlling stockholders and inside directors of foreign parent corporations with Canadian subsidiaries.

For example, Superior Oil of Houston is controlled by the Keck family, which holds a third of its shares. It has three large Canadian subsidiaries, all of which are on the list of dominant subsidiaries of foreign corporations: Canadian Superior Oil, McIntyre Mines and Falconbridge Nickel Mines. H.B. Keck is president of the parent corporation while W.M. Keck also sits on its board. Others, however, hold the inside director positions in the three large Canadian subsidiaries: A.E. Feldmeyer, M.A. Cooper and R.B. Fulton are the presidents of Canadian Superior Oil, McIntyre Mines and Falconbridge respectively. Feldmeyer, Cooper and Fulton are part of the nucleus of the comprador bourgeoisie, while the Kecks belong to the foreign bourgeoisie.

The *organic intellectuals* are the corporate lawyers, financial consultants, consulting engineers and other experts who are neither full-time employees nor major stockholders of a company, but sit on its board as outside directors. Thus there are two lawyers on the board of Canadian Superior Oil, D.E. Lewis and A.W. Hendricks, who hold only a few shares of the company and are only outside directors.

The questions that are posed here concerning the relationships among the different segments of the bourgeoisie indicate why it is important to distinguish between owners and consultants. Are the comprador bourgeoisie and the internal Canadian bourgeoisie surrounded by the same group of organic intellectuals or does each section have its own intelligentsia — its own cohort of advisers? Clement has pointed out the existence of interlocking directorships between subsidiaries of foreign corporations and Canadian-controlled companies. Are these interlocking directorships held only by advisers or by owners as well? Do members of the foreign bourgeoisie send their advisers to Canada to sit on the boards of their subsidiaries or do they make the trip themselves? In other words, what is the extent of the split between the comprador bourgeoisie and the internal bourgeoisie? Does the rift exist only at the level of ownership, or is it a broader social phenomenon that touches a much broader group of intellectuals? One can answer these questions by abandoning the shaky theory of "elites" and adopting instead the much more solid Marxist perspective of a ruling class based on ownership (whatever the legal forms), surrounded by a broader group of organic intellectuals.

The inquiry described here is based on a list of some 130 foreign-owned corporations operating in Canada with assets of more than $100 million as of the end of 1975. This date was chosen to make the list directly comparable with the list of Canadian-owned companies on which *The Economy of Canada* was based, and to make it possible to use Statistics Canada figures on foreign ownership, which are always a few years out of date.

The list includes virtually all the foreign-owned public companies operating in Canada with assets of more than $100 million that are referred to in sources such as: the yearly *Financial Post* surveys (published in Toronto) and Moody's manuals (published in New York), the reports of the superintendents of insurance of Canada, Quebec and Ontario, the *Financial Post*'s annual list of the largest companies, and the Financial Post Corporation Service. The *Financial Post Directory of Directors* was used to classify the members of the boards of directors of these subsidiaries according to their status on the board and main occupation; in the case of lawyers, these data were supplemented with information from the *Martindale-Hubbell Law Directory*.

The "list of 130" is broadly representative of foreign capital in Canada. The 105 non-financial corporations included had total assets of $40.421 billion at the end of 1975. According to Statistics Canada's Corporations and Labour Unions Returns Act publication for 1978 (Catalogue no. 61-210), total assets of foreign-owned non-financial corporations in 1965 were $80.881 billion. Thus, the subsidiaries on the list account for 50 per cent of the assets of foreign-owned non-financial corporations in Canada. For the sensitive industrial sector, the sample is even more representative. The eighty-nine manufacturing and mining enterprises on the list had total assets of $33.328 billion at the end of 1975, or 56 per cent of the total assets of foreign-owned corporations in the industrial sector ($59.672 billion) reported for 1975 by Statistics Canada. Unfortunately, it is impossible to obtain a precise figure for the percentage of total foreign-controlled assets in the Canadian financial system represented by the twenty-five subsidiaries in the financial sector on the list, but one can state that it is well over 50 per cent. The list includes the only foreign-controlled chartered bank as well as all the major federally- or provincially-chartered foreign life insurance companies.

With the list of subsidiaries drawn up, an attempt was made to determine the parent corporation of each subsidiary and find out who controls it and who sits on its board. The same sources that were used to compile the list of 130, along with the Statistics Canada publication *Inter-Corporate Ownership* for 1975, served to determine control of the subsidiaries. A number of sources were used to determine control of the parent corporations. For each American company, proxy statements for the 1975 annual meetings on file at the New York Stock Exchange were consulted. These statements contain a list of all stockholders owning more than 10 per cent of the shares of the company (whether or not they are on the board of directors), the number of shares held by each director and officer, and the number of shares held by pension funds. Issues of *Fortune* and *Forbes* magazines from 1970 to 1977 were consulted to supplement this information. The sources used were thus the ones from which the authors who are most often cited (Jean-Marie Chevalier and Philip Burch) determined the control of large American corporations for 1965.[6]

For France, it was possible to use a very detailed study, François Morin's latest work, which uses similar sources and methods and contains information for the same date.[7] For Britain, the two major financial periodicals that published data on the control of large British firms, *Investors Chronicle* and *The Economist*, were used. For the European continent, the *Répertoire permanent des groupes financiers et industriels*, published in Brussels by the Centre de Recherche et d'Information Socio-Politiques, was used. Finally, a number of the foreign parent corporations are listed on the Toronto Stock Exchange and, as a result, are required to divulge the same information as Canadian corporations that are traded there. The bulletins of the Ontario Securities Commission were used to obtain information on their control, as they were for Canadian-controlled corporations. The boards of directors of parent corporations were obtained from the 1976 edition of *Standard and Poor's Register of Corporations*, published in New York. Various Statistics Canada publications helped in determining the changes in foreign direct investment in Canada during the 1970s. Annual financial surveys (such as the *Financial Post* and the *Moody's* series) and the business press (such as the *Financial Post*, the *Wall Street Journal* and the *Financial Times*) were useful in studying changes in the control of large Canadian corporations in the same period.

It will be recalled that *control* means the legal ability to elect the board of directors of a joint-stock company (or a majority of its members). This power is held by individuals, partnerships or families who own enough stock to impose their choices. Control can be absolute (when the leading stockholder owns 100 per cent of the voting shares), majority (when the percentage is between 50.1 and 99 per cent), minority (between 5 and 49 per cent) or internal (when there is no block of shares larger than 5 per cent and power devolves to members of the board of directors). Official Canadian statistics use a threshold of 50 per cent to determine whether a corporation is foreign-controlled, thus ignoring the possibility of minority foreign control. Fortunately, instances of corporations under minority foreign control are rare. Only 14 per cent of the companies on the list of the 130 largest foreign-controlled corporations in Canada are minority foreign-controlled, so that the figures here are comparable with those of Statistics Canada.

The Control of Foreign-owned Companies

The distinction is made here between initial control and final control of a corporation. Initial control is the degree of control (absolute, majority or minority) exercised by a parent corporation over its subsidiary. Final control is the degree of control of the parent corporation itself. The Ford Motor Company, the American parent of the Ford Motor Company of Canada, holds 88 per cent of the stock of its subsidiary, so that initial control of the Ford Motor Company of Canada is majority. However, the Ford family controls the Ford Motor Company with 40 per cent of its stock, so that final control of the parent corporation, and thus of the subsidiary, is minority.

In classifying parent corporations, it was necessary to adopt an additional category, "family" control, with the degree of control remaining unspecified because of the absence of data. Tate and Lyle Ltd. of London is an example. Four members of the Tate family and three members of the Lyle family are directors of this sugar and foodstuffs multinational, which owns Redpath Industries in Canada. All writers and financial periodicals agree that the two families control the corporation, but no author or source is willing to venture an estimation of the *degree* of control. As a result, it was preferable to classify Tate and Lyle as a company under "family" control without specifying the percentage of the vote held by the controlling families.

The data on initial and final control of the 130 foreign-owned corporations on the list, by degree of control and country of control, are summarized in tables 5-1 and 5-2.

Seventy per cent of the companies on the list of 130 were American-controlled as of 1975, 19 per cent were British-controlled and the re-

TABLE 5-1

Dominant Subsidiaries of Foreign Companies in Canada: Degree of Initial Control by Country of Origin of Immediate Parent Corporation, 1975

Degree of Control	U.S.A.	U.K.	France	Others	Total
Absolute	53 (58%)	6	1	1	61 (47%)
Majority	27 (29%)	18	2	4	51 (39%)
Minority	11 (13%)	1	2	4	18 (14%)
TOTAL	91 (100%)	25	5	9	130 (100%)

Source: Appendix 8.

TABLE 5-2
Dominant Subsidiaries of Foreign Companies in Canada: Degree of Final Control by Country of Origin of Immediate Parent Corporation, 1975

Degree of Control	U.S.A.	U.K.	France	Others	Total
Absolute	1	—	—	—	1 (1%)
Majority	—	—	—	—	—
Minority	29	3	—	3	35 (27%)
Internal	61	10	2	2	75 (58%)
Family (not specified)	—	11	—	3	14 (11%)
Government	—	1	3	—	4 (3%)
Unknown	—	—	—	1	1 (1%)
TOTAL	91	25	5	9	130 (100%)

Source: Appendix 9.

mainder were controlled by French, Belgian, Swiss and South African interests. Subsidiaries of American corporations are the most likely to to be absolutely controlled by their parents, while European and South African companies prefer to run their subsidiaries through majority control.

But there is a constant that cuts across the different countries: cases of control being shared by two or more sets of interests are very rare. Only one corporation under majority or minority foreign control was found in which a substantial block of shares was held by Canadian capitalists. In *The Economy of Canada,* only four corporations were found to be under shared control: Simpsons/Sears (of which Simpsons Ltd. owned 50 per cent and Sears Roebuck owned the other 50 per cent), B.C. Forest Products (of which 6.6 per cent was held by Argus Corp., 28.5 per cent by Noranda Mines, 28.4 per cent by the Mead Corporation of Ohio and 13.2 per cent by the Scott Paper Co. at the end of 1975), Alcan and Inco (each of which was apparently under the control of a joint group of Canadian and American directors). *This clear division between countries of control is the foundation for the split between the indigenous and comprador bourgeoisies.* The domestic bourgeoisie controls a certain number of companies, while the comprador bourgeoisie (a motley assortment of directors of multinational corporations of diverse origins) dominates others. The two groups don't mix in the essential area of corporate control. The rift between the indigenous and comprador bourgeoisies occurs at the very heart of their relation to production, in the economic sphere. These two large sections of Canada's ruling class are separated at the level of the ownership of the means of production.

An analysis of the final control of subsidiaries of foreign companies introduces problems of a very different order. In part, it brings one back to the theoretical debates about corporate control that were discussed in the three main chapters of *The Economy of Canada*. Who controls the parent corporations? Are they under banker or financier control? Have they been affected by the "managerial revolution"? The sample used here does not allow one to generalize about any of these forms of control with respect to the United States, Britain or France. However, it is possible to classify the subsidiaries on the list of 130 by level of final control and compare the results to the literature on the subject for the countries concerned. The results of this classification of the 130 subsidiaries by country of origin and degree of *final* control (that is, assigning to them the degree of control of the parent corporation) are presented in table 5-2.

According to the sources used, about 60 per cent of the parent corporations of Canadian subsidiaries seem to be controlled by career executives, while 40 per cent are under the known control of a family, individual or partnership, most often held through a minority of shares. A look at a few examples of the people who ultimately control foreign-owned companies in Canada is worthwhile. There is the Ford family, which through the Ford Motor Company controls three large Canadian subsidiaries: the Ford Motor Company of Canada, the Ford Motor Credit Company of Canada and Ensite Ltd. There is the Keck family, which controls Superior Oil Co. of Houston, which in turn owns three dominant Canadian subsidiaries: Canadian Superior Oil, McIntyre Mines and Falconbridge Nickel Mines. Also worth noting is the South African millionaire Harry Oppenheimer, who, through the Anglo-American Corporation of South Africa, owned three dominant subsidiaries in Canada as of 1975: the Anglo-American Corporation of Canada, the Hudson's Bay Mining and Smelting Co. and Francana Oil and Gas.

Among other important families in Canada's "foreign" or "parasite" bourgeoisie were the Pew, Mountain and Rothchild families. J. Howard Pew and his family controlled the Sun Co. in the United States, which had two subsidiaries on the list of 130: Sun Oil Co. and Great Canadian Oil Sands. The Mountains are an aristocratic London family who control the Eagle Star Insurance Co. of London, which is effectively a holding company and controls two of the largest real estate corporations in Britain: English Property Corp. (which in 1975 owned Trizec of Canada) and MEPC Ltd. (the owner of MEPC Canadian Properties). Finally, the French Rothchilds controlled Rio Tinto-Zinc Corp. of London, which owned three major subsidiaries in Canada, all in the natural resources sector: Rio Algom Ltd., Indal Ltd. and Preston Mines.

In addition to controlling their subsidiaries through ownership, parent corporations keep a close watch on the boards of directors of their daughter corporations. The subsidiaries on the list of 130 have an average of 10.5 directors; a third of these (3.2) come from the foreign parent corporations, and these are often the people who control the parent corporations. Table 5-3 is a list of major international capitalists

TABLE 5-3
Controlling Stockholders of Foreign Parent Corporations Who Are Directors and/or Officers of Canadian Subsidiaries, 1975

Subsidiary	Controlling Stockholders Who Are Directors and/or Officers
Algoma Central Railway	I.P. Lowson
Anglo-American Corp. of Canada	H.F. Oppenheimer
Beneficial Finance Co. of Canada	C.M. Benadom (chm. of bd.), R.A. Tucker
Blackwood Hodge (Canada)	W.A. Shapland (chm. of bd.)
Canadian Reynolds Metals	R.S. Reynolds, Jr. (chm. of bd.) L.J. Reynolds (v.-chm. of bd.) W.G. Reynolds
Canadian Superior Oil	H.B. Keck, W.M. Keck, Jr.
Falconbridge Nickel Mines	H.B. Keck (chm. of bd.)
Ford Motor Co. of Canada	Henry Ford II
Ford Motor Credit Co. of Canada	B. Ford, W.C. Ford
Gamble Canada	B.C. Gamble
Husky Oil	G.E. Neilson (chm. of bd.) J.E. Neilson (pres.)
Kaiser Resources	E.F. Kaiser (chm. of bd.) E.F. Kaiser, Jr. (pres.)
S.S. Kresge Co.	S.S. Kresge
Maple Leaf Mills	B.A. Norris
McIntyre Mines	H.B. Keck, W.M. Keck Jr.
Redpath Industries	C. Lyle, D.A. Tate, H.S. Tate
Reed, Shaw, Osler	J.G. Stenhouse

who sit on the boards of their Canadian subsidiaries. The names of the Reynolds brothers, the Fords, the Kaisers, Harry F. Oppenheimer, the Tates and Lyles and Kecks stand out. Most often, however, the parent corporation is represented by lesser-known inside directors who come to Canada for monthly board meetings of the Canadian subsidiary. The relative obscurity of these officers doesn't make their leadership any less effective. Boards of directors made up in this way ensure the subordination of the comprador bourgeoisie to the foreign bourgeoisie and to major decisions taken by the parent corporation.

It should not be concluded from these data that the "managerial revolution" is very far advanced in the United States or Canada. There is a "family element" on the board of directors of a number of corporations on our list, which could indicate hidden family control. One example is Philip Morris Inc., which controls Benson & Hedges (Canada) Ltd. Using information from the business press in 1965, both Jean-Marie Chevalier and Philip Burch classified this American tobacco multinational as being under the minority control of the Cullman family, which owned at least 5 per cent of its shares. There are still two Cullmans on the Philip Morris board. According to their declarations, they own about 1 per cent of the shares of the company; if other members of the family who are not directors own substantial blocks of shares, Philip Morris could be under Cullman control. Incidentally, Hugh and Joseph Cullman are also on the board of the Canadian subsidiary.

Another example is Ingersoll Rand of New Jersey. According to Burch and Chevalier, this company was under the minority control of the Phipps-Grace family in 1965. In 1975 four family members on the Ingersoll Rand board held 2.7 per cent of the company's shares. There may be other family members who held stock but did not sit on the board, in which case the parent corporation of Canadian Ingersoll Rand could have been under the control of the Phipps-Grace family.

Studies of the control of large American corporations disagree about the existence or even the possibility of control by financial institutions. Two famous studies, both taking 1965 as their reference year but based on different sources, come to more or less opposite conclusions. According to Philip Burch, banker control is not even possible. Basing his study on the business press, he concluded that family control was much more widespread in the United States than the "managerial" school had led people to believe. Jean-Marie Chevalier, on the other hand, concluded that although family control was a significant phenomenon, it was becoming more and more common for large non-financial corporations in the United States to be controlled by banks. In 1970-71, a debate on the subject pitted Robert Fitch and Mary Oppenheimer, on one side, against Paul Sweezy and James O'Connor on the other.

Fitch and Oppenheimer agreed with Chevalier that the accumulation of stock by pension funds managed by commercial banks gave the banks control of large industrial corporations. Sweezy and O'Connor didn't deny that this accumulation was taking place, but took issue with the idea that the banks acted as controlling stockholders, maintaining instead that they behaved simply as investors.[8]

More recently, there has been a growing number of contributions to both sides of the question. In one of the most detailed studies of the recent control of large American corporations, David M. Kotz presents his own case for the Chevalier thesis.[9] Using data from congressional documents on stockholdings of large corporations, indebtedness and the composition of boards of directors for the years 1967-69, Kotz concluded that 6.5 per cent of the 200 largest non-financial corporations in the United States were under the "full control" and 23 per cent were under the "partial control" of financial institutions. For 46.5 per cent of the corporations, he concluded that no external control seemed to exist, leaving open the possibility of hidden family control.

This study's data was compared with Kotz's and, taking into account the differences in sources and reference years (data here are for 1975), the results are almost identical. Fifty-two corporations on our list were also on Kotz's. In forty-two of these cases, either the same controlling stockholder was identified in both studies, or else no controlling stockholder was detected in either. In one case (Rockwell International), Kotz detected no external control, while declarations on file with the Ontario Securities Commission made it possible to attribute control to the Rockwell family along with two associates. In another case, Kotz correctly attributed control of W.T. Grant & Co. to W.T. Grant, while in 1975 this was no longer the case since the company was in bankruptcy and liquidation. Gulf Oil was controlled by the Mellon National Bank in 1967, while according to the proxy statement for 1975 it was under Mellon family control. Finally, in seven cases (Celanese Corp., B.F. Goodrich, International Paper, Philips Petroleum, Safeway Stores, Standard Oil of Indiana and United Aircraft) for which Kotz found that a bank owned more than 5 per cent of the company's stock and attributed control to that bank, it was not possible to learn whether Kotz's results still held for 1975. In any case, the process on which Chevalier and Kotz based their thesis, the concentration of corporate shares in the hands of bank-administered pension funds, seems to be declining in importance.

This process depended on both the growth of pension funds managed by banks and the massive investment of these funds in corporate shares, and since 1972 neither of these phenomena has been occurring. The 1973-74 recession and the less than glittering performance of the

American economy since then have strongly affected stock prices. Banks had invested most of their funds in stocks and several of them suffered substantial losses. They were thus forced *by the market* to take refuge in fixed-income securities, such as mortgages or government bonds. As well, the Employee Retirement Income Security Act of 1974 requires pension fund managers to make sure that pensioners are paid the real value of their pensions and to index pensions to the cost of living. Since then, pensions fund trustees have disposed of a large proportion of their corporate stocks. For example, Morgan Guaranty Trust let it be known that it had managed to sell $6 billion worth of stock in 1978, replacing it with fixed-income securities.[10] In addition, the poor performance of pension funds administered by commercial banks has allowed a new kind of pension fund manager to emerge — the independent financial consultant, who manages a smaller number of large funds which obtain much higher annual yields than the bank. *Since 1972, almost all the large commercial banks have lost clients and pension funds in absolute terms to financial consultants.*

In this writer's opinion, this double process confirms the hypothesis advanced by Sweezy, O'Connor and Edward S. Herman — the banks must behave as institutional investors or else they lose their clients. If in some cases they deviated from the rule of maximizing profit in investing pensions funds, both the market and the law have forced them to resume acting purely as investors. One might note in passing that a similar process has been occurring in Canada, where the main institutional managers of pension funds, the trust companies, are divesting themselves of their corporate stocks and replacing them with fixed-income securities.[11] The "return of banker and financial control" has not lasted very long, either in Canada or in the United States.

The British companies on the list of 130 were mostly (fourteen companies out of twenty-five, or 56 per cent) controlled by their owners, either families or individuals, while 40 per cent (ten companies out of twenty-five) appeared to be under internal control. Among the dominant families were the Tates and Lyles, owners of Tate and Lyle, which in 1975 controlled Redpath Industries in Canada; the Hambros, owners of Hambros Ltd., which controlled Ontario Trust; and the Shaplands and Sunleys, who owned Blackwood Hodge and thus controlled the Canadian company of the same name. Another prominent family was the Mountains, owners of Eagle Star Insurance, in reality a holding company through which in 1975 they controlled English Property Corporation (and its Canadian subsidiary Trizec) and MEPC Ltd. (and its Canadian subsidiary MEPC Canadian Properties) and shared control of United Dominion Trust and its Canadian subsidiary of the same name.

All these families, except for the Shaplands and Sunleys, belong to the British aristocracy. Their control of the corporations in question has been an open secret, as is the fact that Rio Tinto-Zinc. Corp., the giant London-based mining conglomerate, is controlled by the French branch of the Rothchild family.

A mutual life insurance company (Standard Life Assurance) and a number of large industrial corporations were classified as being under internal control. Some of these could be under family control if the founding families exercise their vote through designated directors who represent them. An example of this is Imperial Chemical Industries, in which the Mond and Brunner families still hold substantial blocks of shares.[12] The role played by a number of large insurance companies as institutional investors and virtual holding companies is very characteristic of British capitalism. As far as Canada is concerned, the most important of these is Eagle Star Insurance Co., owned by the Mountain family. The company was purchased in 1917 by Sir Edward Mountain, who was succeeded as chairman of the board by his son, Sir Brian Mountain, in 1948 and by Sir Brian's son, Sir Denis Mountain, in 1974.

In Britain, however, the largest of these insurance companies is the Prudential Assurance Co., which operates under the same name in Canada. Apparently under internal control, the Prudential holds more than 10 per cent of the shares of some fifty companies. While it doesn't participate directly in running these companies, the Prudential exercises a definite influence on them through its "suggestions."[13] Both insurance companies, the most important institutional investors, and the pension funds deny exercising more than "influence" in the companies in which they hold stock.

Among the foreign corporations with substantial interests in Canada, special reference should be made to the South African companies. The Oppenheimer group consists in Canada of three large corporations: Anglo-American Corporation of Canada, its subsidiary Hudson's Bay Mining and Smelting, and a subsidiary of the latter company, Francana Oil and Gas. This group is dominated by Harry F. Oppenheimer, the most powerful South African capitalist, and is the largest producer of gold, diamonds and platinum in the non-communist world, as well as one of the major world producers of copper, coal, uranium and other minerals. In 1973, it had non-financial assets of $6 billion, of which $500 million were in Canada. The share capital of the parent corporation, Anglo-American Corp. of South Africa, amounted in 1973 to about $1.4 billion; 10 per cent of it belonged to Harry F. Oppenheimer.[14]

The other major South African capitalist with a corporate presence in Canada was Anton Rupert. He controls one of the major world tobacco companies, the Rothmans group, which has a dominant subsidiary in Canada, Rothmans of Pall M. ll. Rupert also owns 25 per cent of a South African mining conglomerate, Federale Mynbou, which controls 57.5 per cent of the stock of General Mining. In turn, General Mining owns 30 per cent of Union Corporation, a company in the financial sector, which controls Capital & Counties Property Co. This is one of London's largest real estate companies, and as of 1975, it had a dominant subsidiary in Canada, Abbey Glen Property Corporation.[15]

Among the continental European groups is the Empain group, represented in Canada by Canadian Hydrocarbons Ltd., an oil company. The group is controlled by a Belgian baron, Edouard-Jean Empain.[16] The Société Générale de Belgique, apparently under internal control, had as of 1975 a dominant subsidiary in Canada, Genstar Ltd. It was also the largest shareholder in Petrofina S.A., the parent corporation of Petrofina Canada, sharing control with the Compagnie Bruxelles Lambert (owned by the Lamberts, a Belgian family) and Imperial Continental Gas, a British company.[17] Another Belgian family, the Solvays, owns about 10 per cent of Allied Chemicals, an American company that has a subsidiary of the same name in Canada. Jacques E. Solvay has been a director of the American parent corporation, which is part of the worldwide empire of the Brussels-based multinational Solvay et Cie.

A number of large subsidiaries in Canada were controlled by European government-owned corporations as of 1975. British Petroleum had two dominant subsidiaries in Canada, BP Canada and Total Petroleum (North America), both oil companies. The Banque Nationale de Paris, one of France's nationalized deposit banks, owned a finance company in Canada, BNP Canada. The Société Nationale des Pétroles d'Aquitaine, a French government-controlled company, also had a major subsidiary in Canada, Aquitaine Co. of Canada Ltd.*

Is there a prevalent form of control in the parent corporations of the subsidiaries on the list? It does seem as if internal control (or at least "unknown" control, to use David M. Kotz's expression) suits the majority of cases. However, one shouldn't jump to the conclusion that there is a worldwide trend towards this form of control. First of all, more complete sources might shorten the list of internally-controlled companies considerably. Second, the current wave of mergers and movement towards the formation of conglomerates has led to smaller companies taking over large corporations that appear to be dominated by career executives. For the large corporation, this means a reversion to control by its legal owners. This generally occurs in one of two ways.

One way is the reverse takeover. A middle-sized company controlled

---

*In 1981 Aquitaine was sold to the CDC.

by an individual, family or partnership exchanges its shares for a sub-stantial block of shares of a large internally-controlled company. As a result, the owners of the middle-sized company become the controlling stockholders of the large one. For example, General Dynamics (the American parent company of the Asbestos Corporation) fell under the control of Chicago financier Henry Crown in 1959 when it absorbed his family company, Material Services Corporation, in a share ex-change.[18] After being rebuffed several times, Henry and Lester Crown gained control of General Dynamics by entering into partnership with another financier, Nathan Cummings. Avco Corp., which has a dominant Canadian subsidiary, Avco Financial Services Co. of Canada, changed hands in the same type of reverse takeover. In 1968, Avco, a Connecticut finance company, absorbed an insurance company in neighbouring Massachusetts, the Paul Revere Corp., which had been controlled by the Harrington family. The Harringtons thus became the principal stockholders in Avco.[19] Similar manoeuvres have occurred in England. In 1972, Bowater Corp.'s absorption of Ralli International in a share exchange led to its takeover by James D. Slater and Malcolm Horsman. Bowater has a pulp and paper subsidiary in Canada, Bowater Paper Corp.[20]

The other major process through which middle-sized corporations, controlled by an individual or family, can take over much larger com-panies, in which share ownership is dispersed, is the pyramid. Two of South Africa's leading capitalists, Anton Rupert and Harry F. Oppen-heimer, are masters of the art of controlling vast conglomerates through investments that are fairly small in relation to the assets of the companies they dominate. Figure 5-1 illustrates the pyramid through which Rupert controlled one of his Canadian companies, Abbey Glen Property Corp.

Large companies are thus not immune to takeover attempts by smaller companies. And as the abundant literature on finance capital suggests, they are similarly not sheltered from a takeover by financial institutions such as British insurance companies, American commercial banks or brokerage houses, or European *banques d'affaires*. Without venturing onto the treacherous ground of analysing "influences" (where there are many "theories" but few hard facts), it is possible to state with some confidence that, in some cases, influence borders on control. However, it is less clear that this is a general trend, as pro-ponents of finance-capital theories maintain. It has been seen that while on the whole, large insurance companies in Britain deny seeking control of the corporations in which they own stock, some of these com-panies, notably Eagle Star Insurance, openly aim for control in their investments.

FIGURE 5-1

The Genmin-Uni Corp. Group, 1975

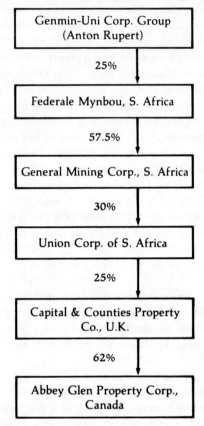

In the United States, no cases were found in which a commercial bank controls any of the industrial parent corporations on the list of 130, but in one case an investment bank exercises a strong influence on an industrial corporation — the Johns-Manville Corp., which controls Canadian Johns-Manville in Quebec. In 1927, H.E. Manville, who owned Johns-Manville, sold a controlling interest in the Company to the largest investment firm in New York, J.P. Morgan & Co., which also became its broker. J.P. Morgan & Co. split in two in 1933, with Morgan Guaranty Trust taking over its commercial activities and Morgan, Stanley & Co. inheriting its brokerage division. Since then, Morgan Guaranty has continued to have a director on the Johns-Manville board, while Morgan Stanley has remained the broker in charge of its stock issues. In 1976, Johns-Manville's president, a career executive named W.R. Goodwin, proposed that Morgan Stanley no longer be the sole manager of its financial syndicate. The Morgan

Guaranty representative on the Johns-Manville board called a board meeting in Goodwin's absence, Goodwin was dismissed, and Morgan Stanley remained the manager of Johns-Manville's financial syndicate.[21]

A third reason for doubting whether internal control is as prevalent as it appears to be is that numerous cases turn up in the business press in which blocks of stock smaller than 5 per cent (the minimum adopted here for minority control) constitute something resembling control of very large companies. Thus, for example, all indications are that United Aircraft was controlled in 1975 by three directors — W.F. Probst, P.W. O'Malley and O.W. Jorgensen — who held only 3 per cent of the voting shares. Armand Hammer owns about 2 per cent of the shares of Occidental Petroleum (parent corporation of Canadian Occidental Petroleum); he is the principal stockholder and appears to control the company. Martin Seretean became the principal stockholder in RCA Corp. with 1.2 per cent of the shares when RCA absorbed his company in 1971. Seretean is not on the RCA board, but the board submits all important decisions to him before they are made final.[22] It is very likely that the 5 per cent threshold is too high for large companies, given that a 1 or 2 per cent block worth at least $100 million can confer effective control.

Fourth, in a number of corporations, the same family names have appeared on the board of directors from generation to generation. Judging from this, some of these corporations would be classified as being under family control if a complete list of stockholders and proxies was available.

Finally, a description in terms of internal control does not account for the fact that even career executives become major stockholders (even if their holdings are negligible compared to those that are passed down by inheritance), and their six-figure salaries place them squarely in the ranks of the bourgeoisie.

In conclusion, this writer believes that final control of large subsidiaries in Canada is in the hands of rich individuals, families and partnerships as well as of career executives, who constitute a dependent and subordinate section of the capitalist class. There is no hard evidence that either internal control or control by financial institutions is becoming more widespread. As far as internal control is concerned, the size of the parent corporations on the list of 130 should be taken into account. These corporations are among the largest in their respective countries, and if a substantial proportion of them appear to be run by career executives, this is not representative of the proportion in industry as a whole. As for financial control, the trend detected by Chevalier has been reversed since 1972. American commercial banks are losing ground in absolute terms to individual managers of pension funds, while all pension fund trustees are changing the composition of their investments by increasing the proportion of fixed-income securities, such as bonds and mortgages, which are not vehicles for corporate control.

Division of Labour and Partnership

Foreign capital has always been well received in Canada. But there was never a stable division into spheres of investment between British capital, oriented more towards portfolio investment (government and railway bonds), and Canadian capital. By 1914, the watershed year in which Canada turned to the United States as a source of capital, the Canadian capitalist class was well entrenched in the financial, commercial and transportation sectors. The United States emerged as the world's greatest industrial power and American manufacturing corporations began to establish subsidiaries in foreign countries. By 1930, according to K. Buckley, American interests owned and controlled roughly 40 per cent of all the capital invested in manufacturing, mining and smelting in Canada.[23] The other sector where there was significant penetration by foreign capital was the utility sector in which, according to Buckley, 45 per cent of the total invested capital was American or British.

In 1975 there were two sectors, mining and manufacturing, in which foreign control amounted to more than 50 per cent. According to Corporations and Labour Unions Returns Act (CALURA) data, 57 per cent of mining assets and 56 per cent of manufacturing assets were foreign-controlled. The foreign-controlled proportions were smaller in all other sectors: 7.7 per cent of the assets in the utility sector, 14.3 per cent in construction, 23.3 per cent in services and 24.9 per cent in the commercial sector. There is a simple explanation for this situation. Canadian companies were confronted with insurmountable technological, commercial and financial barriers in the mining and manufacturing sectors, and remained confined to more traditional and accessible spheres: finance, commerce and services. This led to a division of labour that has been the *sine qua non* of the partnership between the indigenous and comprador bourgeoisies. This partnership, as will be seen, is not free of tensions and conflicts.

Contacts with the Domestic Bourgeoisie

In the earlier discussion of Mills, this leading writer was criticized for not having distinguished owners from organic intellectuals (lawyers, financial consultants, consulting engineers, etc.). It is highly possible that the interlocking directorships between foreign-owned and Canadian companies, to which Wallace Clement has referred, indicate links between the comprador bourgeoisie and the "organic intellectuals" of the ruling class, and not between the comprador bourgeoisie and the indigenous bourgeoisie. This question was looked at more closely by examining first the possible links between the comprador bourgeoisie and the Canadian indigenous bourgeoisie, and then the relationship between the comprador bourgeoisie and the group of intellectuals.

In examining the first set of possible links, a number of indicators were employed. First, the question of who is in charge of securities issues for subsidiaries in Canada was addressed. It is known that the brokerage industry is almost wholly controlled by the Canadian indigenous bourgeoisie, and that a number of subsidiaries do not issue any debt securities on the Canadian market, especially the giant car manufacturers and the insurance companies. If subsidiaries chose foreign brokers or Canadian subsidiaries of foreign brokerage houses, it would indicate weak financial links with the Canadian internal bourgeoisie. Table 5-4, however, shows that this is not the case.

It was possible to obtain the names of the brokers employed by sixty of the companies on the list of 130; in addition, one can say that another thirty companies do not employ a Canadian broker as they do not issue any securities in Canada. This is true of Canadian International Paper, Cyprus Anvil Mining Corp., McIntyre Mines, Canadian General Electric and Allied Chemical Canada, among others. On the whole, however, the data indicate fairly close business contacts between the Canadian financial bourgeoisie and the comprador bourgeoisie. Interlocking directorships offer further evidence of these contacts. Canadian investment dealers sit on the boards of directors of a number of subsidiaries of foreign companies. For example, in 1975 D.N. Stoker, vice-president of Nesbitt Thomson, was a director of Ultramar Canada and MEPC Canadian Properties; C.F.W. Burns, of Burns Bros. & Denton, was on the board of the Algoma Central Railway; D.L. Torrey, vice-president of Pitfield Mackay Ross, was on the board of Anglo Canadian Telephone; P. Kilburn, president of Greenshields, was on the board of Zellers; D.B. Weldon, chairman of the board of Midland Doherty, was a director of Commonwealth Holiday Inns of Canada; and D. Dawson, vice-chairman of the board of Greenshields, was on the board of BNP Canada.

The links between subsidiaries of foreign companies and the domestic bourgeoisie are not limited to the brokerage houses. Interlocking directorships between an industrial corporation and a chartered bank often indicate a commercial relationship between the two (although not control); the corporation may use the bank's commercial credit

TABLE 5-4
Subsidiaries of Foreign Companies
and Their Brokers as of January 31, 1979

Subsidiary	Broker
Mercantile Bank	Wood Gundy, McLeod Young Weir
GM Acceptance Corp.	Wood Gundy, Dominion Securities
Ford Motor Credit Co. of Canada	Wood Gundy, Dominion Securities
Canadian Acceptance Corp.	McLeod Young Weir, Burns Fry
Avco Financial Services Canada Ltd.	Greenshields, Wood Gundy, A.E. Ames, Midland Doherty
Metropolitan Trust	McLeod Young Weir, A. E. Ames
Crédit Foncier*	A.E. Ames
Rio Algom	Nesbitt Thomson, Wood Gundy, McLeod Young Weir, *Morgan Stanley Canada*
Falconbridge Nickel Mines	Dominion Securities
Hudson's Bay Mining and Smelting	Wood Gundy
Kaiser Resources*	A.E. Ames, *First Boston,* Wood Gundy, Pemberton Securities
Asbestos Corp.	Greenshields, Dominion Securities
Reed Paper	Wood Gundy
Crown Zellerbach Canada	Wood Gundy, McLeod Young Weir
Weldwood of Canada	Nesbitt Thomson, Richardson Securities
Ashland Oil Canada	Greenshields, Wood Gundy
Canadian Superior Oil	Richardson Securities
Aquitaine Co. of Canada*	Dominion Securities, Greenshields
Murphy Oil Co.	Dominion Securities
Union Oil of Canada	Dominion Securities
Canadian Hydrocarbons	Greenshields
Hudson's Bay Oil & Gas*	Dominion Securities, Richardson Securities
Canadian Occidental Petroleums	Burns Fry, McLeod Young Weir, A.E. Ames
Imperial Oil	Wood Gundy, McLeod Young Weir, Dominion Securities, A.E. Ames
Shell Canada	Wood Gundy, A.E. Ames, McLeod Young Weir
Gulf Canada	Wood Gundy, Dominion Securities
Texaco Canada	Wood Gundy, McLeod Young Weir, A.E. Ames, Dominion Securities

Subsidiary	Broker
BP Canada	Greenshields, Wood Gundy
Husky Oil*	McLeod Young Weir
Pacific Petroleum*	A.E. Ames, Wood Gundy, McLeod Young Weir
Ultramar Canada	Dominion Securities
Total Petroleum (N. America)	Pitfield Mackay Ross, *Morgan Stanley*
Canadian Industries Ltd.	A.E. Ames, Dominion Securities
DuPont of Canada	Wood Gundy, A.E. Ames
Indal	Wood Gundy
Canada Cement Lafarge	Wood Gundy, Dominion Securities, Lévesque Beaubien
IBM Canada	Wood Gundy, Dominion Securities
International Harvester of Canada	Dominion Securities
Westinghouse Canada	A.E. Ames
Goodyear Canada	Dominion Securities, A.E. Ames
Hawker Siddeley Canada	Wood Gundy
Continental Group of Canada	Wood Gundy
B.F. Goodrich Canada	McLeod Young Weir
Maple Leaf Mills*	Dominion Securities
General Foods	Wood Gundy
Kraft	Dominion Securities
Standard Brands	Burns Fry
Redpath Industries	Wood Gundy
Imasco	Greenshields
Rothmans of Pall Mall Canada	McLeod Young Weir, *Merrill Lynch,* Lévesque Beaubien
Interprovincial Pipeline	Wood Gundy, McLeod Young Weir
Westcoast Transmission*	McLeod Young Weir, Pitfield Mackay Ross
Genstar	Wood Gundy, Pitfield Mackay Ross, Greenshields
F.W. Woolworth	Wood Gundy, McLeod Young Weir, Dominion Securities, Burns Fry
Zellers Ltd.*	Greenshields
B.C. Telephone	Pitfield Mackay Ross
Quebec Telephone	Pitfield Mackay Ross
Algoma Central Railway	Burns Fry, McLeod Young Weir
Trizec*	Greenshields, Dominion Securities

*Company has become Canadian-controlled since 1975.
Foreign or foreign-controlled brokerage houses in italics.
Source: *Financial Post,* February 17, 1979, p. 30.

facilities or keep its cash holdings on deposit with the bank. Inside directors of Canadian chartered banks often sit on the boards of subsidiaries of foreign companies. Thus, in 1975 W.D.H. Gardiner, vice-president of the Royal Bank, was on the board of Canadian Utilities; J.E. Richardson, vice-president of the Canadian Imperial Bank of Commerce, sat on the board of B.C. Telephone; another vice-president of the same bank, J.C. Lofquist, and its president, R.E. Harrison, were directors of United Dominion Corp. (Canada).

The process works in the reverse as well, and leading members of the comprador bourgeoisie are invited to sit on the boards of directors of the Canadian chartered banks. In 1975 the president of Gulf Oil Canada was on the board of the Bank of Nova Scotia, the president of Imperial Oil was on the board of the Royal Bank, the chairman of the board of Canadian General Electric was on the board of the Canadian Imperial Bank of Commerce, etc.

Moreover, the comprador bourgeoisie's contacts with the indigenous bourgeoisie are not restricted to the financial sector; important Canadian industrial capitalists are invited to sit on the boards of subsidiaries of foreign companies. J.P. Gordon, president of Stelco, and Alfred Powis, president of Noranda Mines, were both directors of Gulf Oil Canada in 1975; Hervé Belzile, president of Alliance-Vie, and Antoine Turmel, chairman of the board of Provigo, were on the board of Quebec-Telephone. L.C. Bonnycastle, vice-chairman of the board of Canadian Corporate Management, was a director of the National Life Assurance Co. of Canada; Lucien G. Rolland, president of Rolland Paper, was on the board of Standard Life Assurance Co.; etc.

The Intelligentsia and the Comprador Bourgeoisie

As has been seen previously, there are many points of contact between the domestic and comprador bourgeoisies. In *The Economy of Canada: A Study in Ownership and Control*, it was established that the domestic capitalist class is surrounded by a group of intellectuals (lawyers, financial consultants, consulting engineers) who sit on the boards of large companies and often form a majority on the board of a company, even though they are neither large stockholders in the company nor employees of it. In relation to the present subject, one can ask whether there is a specific group of intellectuals tied to the comprador bourgeoisie, distinct and separate from the one that surrounds the domestic bourgeoisie. It should be remembered that there are significant "ethnic" cleavages within the domestic bourgeoisie (Anglo-Saxon, French Canadian and Jewish) and the owner of a corporation generally recruits his advisers from within his own ethnic group. Where, then, do members of the comprador bourgeoisie recruit their advisers?

Lawyers constitute the most important group of outside advisers. The subsidiaries on the list of 130 had an average of one lawyer on their boards of directors, although 44 per cent of them had no lawyers on their boards. An examination of the names of the lawyers sitting (and firms represented) on the boards of subsidiaries of foreign companies reveals that *these are the same lawyers and the same firms that advise Canadian-controlled companies.* There were approximately 100 lawyers who sat on the boards of the companies on the list of 130; many of them were on two or three of these boards. Among the most sought after of these lawyers were John B. Aird* of Aird Berlis and Zimmerman (a Toronto firm), on the boards of Reed Shaw Osler, the Algoma Central Railway and National Life Assurance; John P. Robarts of Stikeman, Elliott, Robarts and Bowman (Toronto), on the boards of Reed Shaw Osler, Commonwealth Holiday Inns and Metropolitan Life in 1975; Jacques de Billy of Gagnon, de Billy, Cantin, Dionne, Martin, Beaudoin and Lesage (Quebec City), on the boards of Union Carbide of Canada, Shell Canada and Canadian International Paper; and F.M. Covert of Stewart, MacKeen and Covert (Halifax), on the boards of Petrofina Canada, Trizec Corp. and Standard Brands of Canada. Each of these lawyers, like most of the others on the list, were directors of Canadian-controlled corporations as well.

A number of other characteristics of this group of lawyers are worth mentioning. First, only fifteen of the ninety-five were French Canadians (16 per cent) and only two were Jewish (Lazarus Phillips and his son Neil). *Almost all lawyers (82 per cent) who sit on the boards of subsidiaries of foreign companies are Anglo-Saxon Protestants.* French and Belgian companies do not give priority to French Canadians. In other words, the attitude of subsidiaries of foreign companies to francophone advisers is not significantly different from that of English Canadian corporations; on the whole, they choose Anglo-Saxon firms to advise them.

Second, lawyers hold few, if any, shares of the companies of which they are directors; nor are they inside directors of these companies. There were a few cases in which a lawyer is chairman or vice-chairman of the board of directors, but that is all. Third, the same law firms that are most often represented on the boards of Canadian-owned companies, and the same partners of these firms, are also represented on the boards of subsidiaries of foreign companies. *There are no law firms that specialize exclusively in the legal counselling of Canadian subsidiaries of foreign companies.*

Fourth, companies that have a number of lawyers on their boards generally recruit these lawyers from different firms. Among some thirty subsidiaries that have two or more lawyers on their boards, only

---

*Appointed Lieutenant-Governor of Ontario in 1980.

five have two or more lawyers from the same firm. The most remarkable of these exceptions was Genstar Ltd., whose board of directors
includes five partners of the largest law firm in Montreal — Oglivy,
Cope, Porteous. A more representative case was Canada Cement La-
farge, whose board in 1975 included George Marler, a former Quebec
Liberal cabinet minister and a partner in McLean, Marler, Tees, Watson,
Poitevin, Javet and Roberge of Montreal; Sen. Jacques Flynn (federal
minister of justice in the Conservative government in 1979-80), of
Flynn, Rivard, Cimon, Lessard and Lemay (Quebec City); André
Monast, of St-Laurent, Monast, Walters, Gagné and Vallières (Quebec
City); R.F. Elliott of Stikeman, Elliott, Tamaki, Mercier and Robb
(Montreal); and Mr. Thompson of Thompson, Dorfman and Sweatman
(Winnipeg). In all, there were six lawyers from six different firms —
and two political parties — on the board of Canada Cement Lafarge.

Aside from the lawyers, there were also approximately twenty financial consultants, consulting engineers, actuaries and geologists on the
boards of subsidiaries on the list of 130. Among the better-known of
these non-legal advisers are: J.H. Coleman, a director of Hawker Siddeley Canada, Imasco and Chrysler Canada; S.E. Nixon, a director of
Trizec Corp. and Celanese Canada; Claude Castonguay, an actuary,
former Quebec minister of social affairs and director of Imasco; Marcel
Bélanger, an accountant with the firm of Bélanger, Dallaire, Gagnon et
Associés and a director of Pratt & Whitney Aircraft. These same consultants also serve Canadian-owned companies. In short, there is no
separate group of consultants associated with foreign companies doing
business in Canada, just as there is no separate group of lawyers. *There is
only one group of organic intellectuals in Canada for both major segments of the bourgeoisie — the internal segment and the comprador segment.* This helps to explain
the interlocking directorships between large Canadian-controlled
companies and large subsidiaries of foreign corporations.

The Canadian Bourgeoisie and the Comprador Bourgeoisie

According to CALURA data for 1978, there were some 272,000 non-
financial companies in Canada in that year, of which only 5,880 were
classed as foreign. Nonetheless, this group of subsidiaries of foreign
companies accounted for 29 per cent of the assets, 34 per cent of the
sales and 37 per cent of the profits of all non-financial corporations in
Canada. In 1970, these proportions were 37 per cent of the assets, 36
per cent of the sales and 45 per cent of the profits. In other words, in the
first eight years of the 1970s, foreign corporations lost ground significantly in terms of assets and profits, but maintained their position in
terms of sales.

The significance of foreign-owned corporations in the economy is less than it would appear from these figures, since the financial sector is the stronghold of the domestic bourgeoisie. No estimate is available for the proportion of assets under Canadian control in this sector, but it can be stated that foreign ownership does not exceed 15 per cent of total financial assets. Canadian-controlled chartered banks held 99 per cent of the assets of all chartered banks in Canada in 1975. The investment brokerage industry is almost wholly in Canadian hands and most of the assets of other financial institutions are also Canadian-controlled. The existence of major government-owned financial institutions, both federal and provincial, such as the Bank of Canada, the Farm Credit Corporation, or the Caisse de Dépôt et de Placement du Québec, must also be taken into account. If the financial sector were included, the figure of 30 per cent for assets under foreign control would have to be substantially reduced.

In addition, the process of repatriating the Canadian economy did not end in 1978. Between 1970 and 1975, foreign direct investment in Canada averaged $710 million per year, but in 1976 it fell to minus $260 million, and in 1977 it made only a tentative comeback, reaching $500 million. Throughout the 1970s, there has been a clear tendency for foreign direct investment to decline. One likely factor in this was the American withdrawal from Indochina and the end of the war in Vietnam in 1975, although this factor should be viewed in the wider context of the slowdown in the American economy that began in 1968. Concurrently with the decline of foreign investment, there were clear signs of a growth in Canadian economic nationalism. A look at some of the highlights of this development follows.

Early in the decade, the proposal to set up a Canada Development Corporation was revived and implemented (1970-71), the Gray Report on foreign investment was published (1972) and the Foreign Investment Review Agency was established (1972). In 1973 the CDC took over Texasgulf, a large foreign corporation operating in Canada; this takeover involved confrontations with New York financial circles and the American legal system.[24] With total assets of $1.175 billion in 1975, Texasgulf is one of the largest Canadian-controlled industrial corporations. In 1975, the government created Petro-Canada, which took over Atlantic Richfield in 1976 and Pacific Petroleum, along with its subsidiary, Westcoast Transmission, in 1978. All three of these companies had assets well over the $100 million mark.*

A number of provincial crown corporations also played their part in buying back the Canadian economy during the 1970s. The most im-

---

*A subsequent important acquisition was the purchase of Petrofina Canada in 1981.

portant of these is the Potash Corporation of Saskatchewan, which
was established in 1975 by that province's NDP government. It subsequently took over a number of Saskatchewan's foreign-controlled
potash companies and turned them into a publicly-owned corporation
with assets of more than one billion dollars.[25] The joint private-public
corporation Alberta Gas Trunk Line bought a controlling interest in
Husky Oil in 1978-79, bringing another important oil company under
Canadian control.[26] And the Quebec government was negotiating to
buy the Asbestos Corp. so that it could put its planned asbestos company, the Société Nationale de l'Amiante, into operation.

In the meantime, Canadians gained control of another major
Montreal chain of retail stores, was controlled by W.T. Grant & Co.,
a New York-based company in the commercial sector, until 1975.
When W.T. Grant failed, its Canadian subsidiary was put up for sale,
and Joseph Segal of Vancouver acquired 13 per cent of its stock in
1976. Two years later, the Hudson's Bay Company gained control of
the Montreal chain. The Bay also took over Simpsons Ltd.[27] after a
battle with Sears-Roebuck which lasted several months and which the
Bay finally won in January 1979.*

In the meantime, Canadians gained control of another major
foreign financial institution, the Crédit Foncier Franco-Canadien, in
1978-79. In December 1978, Central and Eastern Trust of Moncton
made an offer to purchase the Banque de Paris et des Pays Bas's controlling block of shares in the Crédit Foncier's Montreal mortgage
company. However, Quebec blocked the sale of the Crédit Foncier to
the New Brunswick group that controls Central and Eastern and a
month later, the Montreal City and District Savings Bank announced
that it now held more than 50 per cent of its shares.[28] The Crédit
Foncier was the sixth largest foreign-controlled financial institution
in Canada, following the Mercantile Bank, General Motors Accept-
ance Corp. of Canada and three insurance companies.

Canadians also took over two major foreign-owned real estate
companies between 1976 and 1979. In April 1976 English Property
Corp. sold part of its holding in Trizec Corp., the largest real estate
company in Canada, to Edward and Peter Bronfman. Through a holding company, Carena Properties, the Bronfmans now nominally held
50.01 per cent of the votes in Trizec, but real control remained with
English Property. In 1979 the Bronfmans took definitive control of
Trizec. Meanwhile, Pensionfund Properties Ltd., a private Ontario
company, bought all the shares of MEPC Canadian Properties from
MEPC Ltd. of London.[29]

---

*Another such development took place in 1980 when Atco Industries of
Calgary bought Canadian Utilities Ltd. from American interests.

The process of economic repatriation is thus well underway in Canada and the events just cited indicate that it has assumed considerable proportions. However, it is important to realize that this process has had ramifications outside the purely economic sphere as well. Public authorities, both federal and provincial, have played a determining role in it. It has been noted that the Canada Development Corporation and Petro-Canada bought back four major subsidiaries of foreign companies during the 1970s. NDP provincial governments, especially in Saskatchewan, and the Parti Québécois government of Quebec have been involved as well, notably with the Potash Corporation of Saskatchewan and the Société Nationale de l'Amiante du Québec. This process goes well beyond the establishment of government-controlled corporations. The federal Liberal government has since 1969-70 implemented a variety of policies aimed at limiting and reducing foreign control of the Canadian economy. Federal government activity towards this end began in 1969 when Ottawa blocked the sale of Denison Mines, one of Canada's major private mining companies, to foreign interests. This was followed by the appointment of the Gray Commission and the establishment of the CDC in 1971 and FIRA in 1972.*

The provinces have followed in Ottawa's footsteps. The Conservative government elected in Alberta in 1971 bought back a number of foreign companies, Husky Oil being the most significant. NDP governments developed publicly-owned corporations in a number of sectors (including insurance, pulp and paper, and mining), almost always at the expense of foreign-owned companies. The most spectacular of the NDP projects, the potash takeover in Saskatchewan between 1976 and 1979, is conclusive on this point — only subsidiaries of foreign companies were bought out, and Canadian corporations were not touched.

The PQ government's policy has been similar, but with one difference — it has intervened specifically to help the francophone bourgeoisie of Quebec. Its intervention in the case of the Crédit Foncier is typical in this regard.

It has been shown that several political parties have acted as vehicles for nationalism. From the Conservatives in Alberta to the NDP in Saskatchewan, Manitoba (1969-77) and British Columbia (1972-75) to the PQ in Quebec is a fairly broad political range. But all these governments have had one thing in common — they have intervened to strengthen the indigenous bourgeoisie (private and public) and weaken the comprador bourgeoisie by placing the economic power and legal

---

*More recently the National Energy Policy has become an effective instrument in the Canadianization of the oil industry.

authority of the state at the service of the domestic ruling class. This has occurred even though these various political parties represent different social classes: Alberta business circles, a section of the Canadian capitalist class, the Quebec petty bourgeoisie, and organized labour in western Canada. Without trying to analyse the Canadian political process, let us simply say that the Canadian and regional bourgeoisies were able to influence governments of any political stripe through a variety of means. Through party financing, ownership of the mass media, quasi-official planning and consulting bodies (such as the Canadian-American Committee or the General Council of Industry of Quebec), control of investment and consequently of employment, the dominant class rules even when it does not reign.

This writer agrees with Philip Resnick that nationalist policies are favoured by only a minority of the Canadian bourgeoisie, for which Walter Gordon is the most prominent spokesman.[30] It should not be forgotten, however, that the New Deal was implemented under Roosevelt in the 1930s, although it was supported by only a minority of the American bourgeoisie. It was also a minority which established American business's policy of working together with the labour movement towards the end of the First World War.[31] The nationalist section of the Canadian bourgeoisie won a new victory in early 1980 with the re-election of the Liberal government and the appointment of Herb Gray as minister of industry, trade and commerce.

Conclusion

An attempt has been made to provide a sketch of the economic and social contours of Canada's comprador bourgeoisie, trace its links with the indigenous bourgeoisie and the group of business intellectuals, and to follow some recent developments in its relationship with the indigenous bourgeoisie.

It has been shown that a comprador bourgeoisie exists and that it is especially prominent in the manufacturing and mining industries. This group is composed of the inside directors of subsidiaries of foreign companies. On the boards of directors of these subsidiaries, they are joined by representatives of their parent corporations (constituting about 30 per cent of the directors), representatives of the domestic bourgeoisie and organic intellectuals who serve Canadian business. It was established that the comprador bourgeoisie does not surround itself with a specific group of advisers but the lawyers, financial consultants and consulting engineers who are directors of subsidiaries of foreign companies are the same ones who sit on the boards of large domestically-owned corporations.

However, there are distinct economic boundaries to the comprador bourgeoisie. There are very few corporations where the Canadian and foreign bourgeoisies share control. It was established that 40 per cent of the foreign parent corporations on our list — and therefore their Canadian subsidiaries — are under the ultimate control of a family, individual or partnership. Moreover, this percentage would be somewhat larger if more complete data on the stock ownership of American and British companies were available.

The indigenous Canadian bourgeoisie consolidated its position during the 1970s, as a result of both the relative decline of the American economy and the growth of Canadian economic nationalism. Advocated by a politically influential minority within Canadian business, economic nationalism has been put into practice in a variety of federal and provincial government measures in the last few years. Such measures have resulted in a reduction of foreign control of the economy and consequently in the decline of the comprador bourgeoisie.

Conclusion

In the course of the nineteenth century, as Canadian society matured within the British Empire, a ruling class with distinctly colonial characteristics grew up. The disproportionate growth of the resource extraction, commercial and financial sectors gave rise to an indigenous bourgeoisie based in these activities; the relative weakness of the industrial sector is a constant of Canada's economic history. Canada's economic dependency with respect to the world's two industrial leaders (England prior to 1914, the United States since then) makes it easy to understand why the industrial sector has been the poor relation among Canada's ruling classes.

Other factors besides dependency have also contributed to Canada's industrial underdevelopment: a limited domestic market, a population scattered over a huge territory, technological backwardness, and the economic, social and political power of the merchant and financial bourgeoisie. Under these conditions, the financial sector preferred to finance the production, transportation, and trade of staples rather than resource processing and manufacturing. The absence of banking or financial control of Canadian industry can be explained by the banks' failure to finance manufacturing. Canada's industrial takeoff came too late in the twentieth century at a time when large American manufacturing corporations were becoming multinational. The works of Mira Wilkins have shown that Canada was one of the first host countries for foreign investment by large American industrial corporations.[1] American corporations were technologically up-to-date, already fairly large and solidly based commercially and financially, making it difficult for Canadian companies to enter advanced industrial sectors.

The barriers that define the forbidden zone for the Canadian bourgeoisie are technological (patents, "know-how," research costs), commercial (access to export markets) and financial (industrial financing). For its part, the Canadian bourgeoisie has built legal barriers to prevent easily entered sectors from falling under foreign control. These two sets of barriers define the boundaries of the two major sections of Canada's bourgeoisie, and restrict capital flows to within each of these two relatively self-contained zones.

There have been several stages in the development of Canada's bourgeoisie. The first was the era of the growth and concentration of banks, railways and export trade (1867-1914). It was followed by a stage in which a domestic financial market was created and a transferable securities industry was born. This second stage (1914-1940) was also the heyday of the pulp and paper industry and its energy source, hydro-electricity, and the era in which exploitation of the new mineral staples began under foreign control and gave a boost to the emerging comprador bourgeoisie. But it was in the next period (1940-1970) that foreign investment reached its zenith, especially in the oil and gas, iron ore and automobile industries. At the same time, the Canadian business interests expanded into retail trade, real estate, new financial industries, the mass media and road transport. Since 1970, the slowdown of the American economy has led to a decline in foreign investment and the Canadian government has intervened more openly and consistently to help the indigenous bourgeoisie.

As the twentieth century has progressed, industrial and then financial activities in Canada have gradually become concentrated in Ontario. For some time, provincial governments have been reacting against this process and trying to promote capital accumulation within their respective zones of jurisdiction. Struggles between the Canadian bourgeoisie — increasingly an Ontario bourgeoisie — and regional bourgeoisies have had their political effect in heightened federal-provincial tensions.

Since the Second World War, economic diversification has allowed "ethnic bourgeoisies" to blossom alongside the old Anglo-Saxon capitalist class. Except for the Bronfmans,[2] the emergence of a Jewish capitalist class in Canada is a postwar phenomenon, and most of the companies it controls are still run by the businessmen who founded them or their children.

Eighty per cent of large Canadian-controlled corporations are owned by Anglo-Saxon Protestants and only 10 per cent by French Canadians. The emergence of a francophone establishment was examined in chapter 3. It suffices to say here that "ethnic" cleavages are not figments of the imagination. Ethnic divisions within the Canadian bourgeoisie are visible in several areas: the tendency of controlling stockholders of corporations to choose advisers (outside directors) of the same ethnic background, a preference for marriage within one's ethnic group, preferential business ties, etc.

The Francophone Bourgeoisie

Historically confined to agricultural and wage-earning activities, the francophone population of Canada (and especially of Quebec) underwent a process of increasing social differentiation after the Second World War. Urbanization, education, the growth of the welfare state, and the affluence brought about by wartime and postwar economic growth led to a substantial increase in personal income and transformed French Canadians into an affluent market for new goods and services. Quebecers became consumers of insurance, trust services and urban dwellings, and customers for new retail outlets. There are no barriers to entry in these sectors and a number of them developed under francophone ownership. For example, there are substantial French Canadian interests in insurance (Desjardins, Commerce, La Laurentienne, Sodarcan), real estate (Allarco Developments, Campeau Corporation), retailing (Provigo), transportation (La Vérendrye group), etc. French Canadian participation in large-scale industry is more marginal, being limited to a few companies in the Power Corp. and Bombardier groups.

The rise of the francophone bourgeoisie is not exclusively a Quebec phenomenon; Franco-Ontarians such as Paul and Louis Desmarais and Robert Campeau, Franco-Albertans such as Charles Allard and Acadians such as Jean-Louis Lévesque are examples of the participation of French Canadians from outside Quebec in the development of French Canadian corporations. In addition, French Canadian-controlled companies, whether large (assets of more than $100 million in 1975) or middle-sized ($10 million to $100 million), have investments and markets across Canada. The owners of these companies sit on the boards of federal crown corporations and large English Canadian companies. This is why this segment of the Canadian bourgeoisie was called a "French Canadian" and not a "Quebec" entity.

This Canadian dimension also explains the francophone bourgeoisie's support of the federal and provincial Liberal parties, which it demonstrates both financially and through direct participation in leading Liberal circles. The economic and social division between the French Canadian bourgeoisie and Canada's WASP bourgeoisie is also found at the political level; francophone businessmen are Liberal (like their Jewish counterparts), while Anglo-Saxon business is old-stock Conservative. The interpretation proposed by Pierre Fournier, Gilles Bourque and others, which views the francophone bourgeoisie as an emerging national bourgeoisie which is likely to form an alliance with the Parti Québécois, must therefore be rejected.

The francophone bourgeoisie developed with the help of the Quebec government. This brings us to an examination of crown corporations, both federal and provincial.

Is There a State Bourgeoisie?

Socialist answers to the question of who controls government-owned corporations have generally not been free from confusion. Some see publicly-owned corporations as being controlled by elected officials with executive power; others see them as being controlled by a group of public managers, which they call the "state bourgeoisie"; still others argue that they are controlled by private-sector businessmen. Some writers (notably Paul Baran and Paul Sweezy) solve the problem by wishing it away — they regard publicly-owned enterprises as unimportant and identical to the private sector and simply exclude them from their analysis.

The analysis of state capitalism in Canada is at an embryonic stage. To shed some light on the question, a list was compiled of the largest federally- and provincially-owned corporations and an analysis was undertaken of how they are controlled. It was established that public authorities delegate to the boards of directors of crown corporations most of the prerogatives characteristic of the boards of private companies. In essence, publicly-owned corporations in Canada are controlled by their boards of directors and these are generally composed of Canadian businessmen and their advisers along with a few government officials appointed by the department responsible for the corporation. Aside from some exceptional cases, appointments to boards of directors of crown corporations are for periods ranging from three to ten years, which renders the formation of a group of "public managers" impossible.

Methods and sources of recruitment lead one to favour a description of publicly-owned corporations as being controlled by the indigenous private-sector bourgeoisie (foreigners being excluded by law). The keys to an explanation of how government-owned corporations function, how they have grown and how they are controlled are the regional disparity of Canada's development (as a result of which economic activity tends to become concentrated in Ontario) and its belated industrialization. These two factors explain the compensatory development of provincial crown corporations and the proliferation of publicly-owned corporations designed to encourage domestic entrepreneurship, such as the Canada Development Corporation, the Quebec General Investment Corporation and the British Columbia Resources Investment Corporation.

The Comprador Bourgeoisie

The last chapter explored the control of foreign companies operating in Canada. These companies are among the largest in the country. They account for a third of the assets of non-financial corporations and 15 to

20 per cent of the holdings of financial corporations. They are especially significant in the manufacturing and mining sectors, where they hold nearly 50 per cent of the assets of all companies. The foreign parent corporations usually hold majority or absolute control of their Canadian subsidiaries. These parent corporations are generally controlled internally or by a family. Cases of final control by financial institutions are rather rare, and the theory of finance capital can be definitively discarded in the Canadian context.

The comprador bourgeoisie has many points of contact with the indigenous bourgeoisie, which provides it with a variety of financial and commercial services. In addition, subsidiaries of foreign companies invite Canadian advisers to sit on their boards of directors.

The essence of the comprador bourgeoisie's economic power is its control of productive investment in the most modern and dynamic sectors. However, its social and political power is limited because the state apparatus, the political parties and the mass media are in Canadian hands. One saw at the end of the last chapter how levers of state power were used to effect the repatriation of a number of large subsidiaries of foreign companies, either by crown corporations or by private Canadian interests, during the 1970s; no large Canadian company was taken over by foreign interests during the same period.

Contrary to what much of Canadian nationalist literature maintains, the comprador bourgeoisie is not behind Canadian "provincialism." Provincialism is inherent in the evolution of the Canadian economy, which has led to the concentration of industrial activity (and as a result, financial and commercial activity as well) in Ontario. The comprador bourgeoisie is pro-Canadian and actively federalist. But its political weight should not be overestimated; power relationships are not simply a mirror of economic life, and the control of a third of the Canadian economy doesn't necessarily give the comprador bourgeoisie control of the state apparatus. This study's analysis of crown corporations would seem to indicate the reverse.

An Overview

The purpose of this book has been to study the *economic anatomy* of the Canadian bourgeoisie. It has been described as being marked by ethnic cleavages (Anglo-Saxon/Jewish/French Canadian) and strongly affected by the presence of foreign capital, which gives rise to a comprador bourgeoisie.

While each ethnic section of the indigenous bourgeoisie generally recruits its intellectuals from within its own group, the comprador bourgeoisie recruits intellectuals primarily from among Anglo-Saxon business advisers. It is through these advisers, and through corporate lawyers in particular, that the Canadian bourgeoisie is in touch with the political, cultural and ideological worlds. It is much easier for corporate lawyers to go into politics than it is for businessmen who are more comfortable with a balance sheet than with the text of a bill. The careers of Louis St-Laurent, John Turner, Lazarus Phillips, Brian Mulroney, Jacques Flynn and Mitchell Sharp are only a few examples of the ceaseless comings and goings of corporate lawyers between politics and the corporations. Nevertheless, some businessmen have also been active in politics: onetime Prime Minister R.B. Bennett, Liberal ministers such as James Richardson, Walter Gordon and Don Jamieson, and Conservatives such as Sinclair Stevens, John Crosbie and Ronald Huntington (all ministers in Joe Clark's cabinet), to name a few.

Ethnic divisions largely coincide with political ones. The Anglo-Saxon Protestant bourgeoisie is predominantly Conservative. Jewish and French Canadians tend to be Liberal, along with the nationalist minority of the English Canadian bourgeoisie. The Conservative/Liberal split appears in cultural and ideological spheres as well. On one side is the traditional C.D. Howe Institute, advocating Canada-U.S. integration; on the other is the Canadian Institute for Economic Policy, founded by Walter Gordon. Both institutions claim to be apolitical and devoted to scientific research. G.W. Domhoff said of similar agencies in the United States:

> The policy-formation process is the means by which the power elite formulates policy on larger issues. It is within the organizations of the policy-planning network that the various special interests join together to forge, however slowly and gropingly, the general policies that will benefit them as a whole. It is within the policy process that the various sectors of the business community transcend their interest-group consciousness and develop an overall class consciousness.
>
> The staid and dignified policy-formation process is very different from the helter-skelter special-interest process....It is a world where "expertise" and a mild disdain for the special interests are the coin of the realm. "Nonpartisan" and "objective" are the passwords.[3]

There is no doubt that nationalist elements are in the minority in Canadian business circles. Arrayed against the Canadian Institute for Economic Policy, in addition to the C.D. Howe Institute, are a number of other institutions of the same type with continentalist and Conservative tendencies: the Conference Board in Canada (which is a subsidiary of the Conference Board in the United States and was formerly headed by Robert de Cotret), the Canadian-American Committee and the Canada Committee.

How can the relative success of the nationalist minority within Canadian business be explained? First, economic conditions in the 1970s favoured the rise of Canadian nationalism — the American economy slowed down while the Canadian economy, based on natural resources whose prices were rising, grew more rapidly. Under these circumstances it is not surprising that a number of large American multinationals, such as Chrysler and ITT, have faltered, or that some of these have allowed their Canadian subsidiaries to be taken over by the government or private Canadian capital. Second, this writer believes that Canada's economic and political life has always been essentially controlled by Canadians; when foreign capital was invited in a century ago to industrialize the country it did not interfere fundamentally with existing domestic interests, concentrated in the commercial, transportation and service sectors. The indigenous bourgeoisie opened the door to foreign capital. Now that it is stronger, it is closing the door again, at least part way.

Third, since the beginning of the century, nationalist elements in the Liberal party have been able to form an alliance with progressive parties — today represented by the NDP — to push for nationalizations or measures restricting foreign capital, and have gained added strength from this alliance with the subordinate classes. Fourth, not all foreign capital comes from the same country, and domestic capital is able to take advantage of the divisions among different sources of foreign investment. Finally, no social class acts as a whole, and struggles between classes or segments of classes often take the form of struggles between the politically active elements of these broader social groups. As was noted earlier, policies such as the New Deal and "Business Unionism" were brought about by a minority within American business in the face of the indifference — and sometimes even the hostility — of the majority. Nationalist elements within Canadian business are able to win some major battles while still remaining a minority.

Ethnic and political divisions also coincide reasonably well with a regional division — Montreal is the business centre for the French Canadian and Jewish bourgeoisies, while Toronto is the centre for Anglo-Protestant business circles. Montreal is the heart of Canadian Liberalism and St. James Street is its source of funds. Toronto is the soul of Canadian Conservatism and Bay Street is its bank.[4]

According to Domhoff, business activity in the strictly political sphere takes the form of four processes: lobbying (or the expression of immediate interests), long-term public policy formulation, the choice of candidates through party financing, and the formulation of political ideologies. Neither the long-term public planning process nor the formulation of political ideologies has been, to this writer's knowledge, seriously studied in Canada. The works of Paltiel and Mahon, mentioned earlier, examine how candidates are chosen by the people who finance the Liberal and Conservative parties and what the results of this process are in terms of hegemony within the state.

A Last Look at Theory

The state monopoly capitalism school has provided the fullest and most widely known Marxist theoretical treatment of the economic apparatus of the state. It is refuted in each of the last three chapters of this book. According to the theory of state monopoly capitalism, the state is pillaged by the monopolies, public capital is devalued, the state becomes involved in low-return sectors, etc. It was established here that, on the contrary, the Quebec state, through its crown corporations, protects emerging French Canadian business against English Canadian monopoly capital. One saw that provincial governments, again through publicly-owned corporations, support regional bourgeoisies (in Ontario early in the century and currently in Alberta, Nova Scotia, British Columbia and Quebec) in their struggle with large-scale capital. And the federal government protects smaller-scale Canadian capital against large-scale international monopoly capital, both through federal crown corporations and through legislation on foreign ownership.

The federal and provincial governments turn the corporations they run into profitable enterprises and enhance the value of public capital. When the government has bought money-losing companies from the private sector it has made every effort to make a profit on them; the histories of Canadian National, Air Canada, Canadair and De Havilland bear testimony to that.

Moreover, more often than not, the government goes into sectors that either are profitable from the outset or have high growth potential: hydroelectricity, oil, nuclear energy, air transportation, etc. In addition, in a number of these sectors, the government has intervened specifically to combat excessive economic concentration (monopolization) that is harmful to less concentrated forms of capital; electricity and oil are examples of this process.

Only one of the state monopoly capitalism school's hypotheses was confirmed by the research here: there is no state bourgeoisie, or if there is one, it is marginal. But that hypothesis is not central to the theory. The whole question of who controls government-owned corporations is hardly touched on by the school, and the skeletal outlines of at least two different answers are given: Varga's answer in terms of salaried government officials, and Cheprakov's in terms of control by private capital.

However useful it may be in France or Italy, the theory of state monopoly capitalism, like the theory of finance capital, is ill-suited to the Canadian situation.

Appendices

Assets and Controlling Shareholders of Large French Canadian Companies, December 1975

Company	Assets ($ million)	Controlling Shareholder

FINANCIAL

Banks

Banque Canadienne Nationale	4,872	internal[1]
Provincial Bank of Canada	3,059	Desjardins movement (23%)
Montreal City & District Savings Bank	969	internal

Trust Companies

Montreal Trust	757	Power Corp. through Investors Group (50%)
General Trust of Canada	411	J.L. Lévesque (10.6%), Simard family[3]
North West Trust Co.	170	Allarco Financial Corp. (91.9%)
Fiducie Prêt et Revenu	68	Prêt et Revenu group (94%)
Sherbrooke Trust	53	General Trust of Canada (90%)
Société National de Fiducie	37	St.-Jean-Baptiste Society (100%)

Insurance Companies

Great West Life Insurance Co.	2,349	Power Corp.
Imperial Life Assurance Co.	714	Power Corp.
La Solidarité	39	private
La Nationale, Cie de Réassurance	29	Gérard & Robert Parizeau (50%)[4]
La Cie d'Assurances Provinces Unies	25	private (Major family?)
L'Union Canadienne	23	private
L'Unique	12	private (Bélanger family?)

APPENDIX 1 (continued)

Company	Assets ($ million)	Controlling Shareholder
Mutual Funds		
Investors Group	636	Power Corp. (56.2%)
Fonds Mutuel Corp. de Prêt et Revenu	25	Prêt et Revenu group (99%)
Beaubran Corp.	22	Beaubien family?
Canagex Ltd.	15	Banque Canadienne Nationale
Holding Companies		
Power Corp.	579	Paul Desmarais (53%)
Corporation d'Expansion Financière	51	York Lambton Corp. (79%)
York Lambton Corp.	50	Wellington Corp. (66.6%)
F-I-C Fund	39	J.-L. Lévesque (35.9%)
Finance Companies		
Laurentide Financial Corp.	429	Power Corp. (57.9%)
Mortgage Loan Companies		
Imnat Ltd.	29	Banque Canadienne Nationale (50%)

INDUSTRIAL

Company	Assets ($ million)	Controlling Shareholder
Consolidated-Bathurst Corp.	662	Power Corp. (38.1%)
Bombardier Ltd.	145	Bombardier family (75%)
Dominion Glass	107	Consolidated-Bathurst (96%)
Rolland Paper Co.	62	L.G. Rolland and family (54.5%)
East Sullivan Mines	47	Beauchemin family
Normick Perron	40	Normand, Michel & Jean Perron (75%)
Télé-Métropole	37	Héritage J.A. De Sève (82.6%)
Québécor	34	Pierre Péladeau & family (72.8%)
Vachon, Inc.	27	Desjardins movement (83%) Vachon family (17%)
Simard Beaudry Inc.	23	Corporation d'Expansion Financière (100%)
Melchers Distilleries	22	Hon. Paul Desruisseaux (45.9%) S. Marchand (6.5%)
Alfred Lambert Inc.	18	F-I-C Fund (100%)
Télé-Capitale	11	H. Baribeau, J. Pouliot, C. Pratte (75%)

APPENDIX 1 (continued)

Company	Assets ($ million)	Controlling Shareholder
COMMERCIAL		
Provigo	77	A. Turmel, J. Lamontagne, R. Provost & Associates (18%)
UAP Inc.	43	Préfontaine family (100%)
Cassidy's	24	Brodeur family through Continental Manufacturers (61.1%)
Dupuis Frères	21	Marc Carrière (75%)
TRANSPORTATION AND SERVICES		
Canada Steamship Lines	394	Power Corp. (100%)
La Vérendrye Management Corp.	21	officers & directors (32.9%)
Logistec Corp.	21	P. Gourdeau, R. Paquin and associates (30%)
REAL ESTATE		
Campeau Corp.	482	Robert Campeau (62.5%)
Allarco Developments	101	Charles Allard (48.2%)

[1] At the end of August 1977, the Caisse de Dépôt et de Placement and Hydro-Quebec held 10% of the shares, Canadian Pacific 4.5%, Sun Life Assurance Co. 3.7%, General Trust of Canada 3.5%, Canadian National 1.9%, the Desjardins movement 1.8%, and Montreal Trust 1.6% (*La Presse*, September 3, 1977, p. A7).

[2] At the end of January 1977, the Caisse de Dépôt et de Placement held 10% of the shares, Canada Permanent Trust 10%, La Laurentienne 6%, the Crédit Foncier Franco-Canadien 5%, and Trucina 5% (*La Presse*, February 26, 1977).

[3] *La Presse*, September 21, 1974, p. A6.

[4] *La Presse*, November 11, 1975, p. E1.

APPENDIX 2
Place and Date of Incorporation of Large French Canadian Companies, 1975

Company	Date of Incor- poration	Place of Incor- poration
Financial		
Banque Canadienne Nationale	1873	Canada
Provincial Bank of Canada	1861	Canada
Montreal City & District Savings Bank	1871	Canada
Montreal Trust	1889	Quebec
General Trust of Canada	1909	Quebec
North West Trust Co.	1962	Alberta
Fiducie Prêt et Revenu	1961	Quebec
Sherbrooke Trust	1874	Quebec
Société Nationale de Fiducie	1918	Quebec
Great West Life	1891	Canada
Imperial Life	1896	Canada
La Solidarité	1942	Quebec
La Nationale, Cie de Réassurance	1948	Canada
La Cie d'Assurances Provinces Unies	1927	Quebec
L'Union Canadienne	1943	Quebec
L'Unique	1967	Quebec
Investors Group	1940	Manitoba
Fonds Mutuel Corp. de Prêt et Revenu	1957	Canada
Beaubran Corp.	1947	P.E.I.
Canagex Ltd.	1969	Canada
Power Corp.	1925	Canada
Corporation d'Expansion Financière	1957	Quebec
York Lambton Corp.	1926	Canada
F-I-C Fund	1962	Quebec
Laurentide Financial Corp.	1950	B.C.
Imnat	1971	Quebec
Industrial		
Consolidated-Bathurst Corp.	1928	Canada
Bombardier Ltd.	1942	Quebec
Dominion Glass	1913	Canada
Rolland Paper	1880	Quebec
East Sullivan Mines	1944	Quebec

APPENDIX 2 (continued)

Company	Date of Incorporation	Place of Incorporation
Industrial (continued)		
Normick Perron Inc.	1968	Quebec
Télé-Métropole	1960	Quebec
Québécor	1965	Quebec
Vachon	1947	Quebec
Simard-Beaudry	1964	Quebec
Melchers Distilleries	1898	Quebec
Alfred Lambert Inc.	1937	Quebec
Télé-Capitale	1953	Canada
Commercial		
Provigo	1969	Quebec
UAP Inc.	1926	Quebec
Cassidy's	1796	Quebec
Dupuis Frères	1868	Quebec
Transportation and Services		
Canada Steamship Lines	1913	Canada
La Vérendrye	1962	Quebec
Logistec Corp.	1952	Quebec
Real Estate		
Campeau Corp.	1953	Ontario
Allarco Developments	1954	Alberta

Sources: *Financial Post Survey of Industrials* (Toronto), annual, 1928-76; *Financial Post Survey of Funds* (Toronto), annual, 1962-76; Quebec Development of Consumers, Cooperatives and Financial Institutions, Insurance Branch, *Annual Report* (Editeur du Québec, 1976).

APPENDIX 3
Lawyers on Boards of Directors of Large French Canadian Companies, 1975

Company Lawyer	Law Firm
Banque Canadienne Nationale	
W. Bhérer	Bhérer, Bernier, Côté, Ouellet, Dionne, Houle & Morin (Quebec City)
J. Lagassé	Lagassé, Lagassé, Lagassé (Sherbrooke)
R. St-Laurent	St-Laurent, Monast, Walters & Vallières (Quebec City)
Provincial Bank of Canada	
C. Ducharme	Desjardins, Ducharme, Desjardins & Bourque (Montreal)
Hon. J.O. Renaud	Renaud & Renaud (Montreal)
Montreal City & District Savings Bank	
no lawyers	
Montreal Trust (subsidiary of Investors Group)	
M.S. Hannon	Ogilvy, Cope, Porteous, Montgomery, Renault, Clarke & Kirkpatrick (Montreal)
D.A. Berlis	Aird, Zimmerman & Berlis (Toronto)
K.H. Brown	Lafleur & Brown (Montreal)
Hon. J.M. Godfrey	Campbell, Godfrey & Lewtas (Toronto)
Hon. J. Lesage	Howard, McDougall, Ewasew, Graham & Stocks (Montreal)
R. de W. Mackay	Duquet, Mackay, Weldon & Bronstetter (Montreal)
R. de W. Mingo	Stewart, Mackeen & Covert (Halifax)
A.E. Sheperd	Sheperd, Mackenzie, Plaxton, Little & Jenkins (London, Ont.)
Hon. W. Owen	Owen, Bird (Vancouver)
General Trust of Canada	
Hon. Edouard Asselin	independent (Montreal)

APPENDIX 3 (continued)

Company Lawyer	Law Firm
L. Sirois	Sirois & Tremblay (Quebec City)
J.C. Pollack	Létourneau, Stein, Marseille, Délisle & La Rue (Quebec City)
M. Piché	Blain, Piché, Godbout, Eméry & Blain (Montreal)
D.O. Doheny	Doheny, Mackenzie, Grivaker, Gervais & Lemoyne (Montreal)

North West Trust Co.
  no lawyers

Fiducie Prêt et Revenu (subsidiary of Prêt et Revenu group)

J. Taschereau	Taschereau, Grenier, Wright, Grainville & Champagne (Quebec City)
Hon. J. Flynn	Flynn, Rivard, Cimon, Lessard & Le May (Quebec City)

Sherbrooke Trust (subsidiary of General Trust)

J. Lemieux	Lemieux, Royer & Assoc. (Sherbrooke)

Société Nationale de Fiducie
  no lawyers

Great West Life Insurance Co. (subsidiary of Investors Group)

J.B. Macaulay	Aikins, Macaulay & Thoryalson (Winnipeg)

Imperial Life Assurance Co. (sudsidiary of Power Corp.)

J.G. Porteous	Ogilvy, Cope, Porteous, Montgomery, Renault, Clarke & Kirkpatrick (Montreal)
R. St-Laurent	St-Laurent, Monast, Walters & Vallières (Quebec City)

La Solidarité
  no lawyers

APPENDIX 3 (continued)

Company Lawyer	Law Firm

La Nationale Cie de Réassurance
private company — no information available

La Compagnie d'Assurances Provinces Unies
| B.F. Clarke | Ogilvy, Cope, Porteous,
Montgomery, Renault, Clarke &
Kirkpatrick (Montreal) |
| Hon. J. Lesage | Howard, McDougall, Ewasew,
Graham & Stocks (Montreal) |

L'Union Canadienne
no lawyers

L'Unique
| Jules Landry | independent (Montreal) |

Investors Group (subsidiary of Power Corporation)
no lawyers

Fonds Mutuel Corp. de Prêt et Revenu
| Hon. J. Flynn | Flynn, Rivard, Cimon, Lessard &
Le May (Quebec City) |
| J. Taschereau | Taschereau, Grenier, Wright,
Grainville & Champagne
(Quebec City) |

Beaubran Corp.
| R.L. Munro | Ogilvy, Cope, Porteous,
Montgomery, Renault, Clarke &
Kirkpatrick (Montreal) |

Canagex Ltd.
no lawyers

Power Corp.
| W. Bhérer | Bhérer, Bernier, Côté, Ouellet,
Dionne & Morin (Quebec City) |
| P. Genest | Cassels, Brock (Toronto) |

APPENDIX 3 (continued)

Company Lawyer	Law Firm
C.Pratte	Létourneau, Stein, Marseille, Delisle & La Rue (Quebec City)
Hon. J.P. Robarts	Stikeman, Elliott, Robarts & Bowman (Toronto)

Corporation d'Expansion Financière
| J. Guy | Guy, Vaillancourt, Bertrand,
Bourgeois & Laurent (Montreal) |

York Lambton Corp.
P.F. Vineberg	Phillips & Vineberg (Montreal)
J.G. Porteous	Ogilvy, Cope, Porteous, Montgomery, Renault, Clarke & Kirkpatrick (Montreal)
J. Guy	Guy, Vaillancourt, Bertrand, Bourgeois & Laurent (Montreal)
P. Casgrain	Byers, Casgrain & Stewart (Montreal)

F-I-C Fund
no lawyers

Laurentide Financial Corp. (subsidiary of Power Corp.)
no lawyers

Imnat (subsidiary of BCN)
no lawyers

Consolidated-Bathurst Corp. (subsidiary of Power Corp.)
| Hon. J.B. Aird | Aird, Zimmerman & Berlis (Toronto) |
| R.E. Morrow | Ogilvy, Cope, Porteous,
Montgomery, Renault, Clarke &
Kirkpatrick (Montreal) |

Bombardier Ltd.
no lawyers

Dominion Glass (subsidiary of Consolidated-Bathurst)
| Hon. J.B. Aird | Aird, Zimmerman & Berlis (Toronto) |

APPENDIX 3 (continued)

Company Lawyer	Law Firm
Rolland Paper Co. E.J. Courtois Hon. J.B. Aird	Weldon, Courtois, Clarkson, Parsons & Tétreault (Montreal) Aird, Zimmerman & Berlis (Toronto)
East Sullivan Mines C. Beauchemin	independent
Normick Perron no lawyers	
Télé-Métropole M. Piché	Blain, Piché, Godbout, Eméry & Blain (Montreal)
Québécor P.W. Gauthier	Ogilvy, Cope, Porteous, Montgomery, Renault, Clarke & Kirkpatrick (Montreal)
Vachon Ltd. no lawyers	
Simard-Beaudry Inc. (subsidiary of Corpex) J. Guy	Guy, Vaillancourt, Bertrand, Bourgeois & Laurent (Montreal)
Melchers Distilleries no lawyers	
Alfred Lambert Inc. (subsidiary of F-I-C Fund) no lawyers	
Télé-Capitale C. Pratte, R. Létourneau W. Bhérer R. Amyot	Létourneau, Stein, Marseille, Delisle & La Rue (Quebec City) Bhérer, Bernier, Côté, Ouellet, Dionne, Houle & Morin (Quebec City) Amyot, Lesage, de Grandpré, Colas, Bernard & Drôlet (Quebec City)

APPENDIX 3 (continued)

Company Lawyer	Law Firm
Provigo	
J. Lagassé	Lagassé, Lagassé, Lagassé (Sherbrooke)
M. Bélanger	Bélanger, Dallaire, Gagnon & Associés (Quebec City)
UAP Inc.	
C. Ducharme	Desjardins, Ducharme, Desjardins & Bourque (Montreal)
Cassidy's Ltd.	
F.C. Cope	Ogilvy, Cope, Porteous, Montgomery, Renault, Clarke & Kirkpatrick (Montreal)
Dupuis Frères no lawyers	
Canada Steamship Lines (subsidiary of Power Corp.)	
W. Bhérer	Bhérer, Bernier, Côté, Ouellet, Dionne, Houle & Morin (Quebec City)
Hon. J.P. Robarts	Stikeman, Elliott, Robarts & Bowman (Toronto)
La Vérendrye Management Corp. no lawyers	
Logistec Corp.	
R. Amyot	Amyot, Lesage, de Grandpré, Colas, Bernard & Drolet (Quebec City)
Campeau Corp.	
F. Mercier	Stikeman, Elliott, Tamaki, Mercier & Robb (Montreal)
R.W. Macaulay	Macaulay & Perry (Toronto)
Allarco Developments no lawyers	

APPENDIX 4
Assets (end of 1975) in Millions of Dollars of Principal Federal and Provincial Government-owned Corporations

Company	Assets	Balance Sheet Date	Source
Financial			
Bank of Canada	10,496	31/12/75	(1)
Central Mortgage and Housing Corporation	8,266	31/12/75	(1)
Caisse de Dépôt et de Placement du Québec	3,699	31/12/75	(2)
Farm Credit Corporation	2,007	31/03/76	(1)
Alberta Municipal Financing Corporation	1,330	31/12/75	(3)
Federal Business Development Bank	1,278	31/03/76	(1)
Canada Development Corporation	1,278	31/12/75	(4)
Export Development Corporation	1,141	31/12/75	(1)
Quebec General Investment Corporation	276	31/12/75	(2)
Canada Deposit Insurance Corporation	112	31/12/75	(1)
Industrial			
Atomic Energy of Canada Ltd.	1,400	31/03/76	(1)
Sidbec-Dosco	458	31/12/75	(5)
Sydney Steel Corporation	242	31/12/75	(7)
Eldorado Nuclear	118	31/12/75	(4)
Cape Breton Development Corporation	108	31/03/76	(1)
Transportation, Communication & Utilities			
Ontario Hydro	8,593	31/12/75	(3)
Hydro-Quebec	7,068	31/12/75	(3)
Canadian National Railways	4,953	31/12/75	(6)
British Columbia Hydro and Power	4,097	31/03/76	(3)
Manitoba Hydro-Electric Board	1,794	31/03/76	(3)
Air Canada	1,298	31/12/75	(6)
Newfoundland and Labrador Hydro	1,257	31/12/75	(3)
Alberta Government Telephone	961	31/12/75	(3)
Churchill Falls (Labrador) Corporation	859	31/12/75	(4)
New Brunswick Electric Power	842	31/03/76	(3)
St. Lawrence Seaway Authority	794	31/03/76	(1)
Saskatchewan Power Corporation	774	31/12/75	(3)

APPENDIX 4 (continued)

Company	Assets	Balance Sheet Date	Source
Transportation, Communication & Utilities (continued)			
National Harbours Board	661	31/12/76	(1)
British Columbia Railway	645	02/01/76	(6)
Nova Scotia Power Corporation	514	31/03/76	(3)
Manitoba Telephone System	371	31/03/76	(3)
Canadian Broadcasting Corporation	316	31/03/76	(1)
Saskatchewan Telecommunications	308	31/12/75	(3)
Teleglobe Canada	178	31/03/76	(3)
Commercial			
Canadian Wheat Board	2,080	31/07/75	(1)
Canadian Dairy Commission	136	31/03/76	(1)

(1) Canada, Department of Finance, *Public Accounts of Canada 1975-76*, Vol. 3.
(2) *Annual Report*, 1975.
(3) *Moody's Government and Municipal Manuals*, 1976, 1977 and 1978.
(4) *Financial Post Survey of Industrials*, 1976.
(5) *Moody's Industrial Manual*, 1976.
(6) *Moody's Transportation Manual*, 1976.
(7) Statistics Canada, *Provincial Government Enterprise Finance* (Cat. no. 61-204), 1976.

APPENDIX 5

Year of Establishment (or Nationalization) of Principal Federal and Provincial Government-owned Corporations

Corporation	Year	Party Responsible
Financial		
Bank of Canada	1934	C
Central Mortgage and Housing Corporation	1945	L
Caisse de Dépôt et de Placement du Québec	1965	L
Farm Credit Corporation	1944	L
Alberta Municipal Financing Corporation	1956	SC
Federal Business Development Bank	1944	L
Canada Development Corporation	1972	L
Export Development Corporation	1944	L
Quebec General Investment Corporation	1962	L
Canada Deposit Insurance Corporation	1967	L
Industrial		
Atomic Energy of Canada Ltd.	1952	L
Sidbec-Dosco	1964	L
Sydney Steel Corporation	1967	C
Eldorado Nuclear	1944	L
Cape Breton Development Corporation	1967	L
Transportation, Communication & Utilities		
Ontario Hydro	1906	C
Hydro-Quebec	1944	L
Canadian National Railways	1919	C
British Columbia Hydro and Power	1945	L
Manitoba Hydro-Electric Board	1949	LP
Air Canada	1937	L
Newfoundland and Labrador Hydro	1954	L
Alberta Government Telephone	1908	L
Churchill Falls (Labrador) Corp.	1974	C
New Brunswick Electric Power	1920	L
St. Lawrence Seaway Authority	1954	L
Saskatchewan Power Corporation	1929	L
National Harbours Board	1936	L
British Columbia Railway	1918	L
Nova Scotia Power Corporation	1919	L

APPENDIX 5 (continued)

Corporation	Year	Party Responsible
Transportation, Communication & Utilities (continued)		
Manitoba Telephone System	1908	C
Canadian Broadcasting Corporation	1932	C
Saskatchewan Telecommunications	1908	L
Teleglobe Canada	1950	L
Commercial		
Canadian Wheat Board	1935	C
Canadian Dairy Commission	1966	L

C — Conservative
L — Liberal

LP — Liberal Progressive (coalition)
SC — Social Credit

APPENDIX 6

Composition of Boards of Directors of Principal Federal and Provincial Government-owned Corporations, 1975

Corporation	Inside Directors	Outside Directors			Total
		Businessmen	Govt. officials	Others	
Financial					
Bank of Canada	2	10	—	2	14
CMHC	2	1	3	4	10
Caisse de Dépôt	2	3	3	2	10
Farm Credit Corp.	2	—	—	3	5
Alta. Municipal Financing Corp.	2	—	1	4	7
Fed. Business Development Bank	1	8	4	2	15
Canada Development Corp.	3	16	1	1	21
Export Development Corp.	2	5	5	—	12
Quebec GIC	2	6	3	1	12
Canada Deposit Insurance Corp.	1	—	4	—	5
Industrial					
Atomic Energy of Canada	1	4	2	3	10
Sidbec	1	5	2	1	9
Sysco	1	6	2	—	9
Eldorado Nuclear	3	5	—	1	9
Cape Breton Devco	1	3	—	2	6
Transportation, Communication & Utilities					
Ontario Hydro	3	5	—	4	12
Hydro-Quebec	1	—	3	—	4
CN	1	10	—	1	12
B.C. Hydro	1	2	2	1	6
Manitoba Hydro	2	—	2	3	7
Air Canada	—	6	1	2	9
Nfld. & Labrador Hydro	2	—	4	—	6
Alta. Govt. Telephone	6	—	1	—	7
Churchill Falls (Labrador) Corp.	2	4	5	1	12
N.B. Electric	1	4	—	1	6
St. Lawrence Seaway Authority	2	—	—	1	3
Sask. Power Corp.	1	1	4	5	11
National Harbours Board	2	—	—	1	3
B.C. Railway	—	1	1	1	3

APPENDIX 6 (continued)

Corporation	Inside Direc- tors	Outside Directors Busi- ness- men	Govt. offi- cials	Others	Total
Transportation, Communication & *Utilities (continued)*					
N.S. Power Corp.	2	4	—	2	8
Manitoba Telephone	6	—	—	—	6
CBC	1	6	2	6	15
Sask. Telecommunications	—	—	2	6	8
Teleglobe Canada	1	5	1	0	7
Commercial					
Canadian Wheat Board	2	1	—	1	4
Canadian Dairy Commission	3	—	—	—	3
Total	65 (21%)	121 (40%)	58 (19%)	62 (20%)	306

Sources: *Financial Post Directory of Directors,* 1976; biographical dictionaries; annual reports.

APPENDIX 7

Assets in Millions of Dollars of Principal Canadian Subsidiaries of Foreign Companies, 1975

Company	Assets	Source

FINANCIAL

Company	Assets	Source
Banks		
Mercantile Bank of Canada	1,288	(1)
Insurance		
Metropolitian Life Insurance Co. of America	1,558	(2)
Standard Life Assurance Co.	1,285	(2)
Prudential Insurance Co. of America	1,020	(2)
Prudential Assurance Co. of England	637	(2)
Dominion Life Assurance Co.	506	(1)
National Life	442	(1)
Excelsior Life Insurance Co.	402	(1)
Reed, Shaw, Olser	295	(3)
New York Life Insurance Co.	174	(2)
Travelers Insurance Co.	156	(2)
Montreal Life Insurance Co.	101	(1)
Finance Companies		
G.M. Acceptance Corp. of Canada	1,308	(3)
Ford Motor Credit Co. of Canada	740	(3)
Canadian Acceptance Corp.	581	(3)
Avco Financial Services Co. of Canada	546	(3)
Associates Acceptance Co. Ltd. (Canada)	216	(3)
Beneficial Finance Co. of Canada	214	(1)
United Dominion Corp. (Canada)	166	(1)
BNP Canada Inc.	128	(3)
Transamerica Financial Corp. of Canada	117	(4)
Mortgage Loan Companies		
Crédit Foncier Franco-Canadien	813	(3)
Trust Companies		
Metropolitian Trust Co.	361	(3)
Ontario Trust	237	(3)
Holding Companies		
Anglo-American Corp. of Canada	176	(3)

APPENDIX 7 (continued)

Company	Assets	Source
INDUSTRIAL		
Imperial Oil Ltd.	2,950	(3)
Gulf Oil Canada Ltd.	1,727	(3)
Ford Motor Co. of Canada Ltd.	1,591	(3)
Shell Canada Ltd.	1,549	(3)
General Motors of Canada Ltd.	1,107	(3)
Texaco Canada Ltd.	772	(3)
Falconbridge Nickel Mines	763	(3)
Genstar Ltd.	705	(3)
Westcoast Transmission Co.	675	(3)
Pacific Petroleums Ltd.	640	(3)
Hudson's Bay Oil and Gas Co.	613	(5)
Chrysler Canada Ltd.	605	(3)
Canadian General Electric Co.	602	(3)
B.P. Canada Ltd.	553	(3)
Canadian International Paper Co.	550	(3)
Rio Algom Ltd.	541	(3)
Petrofina Canada Ltd.	520	(3)
Hudson's Bay Mining & Smelting Co.	518	(3)
Canada Cement Lafarge Ltd.	516	(3)
Sun Oil Co.	491	(3)
International Harvester Co. of Canada	489	(3)
IBM Canada Ltd.	460	(3)
Husky Oil Ltd.	432	(3)
Union Carbide Canada Ltd.	432	(3)
Dow Chemical Co. of Canada Ltd.	414	(3)
Reed Paper Ltd.	413	(3)
DuPont of Canada Ltd.	411	(3)
Rothman's of Pall Mall Canada Ltd.	403	(3)
Canadian Industries Ltd.	390	(3)
Aquitaine Co. of Canada	367	(6)
Imasco Ltd.	365	(3)
Ultramar Canada Ltd.	354	(3)
Great Canadian Oil Sands	333	(6)
Crown Zellerbach Canada Ltd.	290	(3)
Hawker Siddeley Canada Ltd.	282	(3)
Canadian Johns-Manville Co.	277	(3)
Kaiser Resources Ltd.	262	(5)
Procor Ltd.	261	(3)
Ashland Oil Canada	257	(6)
Goodyear Canada Inc.	245	(3)

APPENDIX 7 (continued)

Company	Assets	Source
Canadian Superior Oil	238	(6)
Procter & Gamble Co. of Canada	237	(3)
Westinghouse Canada Ltd.	223	(3)
McIntyre Mines	218	(5)
Canadian Hydrocarbons Ltd.	214	(3)
Celanese Canada Ltd.	213	(3)
Sherritt Gordon Mines Ltd.	211	(3)
Firestone Tire & Rubber Co. of Canada	209	(3)
Union Oil Co. of Canada	209	(6)
International Minerals & Chemical Corp.	208	(3)
Ensite Ltd.	204	(3)
Weldwood of Canada Ltd.	198	(3)
Total Petroleum (North America) Ltd.	195	(3)
Asbestos Corp.	192	(5)
Contential Can Co. of Canada Ltd.	185	(3)
St. Lawrence Cement Co.	173	(3)
Standard Brands Ltd.	168	(3)
Northwestern Utilities	162	(6)
Pratt & Whitney Aircraft of Canada	155	(3)
Rayonier Canada Ltd.	154	(3)
Bowater Canadian Ltd.	151	(3)
Canadian Occidental Petroleums	151	(6)
Maple Leaf Mills Ltd.	149	(3)
General Foods Ltd.	147	(3)
Redpath Industries Ltd.	146	(3)
PPG Industries Canada Ltd.	142	(3)
Murphy Oil Co.	133	(6)
Kodak Canada Ltd.	131	(3)
Uniroyal Ltd.	131	(3)
Preston Mines	130	(5)
Allied Chemical Canada Ltd.	127	(3)
Canadian Ingersoll Rand Co.	127	(3)
Francana Oil & Gas	127	(6)
Canadian Reynolds Metals	126	(3)
Canadian Western Natural Gas	123	(6)
Bovis Corp.	117	(3)
Lever Brothers Ltd.	116	(3)
Cyprus Anvil Mining Co.	115	(5)
Swift Canadian Co.	115	(3)
Indal Ltd.	113	(3)

APPENDIX 7 (continued)

Company	Assets	Source
Rockwell International of Canada Ltd.	113	(3)
Kraft Foods Ltd.	111	(3)
B.F. Goodrich Canada Ltd.	110	(3)
RCA Ltd.	109	(3)
Cyanamid Canada Ltd.	105	(3)
Fiberglas Canada Ltd.	105	(3)
Benson & Hedges (Canada) Ltd.	104	(3)
GTE Sylvania Canada Ltd.	101	(3)

COMMERCIAL

Canada Safeway Ltd.	436	(7)
F.W. Woolworth Ltd.	330	(7)
S.S. Kresge Co.	190	(7)
Zeller's Ltd.	165	(7)
Gambles Canada Ltd.	139	(7)
Blackwood Hodge	102	(7)

REAL ESTATE

Trizec Corp.	900	(7)
Abbey Glen Property Corp.	388	(7)
MEPC Canadian Properties	180	(7)
Commonwealth Holiday Inns of Canada	160	(7)

UTILITIES

Anglo Canadian Telephone Co.	1,579	(3)
British Columbia Telephone Co.	1,263	(3)
Canadian Utilities	574	(3)
Canadian International Power Co.	362	(3)
Quebec Telephone	207	(3)
Algoma Central Railway	118	(3)

Sources: (1) *Moody's Bank and Finance Manual* (New York), 1976.
(2) *Report of the Superintendent of Insurance for Canada for the Year Ended December 31, 1975* (Ottawa, 1976).
(3) *Financial Post Survey of Industrials* (Toronto), 1976.
(4) Files, Department of Consumer and Corporate Affairs (Ottawa).
(5) *Financial Post Survey of Mines* (Toronto), 1976 and 1977.
(6) *Financial Post Survey of Oils* (Toronto), 1976 and 1977.
(7) *F.P. 300*, July 31, 1976.

APPENDIX 8
Control of Canadian Subsidiaries
of Foreign Companies in 1975

Company	Parent Corporation (Source)

FINANCIAL

Company	Parent Corporation (Source)
Mercantile Bank of Canada	First National City Bank of New York (24.2%) (1)
Metropolitian Life Insurance of America	(*) (4)
Standard Life Assurance Co. of England	(*) (4)
Prudential Insurance Co. of America	(*) (4)
Prudential Assurance Co. of England	(*) (4)
Dominion Life Assurance Co.	Lincoln National Corp., Ind. (100%) (3)
National Life Assurance Co. of Canada	Continental Corp., N.J. (100%) (3)
Excelsior Life Insurance Co.	Aetna Life & Casualty Co., Conn. (100%) (3)
Reed, Shaw, Osler	Stenhouse Holdings, London (50.1%) (3)
New York Life Insurance Co.	(*) (4)
Travelers Insurance Co.	Travelers Corp., Conn. (100%) (3)
Montreal Life Insurance Co.	Guardian Royal Exchange Assurance Group, London (100%) (3)
G.M. Acceptance Corp. of Canada	General Motors Corp., Detroit .(100%) (1)
Ford Motor Credit Co. of Canada	Ford Motor Co., Mich. (100%) (1)
Canadian Acceptance Corp.	C.I.T. Financial Corp., N.Y. (100%) (2)
Avco Financial Services Co. Canada	Avco Corp., Conn. (100%) (3)
Associates Acceptance Co. Ltd. (Canada)	Gulf and Western Industries (100%) (3)

APPENDIX 8 (continued)

Company	Parent Corporation (Source)

FINANCIAL *(continued)*

Company	Parent Corporation (Source)
Beneficial Finance Co. of Canada	Beneficial Corp., Del. (100%) (3)
United Dominion Corp. (Canada)	United Dominion Trust, London (51%) (3)
BNP Canada Ltd.	Banque Nationale de Paris (100%) (2)
Transamerica Financial Corp. of Canada	Transamerica Corp., Del. (100%) (3)
Crédit Foncier Franco-Canadien	Banque de Paris et des Pays Bas (21%) (5)
Metropolitan Trust Co.	Cardigan Holdings, N.V., Curaçao (11%) (2)
Ontario Trust	Hambros Ltd., London (56%) (2)
Anglo-American Corp. of Canada	Anglo-American Corp. of S. Africa (100%)

INDUSTRIAL

Company	Parent Corporation (Source)
Imperial Oil Ltd.	Exxon Corp., N.Y. (70%) (1)
Gulf Oil Canada Ltd.	Gulf Oil Corp., Pitt. (69%) (1)
Ford Motor Co. of Canada Ltd.	Ford Motor Co., Mich. (88%) (1)
Shell Canada Ltd.	Royal Dutch/Shell Group, London (71%) (1)
General Motors of Canada Ltd.	General Motors Corp., Det. (100%) (1)
Texaco Canada Ltd.	Texaco Inc., N.Y. (68%) (1)
Falconbridge Nickel Mines Ltd.	McIntyre Mines (37%) (6)
Interprovincial Pipelines Ltd.	Exxon Corp., N.Y. (23%) (1)
Genstar Ltd.	Société Générale de Belgique and subsidiaries (21%) (1)
Westcoast Transmission Co.	Phillips Petroleum, Okla. (17%) (1)
Pacific Petroleums Ltd.	Phillips Petroleum, Okla. (17%) (1)
Hudson's Bay Oil & Gas Co.	Continental Oil Co., Conn. (53%) (1)
Chrysler Canada Ltd.	Chrysler Corp., Det. (100%) (1)
Canadian General Electric Co.	General Electric Co., U.S.A. (92%) (1)
B.P. Canada Ltd.	British Petroleum Co., London (66%) (1)

APPENDIX 8 (continued)

Company	Parent Corporation (Source)
	INDUSTRIAL (continued)
Canadian International Paper Co.	International Paper Co., N.J. (100%) (1)
Rio Algom Ltd.	Rio Tinto-Zinc Corp., London (51%) (1)
Petrofina Canada Ltd.	Petrofina SA, Belgium (72%) (1)
Hudson's Bay Mining and Smelting Co.	Anglo-American Corp. of Canada (39%) (1)
Canada Cement Lafarge Ltd.	Lafarge SA, Paris (55%) (1)
Sun Oil Co.	Sun Co., Penna. (100%) (1)
International Harvester Co. of Canada	International Harvester Co., Chi. (100%) (1)
IBM Canada Ltd.	IBM Corp., N.Y. (100%) (1)
Husky Oil Ltd.	Nielson family, U.S.A. (21%) (5)
Union Carbide Canada Ltd.	Union Carbide Corp., N.Y. (75%) (1)
Dow Chemical Co. of Canada Ltd.	Dow Chemical Co., Mich. (100%) (1)
Reed Paper Ltd.	Reed International Ltd., London (85%) (1)
Du Pont of Canada Ltd.	E.I. du Pont de Nemours, U.S.A. (75%) (1)
Rothmans of Pall Mall Canada Ltd.	Rupert Foundation (S. Africa) (88%) (1)
Canadian Industries Ltd.	Imperial Chemical Industries, London (73%) (1)
Aquitaine Co. of Canada	Société Nationale des Pétroles d'Aquitaine, France (75%) (1)
Imasco Ltd.	British American Tobacco, London (53%) (1)
Ultramar Canada Ltd.	Ultramar Co., London (100%) (1)
Great Canadian Oil Sands	Sun Co., Pa. (96%) (1)
Crown Zellerbach Canada Ltd.	Crown Zellerbach, S. Francisco (88%) (1)
Hawker Siddeley Canada Ltd.	Hawker Siddeley Group Ltd., London (59%) (1)
Canadian Johns Manville Co. Ltd.	Johns Manville Corp., N.Y. (100%) (1)
Kaiser Resources Ltd.	Kaiser Steel Corp., (48%) (1)
Procor Ltd.	Union Tank Car Co., Chicago (100%) (1)
Ashland Oil Canada Ltd.	Ashland Oil Inc., Ky. (83%) (1)
Goodyear Canada Ltd.	Goodyear Tire & Rubber Co., Akron (89%) (1)

APPENDIX 8 (continued)

Company	Parent Corporation (Source)

INDUSTRIAL (continued)

Company	Parent Corporation (Source)
Canadian Superior Oil	Superior Oil Co., Houston (53%) (1)
Procter & Gamble Co. of Canada	Procter & Gamble Co., Cin. (100%) (1)
Westinghouse Canada Ltd.	Westinghouse Electric, Pitt. (75%) (1)
McIntyre Mines	Superior Oil Co., Houston (41%) (1)
Canadian Hydrocarbons Ltd.	Empain Groups, Belgium (54%) (1)
Celanese Canada Ltd.	Celanese Corp., N.Y. (57%) (1)
Sherritt Gordon Mines Ltd.	Newmont Mining Corp., N.Y. (40%) (1)
Firestone Tire & Rubber Co. of Canada	Firestone Tire & Rubber Co., Akron (100%) (1)
Union Oil Co. of Canada	Union Oil Co., Los Angeles (57%) (1)
International Minerals & Chemical Corp.	International Minerals & Chemicals, Ill. (100%) (1)
Ensite Ltd.	Ford Motor Co., Mich. (100%) (1)
Weldwood of Canada Ltd.	Champion International, N.Y. (74%) (1)
Total Petroleum (North America) Ltd.	Cie Française des Pétroles, France (47%) (1)
Asbestos Corp.	General Dynamics Corp., St. Louis (54%) (1)
Continental Can Co. of Canada Ltd.	Continental Can Co., N.Y. (100%) (1)
St. Lawrence Cement Co.	Holderbank Financière Glaris, Switzerland (48%) (1)
Standard Brands Ltd.	Standard Brands Inc., N.Y. (100%) (1)
Northwestern Utilities Ltd.	Canadian Utilities Ltd. (100%) (8)
Pratt & Whitney Aircraft of Canada	United Aircraft, Conn. (100%) (1)
Rayonier Canada Ltd.	I.T.T., N.Y. (100%) (1)
Bowater Canadian Ltd.	Bowater Paper Corp., London (100%) (1)
Canadian Occidental Petroleums	Occidental Petroleums Ltd. (82%) (8)
Maple Leaf Mills Ltd.	Norris Grain Co., Chicago (73%) (1)
General Foods Ltd.	General Foods Corp., White Plains (100%) (1)
Redpath Industries Ltd.	Tate & Lyle Ltd., London (55%) (1)
PPG Industries Canada Ltd.	PPG Industries Inc., Pitt. (100%) (1)
Murphy Oil Co.	Murphy Oil Corp. Ark. (77%) (1)
Kodak Canada Ltd.	Eastman Kodak Co., N.Y. (100%) (1)

APPENDIX 8 (continued)

Company	Parent Corporation (Source)
INDUSTRIAL (continued)	
Uniroyal Ltd.	Uniroyal Inc., N.Y. (100%) (1)
Preston Mines	Rio Tinto-Zinc Corp., London (81%) (7)
Allied Chemical Canada Ltd.	Allied Chemical, N.J. (100%) (1)
Canadian Ingersoll Rand Co.	Ingersoll-Rand Co., N.J. (100%) (1)
Francana Oil & Gas Co.	Hudson's Bay Mining & Smelting (55%) (8)
Canadian Reynolds Metals Co.	Reynolds Metals Co., Va. (100%) (1)
Canadian Western Natural Gas	Canadian Utilities Ltd. (100%) (1)
Bovis Corp.	P & O Steam Navigation Co., London (62%) (1)
Lever Brothers Ltd.	Unilever Ltd., London (100%) (1)
Cyprus Anvil Mining Co.	Cyprus Mines Corp., Los Angeles (63%) (1)
Swift Canadian Co.	Swift & Co., Chicago (100%) (1)
Indal Ltd.	Rio Tinto-Zinc Corp., London (59%) (1)
Rockwell International of Canada Ltd.	Rockwell International, Pitt. (100%) (1)
Kraft Foods Ltd.	Kraftco Corp., Ill. (100%) (1)
BF Goodrich Canada Ltd.	BF Goodrich Co., N.Y. (100%) (1)
RCA Ltd.	RCA Corp., N.Y. (100%) (1)
Cyanamid Canada Ltd.	American Cyanamid, N.J. (100%) (1)
Fiberglas Canada Ltd.	Owens-Corning Fiberglas Corp., Toledo (100%) (1)
Benson & Hedges (Canada) Ltd.	Philip Morris Inc., N.Y. (100%) (1)
GTE Sylvania Canada Ltd.	General Telephone & Electronics Corp., N.Y. (100%) (1)

COMMERCIAL

Canada Safeway Ltd.	Safeway Stores Inc., Oakland (100%) (1)
F.W. Woolworth Ltd.	F.W. Woolworth Co., N.Y. (100%) (1)
S.S. Kresge Co.	S.S. Kresge Co., Mich. (100%) (1)
Zeller's Ltd.	W.T. Grant Co., N.Y. (50.1%) (1)
Gambles Canada Ltd.	Gamble-Skomo Inc., Minn. (100%) (1)
Blackwood Hodge (Canada) Ltd.	Blackwood Hodge Ltd., London (75%) (2)

APPENDIX 8 (continued)

Company	Parent Corporation (Source)

REAL ESTATE

Trizec Corp.	English Property Corp., London (55%) (1)
Abbey Glen Property Corp.	Capital & Counties Property Co., London (62%) (2)
MEPC Canadian Properties	MEPC Ltd., London (67%) (2)
Commonwealth Holiday Inns of Canada	Holiday Inns Inc. (27%); D. Rubinoff (London, Ont.) (18%) (2)

UTILITIES

Anglo Canadian Telephone Co.	General Telephone & Electronics Corp., N.Y. (84%) (1)
B.C. Telephone Co.	Anglo Canadian Telephone Co. (51%) (2)
Canadian Utilities Ltd.	I.U. International Corp., Phil. (77%) (1)
Canadian International Power Co.	United Corp., Del. (48%) (2)
Quebec Telephone	Anglo Canadian Telephone Co. (55%) (2)
Algoma Central Railway	Estates House Investment Trust, London (18%); Sir D. Lowson (7%) (5)

Sources: (1) *F.P. 300*, 1976.
   (2) *Financial Post Survey of Industrials* (Toronto), 1976.
   (3) *Moody's Bank and Finance Manual* (New York), 1976.
   (4) *Report of the Superintendent of Insurance for Canada for the Year Ended December 31, 1975* (Ottawa, 1976).
   (5) Ontario Securities Commission, *Bulletins* (Toronto).
   (6) *Moody's Industrial Manual* (New York).
   (7) *Financial Post Survey of Mines* (Toronto), 1977.
   (8) *Financial Post Survey of Oils* (Toronto), 1977.

*The parent corporation operates in Canada under the same corporate identity.

APPENDIX 9

Control of Parent Corporations

Company	Type of Control	Details (Source)

FINANCIAL

Company	Type of Control	Details (Source)
First National City Bank of N.Y.	int.*	Board has less than 1% of vote (1)
Metropolitan Life	int.	Mutual
Standard Life	int.	Mutual
Prudential of America	int.	Mutual
Prudential of England	int.	Possible
Lincoln National Corp.	int.	Board has 1.4% of vote (1)
Continental Corp.	int.	Board has less than 1% of vote (1)
Aetna Life Casualty Co.	int.	Board has less than 1% of vote (1)
Stenhouse Holdings	fam.*	Possible, Stenhouse family (2)
New York Life Insurance Co.	int.	Mutual
Travelers Corp.	int.	Board has less than 1% of vote (1)
Guardian Royal Exchange Assurance Group	int.	Possible
General Motors Corp.	int.	Board has less than 1% of vote (1)
Ford Motor Co.	min.*	Ford family has 40% of vote (1)
C.I.T. Financial Corp.	int.	Board has 1% of vote (1)
Avco Corp.	min.	Harrington family has 5.2% of vote (OSC); R.D. and F.A. Harrington are directors
Gulf and Western Industries	min.	Board has 8.9% of vote (1)
Beneficial Corp.	min.	Board has 6% of vote (1)
United Dominion Trust	min.	Prudential Assurance owns 27%; Eagle Star Group 10% (5)
Banque Nationale de Paris	govt.*	(Morin, *La banque*, p. 254)
Transamerica Corp.	int.	Board has 1.6% of vote (1)
Banque de Paris et des Pays Bas	int.	(Morin, *La banque*, p. 255)
Cardigan Holdings, N.V.	?	Curaçao holding company
Hambros Ltd.	fam.	Hambro family (Sampson, *New Anatomy*, p. 493)
Anglo-American Corp. of South Africa	min.	Oppenheimer family, 10% (3)

APPENDIX 9 (continued)

Company	Type of Control	Details (Source)

INDUSTRIAL

Company	Type of Control	Details (Source)
Exxon Corp.	int.	Board has less than 1% of vote (1)
Gulf Oil Corp.	min.	Mellon family has 20% of vote (3)
Ford Motor Co.	min.	See above
Royal Dutch/Shell Group	int.	
General Motors Corp.	int.	See above
Texaco Inc.	int.	Board has less than 1% of vote (1)
McIntyre Mines	min.	Canadian subsidiary of Superior Oil (7)
Exxon Corp.	int.	See above
Société Générale de Belgique	int.	(CRISP, *Répertoire permanent,* 1975, 3rd quarter, p. 2988)
Phillips Petroleum	int.	Board has less than 1% of vote (1)
Continental Oil Co.	int.	Board has less than 1% of vote (1)
Chrysler Corp.	int.	Board has less than 1% of vote (1)
General Electric Corp.	int.	Board has less than 1% of vote (1)
British Petroleum Co.	govt.	*(Moody's Ind. Manual,* 1976)
International Paper Co.	int.	Board has less than 1% of vote (1)
Rio Tinto-Zinc Corp.	fam.	French Rothschilds dominant (3)
Petrofina S.A.	int.	Société Générale, 6.4%; Imperial Continental Gas U.K., 6.4%; Cie Bruxelles Lambert, 2.5%; Cie de Suez, 0.4% (CRISP, *Répertoire permanent,* 1975, p. 3048); Société Générale internally controlled (see above)
Anglo-American Corp. of Canada	min.	Canadian subsidiary of Anglo-American Corp. of South Africa (7)
Lafarge SA	int.	(Morin, *La banque,* p. 234)
Sun Co.	min.	J. Howard Pew family, 18.1% (1)
International Harvester Co.	int.	Board has less than 1% of vote (1)
IBM Corp.	int.	Board has less than 1% of vote (1)
Union Carbide Corp.	int.	Board has less than 1% of vote (1)
Dow Chemical Co.	min.	7 members of Dow family had 5.7% of vote in 1972 (6)

APPENDIX 9 (continued)

Company	Type of Control	Details (Source)

INDUSTRIAL *(continued)*

Company	Type of Control	Details (Source)
Reed International Ltd.	int.	Possible
E.I. du Pont de Nemours	min.	du Pont family has 28% of vote (1)
Rupert Foundation	fam.	Dr. Anton Rupert (*Investors Chronicle*, 5/12/75, p. 701)
Imperial Chemical Industries	int.	(Sampson, *New Anatomy*, p. 601)
Société Nationale des Pétroles d'Aquitaine	govt.	ERAP has 53% of vote (*Moody's Industrial Manual*, 1976)
British American Tobacco	int.	Possible
Ultramar Co.	int.	Board has les than 1% of vote (OSC)
Sun Co.	min.	See above
Crown Zellerbach Corp.	int.	Board has less than 1% of vote (1)
Hawker Siddeley Group Ltd.	int.	Possible
Johns-Manville Corp.	int.	Board has less than 1% of vote (1)
Kaiser Industries	min.	Kaiser family has more than 40% of vote (4)
Union Tank Car Co.	int.	Board has 2.1% of vote (1)
Ashland Oil Inc.	int.	Board has less than 1% of vote (1)
Goodyear Tire and Rubber Co.	int.	Board has less than 1% of vote (1)
Superior Oil Co.	min.	Keck family has 32.5% of vote (3)
Procter & Gamble Co.	int.	Board has less than 1% of vote (1)
Westinghouse Electric Co.	int.	Board has less than 1% of vote (1)
Superior Oil Co.	min.	See above
Empain Group	fam.	Baron Edouard-Jean Empain (4)
Celanese Corp.	int.	Board has less than 1% of vote (1)
Newmont Mining Corp.	int.	Board has 2.8% of vote (1)
Firestone Tire & Rubber Corp.	min.	Firestone family has 19.2% of vote (1)
Union Oil Co.	int.	Board has less than 1% of vote (1)
International Minerals & Chemicals	int.	Board has less than 1% of vote (1)
Ford Motor Co.	min.	See above
Champion International	int.	Board has less than 1% of vote (1)
Cie Française des Pétroles	govt.	British Petroleum, U.K.

APPENDIX 9 (continued)

Company	Type of Control	Details (Source)

INDUSTRIAL (continued)

Company	Type of Control	Details (Source)
General Dynamics Corp.	min.	Henry Crown, Lester Crown and N. Cummings have 19.5% of the vote (1)
Continental Can Co.	int.	Board has less than 1% of vote (1)
Holderbank Financière Glaris S.A.	fam.	Controlled by Max Schmidheiny (Ziegler, *Une Suisse*, p. 28)
Standard Brands Inc.	int.	Board has less than 1% of vote (1)
Canadian Utilities Ltd.	int.	Canadian subsidiary of I.U. International Corp. (7)
United Aircraft Ltd.	int.	Board has 3.5% of vote (1)
ITT Corp.	int.	Board has less than 1% of vote (1)
Bowater Paper Corp.	min.	J.D. Slater has 6% and M. Horsman 1% of vote (3)
Occidental Petroleums Ltd.	int.	Board has 2.2% of vote (OSC)
Norris Grain Co.	abs.*	Private company, Bruce A. Norris pres. & chm. (*Standard Poor's*, 1974)
General Foods Corp.	int.	Board has less than 1% of vote (1)
Tate & Lyle Ltd.	fam.	Tate and Lyle families (Sampson, *New Anatomy*, pp. 601-2)
PPG Industries Inc.	min.	Pitcairn family has 15.7% of vote (1)
Murphy Oil Co.	min.	Murphy family has 38.1% of vote (1)
Eastman Kodak Co.	int.	Board has less than 1% of vote (1)
Uniroyal Inc.	int.	Board has less than 1% of vote (1)
Rio Tinto-Zinc Corp.	fam.	See above
Allied Chemical	min.	Solvay family of Belgium has 9.6% of vote (1)
Ingersoll Rand Co.	int.	Board has less than 1% of vote (1)
Hudson's Bay Mining & Smelting	min.	Canadian subsidiary of Anglo-American Corp. of South Africa (7)
Reynolds Metals Co.	min.	4 Reynolds brothers, directors, have 18% of vote (1)
Canadian Utilities Ltd.	int.	See above

APPENDIX 9 (continued)

Company	Type of Control	Details (Source)

INDUSTRIAL *(continued)*

P&O Steam Navigation Co.	int.	Internal regulations limit stock-holders to a maximum of 20 votes
Unilever Ltd.	min.	Leverhulme Trust has 18.4% of vote
Cyprus Mines Corp.	min.	Mudd family has 22% of vote (1)
Swift & Co.	min.	J.A. Vickers & L. Crown have 8.4% of vote (1)
Rio Tinto-Zinc Corp.	fam.	See above
Rockwell International	min.	Rockwell family has 3.2% of vote, two other directors have 2% (OSC)
Kraftco Corp.	int.	Board has less than 1% of vote (1)
B.F. Goodrich Corp.	int.	Board has less than 1% of vote (1)
RCA Corp.	int.	Board has less than 1% of vote (1)
Owens-Corning Fiberglas Corp.	int.	Board has about 1% of vote (1)
Philip Morris Inc.	int.	Board has 1.4% of vote (1)
General Telephone and Electronics Corp.	int.	Board has less than 1% of vote (1)

COMMERCIAL

Safeway Stores Inc.	int.	Board has less than 2% of the shares (1)
F.W. Woolworth Co.	int.	Board has about 2% of vote (1)
S.S. Kresge Co.	min.	Kresge family: 9.2% of vote (1)
W.T. Grant Co.	int.	In bankruptcy since Oct. '75 (3)
Gamble-Skomo Inc.	min.	Gamble family has 11.6% of vote (1)
Blackwood Hodge Ltd.	fam.	Shapland and Sunley families (2)

REAL ESTATE

English Properties Corp.	fam.	Eagle Star Insurance holds 20.8%; Eagle Star controlled by Mountain family (2)

APPENDIX 9 (continued)

Company	Type of Control	Details (Source)

REAL ESTATE *(continued)*

Company	Type of Control	Details (Source)
Capital & Counties Property Co.	fam.	Union Corp. holds 25%; Union Corp. controlled by Dr. Anton Rupert (2)
MEPC Ltd.	fam.	Eagle Star Insurance holds 7% of vote; Eagle Star controlled by Mountain family (2)
Holiday Inns Inc.	min.	Board has 13.8% of vote (1)

UTILITIES

Company	Type of Control	Details (Source)
General Telephone & Electronics	int.	See above
Anglo Canadian Telephone Co.	int.	Canadian subsidiary of General Telephone & Electronics (7)
I.U. International Corp.	int.	Board has less than 1% of vote (OSC)
United Corp.	int.	Board has 1.5% of vote (1)
Anglo Canadian Telephone Co.	int.	See above
Estates House Investment Trust	fam.	Sir D. Lowson (2)

Sources: (1) New York Stock Exchange, *Proxy Statements* (1975).
(2) *Investors Chronicle* (London), weekly.
(3) *Forbes* (New York), fortnightly.
(4) *Fortune* (New York), monthly.
(5) *Financial Times International Business Yearbook*, 1975 (London).
(6) U.S. Congress, Senate, Government Operations Committee, *Disclosure of Corporate Ownership*, 93rd Congress, 1st Session, 1973.
(7) See appendix 8 and entry under foreign parent corporation in appendix 9 for details.

*int.: internal fam.: family abs.: absolute min.: minority govt.: government

Notes

Introduction

1 Jorge Niosi, *The Economy of Canada: A Study of Ownership and Control* (Montreal: Black Rose Books, 1978).

2 K.Z. Paltiel, *Political Party Financing in Canada* (Toronto: McGraw-Hill, 1970); R. Mahon, "Canadian Public Policy: The Unequal Structure of Representation" in Leo Panitch, ed., *The Canadian State* (Toronto: University of Toronto Press, 1977), pp. 165-98.

3 F.H. Cardoso, *Autoritarismo e democratizaçao* (Rio de Janeiro: Paz e Terra, 1975), especially pp. 16-18, 40-42, 61 and 215; F.H. Cardoso, "Desenvolvimento capitalista e Estado: bases e alternativas", in C.E. Martins, ed., *Estado e capitalismo no Brasil* (Sao Paulo: Ed. Hucitec-Cebrap, 1977), pp. 205-20.

4 Philip Ehrensaft and Warwick Armstrong, "Le capitalisme des Dominions", *Cahiers du Socialisme*, Montreal, no. 3 (Spring 1979).

Chapter 1

1 Rudolf Hilferding, *Le capital financier* (1910; Paris: Minuit, 1970); V.I. Lenin, *Imperialism, The Highest Stage of Capitalism* (1916), in *Selected Works*, 3 vols. (Moscow: Progress Publishers; New York: International Publishers, 1967), 1:673-777.

2 Jean-Marie Chevalier, *La structure financière de l'industrie américaine* (Paris: Cujas, 1970); S. Menshikov, *Millionaires and Managers* (Moscow: Progress Publishers, 1969); Robert Fitch and Mary Oppenheimer, "Who Rules the Corporations?", *Socialist Revolution* (San Francisco) 1, nos. 5-7 (1970); David M. Kotz, *Bank Control of Large Corporations in the United States* (Berkeley: University of California Press, 1978).

3 Olivier Pastré, *La stratégie internationale des groupes financiers américains* (Paris: Economica, 1979).

4 Paul A. Baran and Paul M. Sweezy, *Monopoly Capital: An Essay on the American Economic and Social Order* (New York: Monthly Review Press, 1966); Paul M. Sweezy, "The Resurgence of Financial Control: Fact or Fancy?", *Monthly Review* (New York), November 1971; Edward Herman, *Corporate Control, Corporate Power* (Cambridge: Cambridge University Press, 1981).

5 J. Bouvier, *Un siècle de banque française* (Paris: Hachette, 1973); P. Sargant Florence, *Ownership, Control and Success of Large Companies* (London, 1961); E.P. Neufeld, *The Financial System of Canada: Its Growth and Development* (Toronto: Macmillan of Canada, 1972).

6 Libbie and Frank Park, *Anatomy of Big Business* (1962; Toronto: James Lewis and Samuel, 1973).

7 Statistics Canada, *Trusteed Pension Plans. Financial Statistics* (Cat. 74-201) (Ottawa: Supply and Services, 1976).

8 Canada, Royal Commission on Banking and Finance (Porter Commission), *Report* (Ottawa: Queen's Printer, 1964), p. 194.

9 Adolf A. Berle, Jr., and Gardiner C. Means, *The Modern Corporation and Private Property* (1932; New York: Harcourt Brace & World, 1968).

10 Robert J. Larner, *Management Control and the Large Corporation* (Cambridge, Mass.: Harvard University Press, 1970).

11 E.S. Mason, "The Apologetics of Managerialism", *Journal of Business of the University of Chicago* 31 (January 1958).

12 These companies are Sun Life, Mutual Life, Manufacturers Life, Canada Life, Confederation Life and North American Life.

13 Peter C. Newman, *Flame of Power: Intimate Profiles of Canada's Greatest Businessmen* (Toronto: McClelland and Stewart, 1959), p. 224.

14 C. Wright Mills, *The Power Elite* (New York: Oxford University Press, 1956).

15 See among others: P. Birnbaum, *Les sommets de l'Etat, essai sur l'élite du pouvoir en France* (Paris: Seuil, 1977); Ralph Miliband, *The State in Capitalist Society* (London: Weidenfeld and Nicholson, 1969); G.W. Domhoff, *Who Rules America?* (Englewood Cliffs, N.J.: Prentice Hall, 1967).

16 Ferdinand Lundberg, *The Rich and the Super-rich* (New York: Bantam Books, 1968), pp. 543-46; Paul Sweezy, "Power Elite or Ruling Class", *Monthly Review* (New York), September 1956.

17 These paragraphs summarize the theme of my previous work, *The Economy of Canada: A Study of Ownership and Control* (Montreal: Black Rose Books, 1978).

Chapter 2

1 H.C. Pentland, "The Development of a Capitalistic Labour Market in Canada", *Canadian Journal of Economics and Political Science* 25, no. 4 (November 1959); Leo Johnson, "The Development of Class in Canada in the Twentieth Century", in Gary Teeple, ed., *Capitalism and the National Question in Canada* (Toronto: University of Toronto Press, 1972).

2 For a brief look at the history of United Auto Parts (controlled by the Préfontaine family) and Campeau Corp. (controlled by Robert Campeau), see chapter 3.

3 For an excellent analysis of the forces leading to concentration in the American economy, see J. Blair, *Economic Concentration* (New York: Harcourt Brace Jovanovich, 1972).

4 John A. Guthrie, *The Newsprint Paper Industry* (Cambridge, Mass.: Harvard University Press, 1943), chapter 5.

5 W.J.A. Donald, *The Canadian Iron and Steel Industry* (Boston: Houghton Mifflin & Co., 1915); William Kilbourn, *The Elements Combined* (Toronto: Clarke Irwin & Co., 1960).

6 Canada, Royal Commission on the Automotive Industry, *Report* (Ottawa: Queen's Printer, 1961).

7 E.P. Neufeld, *The Financial System of Canada: Its Growth and Development* (Toronto: Macmillan of Canada, 1972).

8 See E.D. Baltzell, *The Protestant Establishment* (New York: Random House, 1964).

9 W.E. Kalbach and W.W. McVey, *The Demographic Basis of Canadian Society* (Toronto: McGraw-Hill of Canada, 1971), pp. 72-73.

10 Gustavus Myers, *A History of Canadian Wealth* (1914; Toronto: James Lewis & Samuel, 1972), p. 151. K. Buckley calculated the lands given to railways at 47.3 million acres, and financial assistance between 1867 and 1920 at $755 million (K. Buckley, *Capital Formation in Canada 1896-1930* [Toronto: McClelland and Stewart, 1955], pp. 110-11).

11 Neufeld, *Financial System of Canada*, pp. 78-79, 99.

12 *Ibid.,* p. 492.

13 H. Bullock, *The Story of Investment Companies* (New York: Columbia University Press, 1959).

14 Jorge Niosi, *The Economy of Canada: A Study of Ownership and Control* (Montreal: Black Rose Books, 1978).

15 Guthrie, *Newsprint Paper Industry*, chapter 3.

16 K.H. Burley, *The Development of Canada's Staples 1867-1939* (Toronto: McClelland and Stewart, 1970), p. 179.

17 Statistics Canada, *Canada's International Investment Position 1971-73* (Cat. 67-202) (Ottawa: Supply and Services, 1977), p. 135.

18 It was expected that more than 50 per cent of the tonnage through the St. Lawrence Seaway would be iron ore from Ungava and Labrador. See W.T. Easterbrook and H.D. Aitken, *Canadian Economic History* (Toronto: Macmillan, 1956), p. 556.

Chapter 3

1 Maurice Séguin, "La Conquête et la vie économique des Canadiens", in René Durocher and Paul-André Linteau, eds., *Le retard du Québec et l'infériorité économique des Canadiens français* (Montreal: Boréal Express, 1971), pp. 93-111.

2 Paul-André Linteau, "Quelques réflexions autour de la bourgeoisie québécoise 1850-1914", *Revue d'Histoire de l'Amérique Française* 30, no. 1 (June 1976): 55-56.

3 *Commerce* (Montreal), August 1951, pp. 14-20.

4 Errol Bouchette, "Emparons-nous de l'industrie", in R.J. Bédard, ed., *L'Essor économique du Québec* (Montreal: Beauchemin, 1969), pp. 233-73; Errol Bouchette, *L'Indépendance économique du Canada français* (1906; Montreal: La Presse, 1977).

5 Jacques Melançon, "Retard de croissance de l'entreprise canadienne-française", in Bédard, ed., *L'Essor économique du Québec*, pp. 158-76; Norman W. Taylor, "L'industriel canadien-français et son milieu", in Durocher and Linteau, eds., *Le retard du Québec*, pp. 43-74; Fernand Ouellet, *Histoire économique et sociale du Québec 1760-1850* (Montreal: Fides, 1966).

6 *Financial Post Survey of Corporate Securities* (Toronto: Maclean-Hunter Ltd., annual), 1928-46; *Financial Post Survey of Industrials* (Toronto: Maclean-Hunter Ltd., annual), 1947-76; *Financial Post Survey of Mines* (Toronto: Maclean-Hunter Ltd., annual), 1926-76; *Financial Post Survey of Oils* (Toronto: Maclean-Hunter Ltd., annual), 1936-76; *Financial Post Survey of Funds* (Toronto: Maclean-Hunter Ltd., annual), 1962-76; Quebec, Department of Consumers, Cooperatives and Financial Institutions, Inspector of Trust Companies, *Report* (Quebec City: Éditeur du Québec, 1976); Quebec, Department of Consumers, Cooperatives and Financial Institutions, Insurance Branch, *Annual Report* (Quebec City:

Editeur du Québec, 1975).

[7] Quebec Securities Commission, *Bulletin* (Montreal), 1974-77; Ontario Securities Commission, *Bulletin* (Toronto), 1967-77; *Financial Post Directory of Directors* (Toronto: Maclean-Hunter Ltd., annual), 1931-76; *Biographies canadiennes-françaises* (Montreal: Les Editions Biographiques Canadiennes-Françaises, irregular), 1920-76; *Who's Who in Canada* (Toronto: International Press Ltd., irregular), 1912-76; *The Canadian Who's Who* (Toronto: The Trans-Canada Press, irregular), 1912-76.

[8] Jorge Niosi, *The Economy of Canada: A Study of Ownership and Control* (Montreal: Black Rose Books, 1978), chapter 2.

[9] *Commerce* (Montreal), May 1950 and July 1977.

[10] Jean-Marie Chevalier, *La structure financière de l'industrie américaine* (Paris: Cujas, 1970).

[11] "La Caisse de dépôt vendra ses actions", *Le Devoir*, April 11, 1975, p. 17.

[12] *Le Devoir*, April 6, 1976, p. 16.

[13] Niosi, *The Economy of Canada*, chapter 2.

[14] "Sodarcan se lance à la conquête du club international et fermé de la réassurance", *La Presse*, November 11, 1975, p. E1.

[15] Bulletins of the Ontario and Quebec Securities Commissions.

[16] John Porter, *The Vertical Mosaic: An Analysis of Social Class and Power in Canada* (Toronto: University of Toronto Press, 1965); Wallace Clement, *The Canadian Corporate Elite: An Analysis of Economic Power* (Toronto: McClelland and Stewart, Carleton Library no. 89, 1975). For a critique of the theory of elites see J. Heap, *Everybody's Canada* (Toronto: Burns and MacEachern, 1974) and Niosi, *The Economy of Canada*, chapter 3.

[17] *Le Devoir*, April 6, 1976, p. 17.

[18] "Guy St-Pierre, président d'Ogilvie", *Le Devoir*, October 7, 1977, p. 17.

[19] Confederation of National Trade Unions, *La Coopérative fédérée est capitaliste* (Montreal, 1974).

[20] Gilles Bourque and Nicole Laurin-Frenette, "Social Classes and Nationalist Ideologies in Quebec, 1760-1970", trans. P. Resnick and P. Renyi, in Gary Teeple, ed., *Capitalism and the National Question in Canada* (Toronto: University of Toronto Press, 1972), pp. 185-210.

[21] Pierre Fournier, "Les nouveaux paramètres de la bourgeoisie québécoise", in Pierre Fournier, ed., *Le capitalisme au Québec* (Montreal: Ed. A. St-Martin, 1978).

[22] *Ibid.*, pp. 171-72.

[23] *Financial Post Directory of Directors*, 1976-78, and annual reports of companies.

[24] See *Financial Post*, December 9, 1978, p. 3. The Caisse also sold its Power Corp. securities when Desmarais asked it to in July 1977 ("Why the Caisse took cash", *Financial Post*, July 23, 1977, p. 17.

[25] *Financial Post*, December 17, 1977, p. 12.

[26] Fournier, "Les nouveaux paramètres", p. 139.

[27] A. Sales, *La bourgeoisie industrielle au Québec* (Montreal: Presses de l'Université de Montréal, 1979).

[28] See *Le Devoir*, January 18, 1979, p. 15.

[29] See *Le Devoir*, August 31, 1979, p. 1.

[30] See *Le Devoir*, November 30, 1978, p. 19.

³¹ See *Le Devoir*, June 26, 1979, p. 11.

³² See *Le Devoir*, October 2, 1979, p. 15.

³³ See *Le Devoir*, March 24, 1979, p. 17.

³⁴ See *La Presse*, October 3, 1979, p. 1.

³⁵ For an evaluation of the PQ government's first two years see Jorge Niosi, "Le gouvernement du P.Q. deux ans après", *Cahiers du Socialisme*, Montreal, no. 2 (Autumn 1978).

³⁶ The concept of "language workers" was used by Marcel Fournier in his excellent address to the "Un an après" (One year later) conference at the University of Quebec at Montreal, November 10-11, 1977.

Chapter 4

1 Frederick Engels, *Socialism: Utopian and Scientific*, trans. Edward Aveling (Westport, Conn.: Greenwood, 1977), pp. 66-67.

2 *Ibid.*, p. 66.

3 V.I. Lenin, *Selected Works*, 3 vols. (Moscow: Progress Publishers; New York: International Publishers, 1967), 2:263-361, 1:673-777, 2:213-54.

4 Notably in "'Left-Wing' Childishness and the Petty-Bourgeois Mentality", in Lenin, *Selected Works*, 2:685-709.

5 Yevgenii Varga, *The Great Crisis and Its Political Consequences: Economics and Politics, 1928-1934* (New York: International Publishers, 1935).

6 Yevgenii Varga, *Politico-Economic Problems of Capitalism*, trans. Don. Danemanis (Moscow: Progress Publishers, 1968), p. 55.

7 *Ibid.*, p. 67.

8 Paul Boccara, *Études sur le C.M.E. sa crise et son issue* (Paris: Editions Sociales, 1974), p. 31.

9 *Ibid.*, pp. 35-36.

10 Victor Cheprakov, *Le capitalisme monopoliste d'Etat* (Moscow: Editions du Progrès, 1969), p. 128.

11 B. Théret and M. Wieviorka, *Critique de la théorie du* CME (Paris: Maspéro, 1978), p. 91.

12 J. Valier, *Le P.C.F. et le capitalisme monopoliste d'Etat* (Paris: Maspéro, 1976).

13 Paul A. Baran and Paul M. Sweezy, *Monopoly Capital: An Essay on the American Economic and Social Order* (1966; New York, Monthly Review Press, Modern Reader Paperbacks, 1968), pp. 66-67.

14 Frédéric François-Marsal, *Le dépérissement des entreprises publiques* (Paris: Calmann-Levy, 1973), p. 16.

15 Charles Bettelheim, *Les luttes de classes en URSS, 1re période, 1917-1923* (Paris: Seuil/Maspéro, 1974), p. 41.

16 Fernando H. Cardoso, "Desenvolvimento capitalista e estado: bases e alternativas", in C.E. Martins, ed., *Estado e capitalismo no Brasil* (Sao Paulo: Ed. Hucitec-Cebrap, 1977), p. 214.

17 Fernando H. Cardoso, *Autoritarismo e democratização* (Rio de Janeiro: Paz e Terra, 1975).

18 François H. Morin, *La banque et les groupes industriels à l'heure des nationalisations* (Paris: Calmann-Lévy, 1977), especially pp. 76-82.

19 For a discussion of managers in the private sector and the division of labour

within boards of directors of privately-owned corporations, see my earlier work, *The Economy of Canada: A Study of Ownership and Control* (Montreal: Black Rose Books, 1978), chapter 3.

20 See, among others, J. Gillman, *The Falling Rate of Profit* (London: Dobson, 1956); Baran and Sweezy, *Monopoly Capital*; A. Emmanuel, *Le profit et les crises* (Paris: Maspéro, 1974), pp. 113ff.

21 The concept of state capitalism is not referred to in the works of Ralph Miliband, G.W. Domhoff, Harry Magdoff, Harry Braverman or Leo Panitch, to mention only a few of the more representative scholars writing in English. The only significant exception to this general rule is James O'Connor, *The Fiscal Crisis of the State* (San José: St. Martin's Press, 1970). Also, British Communists use the concept regularly; see for example Maurice Dobb, "Some Features of Capitalism since the First World War", in *Papers on Capitalism, Development and Planning* (London: Routledge & Kegan Paul, 1967).

22 The concept is deprived of its analytical precision if it is used to designate a *phase* of private capitalism, a *sector of activity* (the sector of government-owned corporations) and a *mode of production* (describing societies such as the Soviet Union and China) simultaneously. In any case, the state has always played an important role in capitalist societies, although less so in Britain and the United States than elsewhere.

23 *Revised Statutes of Canada*, 1970, chapter F-10.

24 For a complete list of departmental corporations in 1975, see Statistics Canada, *Canada Year Book 1976-77* (Ottawa: Supply and Services, 1977), p. 109.

25 "An agency corporation is defined as a Crown corporation that is an agent of Her Majesty in right of Canada and is responsible for the management of trading or service operations on a quasi-commercial basis or for the management of procurement, construction or disposal activities on behalf of Her Majesty in right of Canada." (*Canada Year Book 1976-77*, p. 109)
"A proprietary corporation is defined as a Crown corporation that is responsible for the management of lending or financial operations, or for the management of commercial or industrial operations involving the production of or dealing in goods and the supplying of services to the public, and is ordinarily required to conduct its operations without parliamentary appropriations." (*Canada Year Book 1976-77*, pp. 109-10)
"Unclassified corporations. The following Crown corporations are not classified in the Financial Administration Act but are governed by their own acts of incorporation: the Bank of Canada, the Canada Council, the Canadian National Railways Securities Trust, the Canadian Wheat Board, and the National Arts Centre Corporation." (*Canada Year Book 1976-77*, p. 110).

26 Canada, Department of Finance, *Public Accounts of Canada 1975-76*, 3 vols. (Ottawa: Supply and Services, 1976), 3; *Canada Year Book 1976-77*, pp. 109-10.

27 C.A. Ashley and R.G.H. Smails, *Canadian Crown Corporations: Some Aspects of Their Administration and Control* (Toronto: Macmillan of Canada, 1965), pp. 3-4.

28 *Ibid.*, pp. 21-27.

29 Canada, Privy Council Office, *Crown Corporations — Direction, Control, Accountability — Government of Canada's Proposals* (Ottawa: Supply and Services, 1977), p. 16.

30 Canada, Parliament, House of Commons, Standing Committee on Public Accounts, *Proceedings and Testimony*, 2nd session, 30th parliament, Issue no. 33, May 17, 1977, Appendix PA-220.

31 *Ibid.*, Issue no. 32, May 10, 1977, p. 32:22.

32 Canada, Central Mortgage and Housing Corporation, *Annual Report 1975*, p. 68.

33 *Public Accounts of Canada 1975-76*, 3:87, 3:80, 3:15 and 3:26.

34 Leonard Tivey, *Nationalization in British Industry* (London: J. Cape Ltd., 1973), p. 17.

35 Rick Deaton, "The Fiscal Crisis of the State in Canada", in Dimitrios Roussopoulos, ed., *The Political Economy of the State* (Montreal: Black Rose Books, 1973), p. 30.

36 See Larry Pratt, "The State and Province Building: Alberta's Development Strategy", in Leo Panitch, ed., *The Canadian State* (Toronto: University of Toronto Press, 1977), pp. 155-56.

37 See L.A. Wood, *Farmers' Movements in Canada* (1924; Toronto: University of Toronto Press, 1975).

38 "Who does what and from whom", *Financial Post*, May 20, 1978, p. 38.

39 "What will save troubled manufacturing?", *Financial Post*, December 17, 1977, p. 36.

40 Kari Levitt, *Silent Surrender: The Multinational Corporation in Canada* (Toronto: Macmillan of Canada, 1970), pp. 145-46; Garth Stevenson, "Federalism and the Political Economy of the Canadian State", in Panitch, ed., *The Canadian State*, p. 82.

41 Canada, Parliament, House of Commons, 3rd Session, 28th Parliament, Bill C-219, "An Act to Establish the Canada Development Corporation", as passed by the House of Commons June 9, 1971.

42 *Canada Year Book 1976-77*, p. 1064.

43 W.R. Plewman, *Adam Beck and the Ontario Hydro* (Toronto: Ryerson Press, 1947).

44 H.V. Nelles, *The Politics of Development: Forests, Mines and Hydro-Electric Power in Ontario, 1849-1941* (Toronto: Macmillan of Canada, 1974), pp. 248-49.

45 "Avant de nationaliser l'électricité. Une étude minutieuse de la question s'impose (Chambre de commerce du Québec)", *Le Devoir*, September 6, 1962, p. 1.

46 "Dans la production et la distribution d'électricité. R. Lévesque: plus grande responsabilité pour l'Etat", *Le Devoir*, February 13, 1962, p. 3.

47 Carol Jobin, *Les enjeux économiques de la nationalisation de l'électricité* (Montreal: A. St. Martin, 1978).

48 *Ibid.*, p. 125.

49 *Ibid.*, pp. 7-8.

50 "Le président de l'Hydro-Québec — Révolution paisible au Québec", *La Presse*, November 21, 1963, p. 41.

51 W.J.A. Donald, *The Canadian Iron and Steel Industry* (Boston: Houghton Mifflin Co., 1915), chapter 1.

52 Canada, Royal Commission on Canada's Economic Prospects, *The Canadian Primary Iron and Steel Industry* (Ottawa, 1956).

53 Canada, Dominion Bureau of Statistics, *Monthly Report on Primary Iron and Steel in Canada*, 1926 and 1941.

54 Royal Commission on Canada's Economic Prospects, *Primary Iron and Steel*.

55 Canada, Privy Council Office, *Steel Profits Inquiry* (Ottawa: Information Canada, 1974), p. 28.

56 Canada, Department of Energy, Mines and Resources, *Iron Ore*, Cat. 148, 1976.

57 N. Voeikoff, "Quelques aspects du projet sidérurgique de Québec", *Commerce* (Montreal), May 1964; D. Leduc, "Quatre grands noms canadiens de l'acier — Sidbec le cinquième?", *Commerce* (Montreal), February 1965.

58 M. Thivierge, "M. Lesage: Québec lancera une société de financement pour établir une sidérurgie", *Le Devoir*, September 2, 1961, p. 1.

59 Quebec, Parliament, Legislative Assembly, *Comité des régies gouvernementales, Débats*, 3rd session, 28th legislature — Sidbec — May 28, 1968, pp. 80-82.

60 *Ibid.*, p. 45.

61 *Ibid.*, p. 44.

62 Quebec, National Assembly, *Commission permanente des finances, des comptes publics et du revenu, Débats — Etude du projet de loi 44*, July 18, 1974.

63 "Sidbec innove au plan technologique", *Le Devoir*, November 15, 1978, p. 15.

64 J.P. Lefebvre, "Etat s'abstenir", *Le Magazine Maclean*, November 1972, p. 43.

65 Canada, Privy Council Office, *Steel Profits Inquiry*, p. 28.

66 "Study may douse steel fires in Cape Breton", *Financial Post*, October 7, 1967, p. 29. Sysco publishes no financial statements, so that it was necessary to glean information from the business press. This section is based on information obtained from the *Financial Post Survey of Industrials*, 1967-69, and articles in the weekly *Financial Post*, especially: "Hawker Siddeley does well despite Dosco's heavy loss", April 28, 1967, p. 4; "How the final straw broke Dosco's back", October 21, 1967, p. 1; "How far should govt. go into business itself?", December 16, 1967, p. 4; "How will Smith deal with Sydney mills?", December 30, 1967, p. 7; "Dosco dissolution offers test for the steel nerved", March 23, 1968, p. 33; "Labor love-in at Sysco almost over", June 21, 1968, p. 7; "Sysco scores point in door die battle", July 13, 1968, p. S-11; "Steel mill future much brighter premier says", October 5, 1968, p. N-1; "Report writes off Sydney steel hope", May 10, 1969, p. 34; "Sysco could break record for output", September 20, 1969, p. 52; "An uneasy time for Sydney Steel Corp.", July 5, 1969, p. S-7; "Sydney Steel hopes to raise exports in a few years to 70% of production", July 4, 1970, p. S-2; "Sidbec and Sysco expand operations," August 8, 1970, p. 12; "Sysco Steel Miracle goes on", October 3, 1970, p. 5; "With no taxes to pay Sysco has $$ to invest", July 3, 1971, p. S-4; "Cape Breton industry problems play havoc with steel mill operation", February 12, 1972, p. 35; "For the want of coke Sysco suffers", June 10, 1972, p. S-6; "SIP may make Sysco a real winner", June 2, 1973, p. S-4; "Financing is big worry at Sysco in Nova Scotia", June 7, 1975, p. D-2; "Uncertainty prolonged at Sysco", June 5, 1976, p. 40; and "Nova Scotia awaits word on Sysco plan", January 6, 1979, p. 1.

67 "Report writes off Sydney steel hope", *Financial Post*, May 10, 1969, p. 34.

68 "Sydney Steel hopes to raise exports in a few years to 70% of production", *Financial Post*, July 4, 1970, p. S-2.

69 "Nova Scotia awaits word on Sysco plan", *Financial Post*, January 6, 1979, p. 1.

70 S. Abranches, "Empresa estatal e capitalismo: una analise comparada", in C.E. Martins, ed., *Estado e capitalismo no Brasil* (Sao Paulo: Ed. Hucitec-Cebrap, 1977), p. 28.

71 *Ibid.*, p. 29.

72 Jacques Melançon, "Rôle et financement d'une banque d'affaires", *L'Actualité Economique*, October-December 1956, pp. 449-73.

73 D. Brunelle, *La désillusion tranquille* (Montreal: HMH, 1978), chapter 2.

74 Quebec General Investment Corporation, *Annual Report*, 1972.

75 Quebec, National Assembly, *Commission permanente de l'industrie et du commerce, du tourisme, de la chasse et de la pêche, Débats*, May 17, 18, 19 and 23, 1972, no. 31, pp. B-1947-52.

76 Quebec, National Assembly, *Commission parlementaire permanente de l'industrie et du commerce, Débats — Etude du projet de Loi 108*, December 7, 1978.

77 Statement by Gordon R. Ball before the Royal Commission on Canada's Economic Prospects, Montreal, February 21, 1956.

78 Walter Gordon, *A Political Memoir* (Toronto: McClelland and Stewart, 1977), pp. 135, 179, 189, 203, 205.

79 Canada, Privy Council Office, *Foreign Ownership and the Structure of Canadian Industry* (Ottawa, 1968), pp. 411-12.

80 "CDC emerges, ready to roar", *Financial Post*, April 11, 1970, p. 1.

81 Michael R. Graham, *Canada Development Corporation*, Corporate Background Report to the Royal Commission on Corporate Concentration (Ottawa, 1976), pp. 14-16.

82 *La Presse*, September 15, 1979, p. A-2.

Chapter 5

1 Cy Gonick, *Inflation or Depression: The Continuing Crisis of the Canadian Economy* (Toronto: James Lorimer & Co., 1975), p. 89.

2 Jim Laxer, "Introduction to the Political Economy of Canada", in Robert M. Laxer, ed., *(Canada) Ltd.: The Political Economy of Dependency* (Toronto: McClelland and Stewart, 1973), p. 35.

3 John Hutcheson, "The Capitalist State in Canada", in R.M. Laxer, ed., *(Canada) Ltd.*, p. 174.

4 See Wallace Clement, *The Canadian Corporate Elite: An Analysis of Economic Power* (Toronto: McClelland and Stewart, Carleton Library no. 89, 1975), especially pp. 33, 36-37, 117-19; Wallace Clement, "The Canadian Bourgeoisie: Merely Comprador?", in J. Saul and C. Heron, eds., *Imperialism, Nationalism and Canada* (Toronto: New Hogtown Press, 1977), pp. 71-84; Wallace Clement, *Continental Corporate Power* (Toronto: McClelland and Stewart, 1977).

5 See Jorge Niosi, "Who Controls Canadian Capitalism?", *Our Generation* Vol. 12, no. 1 (Summer 1977), a preliminary version of chapter 1 of this book.

6 Jean-Marie Chevalier, *La structure financière de l'industrie américaine* (Paris: Cujas, 1970); Philip Burch, *The Managerial Revolution Reassessed* (Lexington, Mass.: D.C. Heath & Co., 1972). Chevalier based his study primarily on the proxy statements for 1965, while Burch used business periodicals including *Fortune* and *Forbes*.

7 François Morin, *La banque et les groupes industriels à l'heure des nationalisations* (Paris: Calmann-Levy, 1977).

8 Paul M. Sweezy, "The Resurgence of Financial Control: Fact or Fancy?", in Paul M. Sweezy and Harry Magdoff, *The Dynamics of U.S. Capitalism* (New York: Monthly Review Press, 1972).

9 David M. Kotz, *Bank Control of Large Corporations in the United States* (Berkeley, Calif.: University of California Press, 1978).

10 "Pension Funds: The Banks Can't Take Anything For Granted Anymore", *Forbes*, April 16, 1979, p. 118.

11 "Big investors on edge", *Financial Post*, March 24, 1977, p. 1.

12 Anthony Sampson, *The New Anatomy of Britain* (London: Hodder and Stoughton, 1971), p. 601.

13 "Eagle Star in the Hall of the Mountain Kings", *Investors Chronicle*, October 8, 1975, p. 889; "The Wise and the Prudent", *Investors Chronicle*, September 24, 1971, p. 1212.

14 "Blacks, Whites and Harry Oppenheimer", *Forbes*, June 15, 1973, p. 38.

15 "Genmin Unicorp — Act two", *Investors Chronicle*, December 5, 1975, p. 701.

16 "The Empain Group", *Fortune*, August 1975, pp. 171-83.

17 Centre de Recherche et d'Information Socio-Politiques, *Répertoire permanent des groupes financiers et industriels* (Brussels, 1975), p. 3048.

18 See *Forbes*, July 1, 1974, p. 30.

19 See *Forbes*, November 1, 1976, p. 61.

20 See *Forbes*, July 15, 1973, p. 28.

21 See *Fortune*, October 1976, pp. 146ff.

22 See *Forbes*, September 15, 1972, p. 82; *Fortune*, November 1976, p. 40.

23 K. Buckley, *Capital Formation in Canada, 1896-1930* (Toronto: McClelland and Stewart, 1974), p. 103.

24 See Michael R. Graham, *Canada Development Corporation*, Corporate Background Report to the Royal Commission on Corporate Concentration (Ottawa, 1976), pp. 32-35.

25 As of June 1979, the Potash Corporation of Saskatchewan owned 45 per cent of the province's production capacity, as compared with 30 per cent for Canadian producers which were not taken over and 25 per cent for remaining foreign companies. Three years earlier the breakdown was 75 per cent foreign, 25 per cent Canadian. (See *Wall Street Journal*, June 16, 1976, p. 12; March 8, 1977, p. 12; July 14, 1977, p. 10; and January 11, 1978, p. 10; and *Financial Post*, May 13, 1978, p. 9; and November 25, 1978, p. 7 [Saskatchewan supplement].)

26 The Nielson family turned over its 20 per cent controlling block in May 1979, but Alberta Gas Trunk Lines had already acquired 35 per cent of Husky's shares in June 1978 (see *Le Devoir*, May 15, 1979, p. 15).

27 See *Financial Post*, January 13, 1979, p. 13.

28 See *Le Devoir*, December 6, 1978, p. 19; December 7, 1978, p. 1; January 18, 1979, p. 15; and January 24, 1979, p. 15.

29 See *Investors Chronicle*, April 30, 1976, p. 411.

30 Philip Resnick, *The Land of Cain* (Vancouver: New Star Books, 1977), p. 133.

31 G.W. Domhoff, *Who Rules America?* (Englewood Cliffs, N.J.: Prentice Hall, 1967), chapter 4; J. Weinstein, *The Corporate Ideal in the Liberal State* (Boston: Beacon Press, 1968).

Conclusion

1 Mira Wilkins, *The Emergence of Multinational Enterprise* (Cambridge, Mass.: Harvard University Press, 1970); Mira Wilkins, *The Maturing of Multinational Enterprise* (Cambridge, Mass.: Harvard University Press, 1974).

2 See Peter C. Newman, *Bronfman Dynasty: The Rothschilds of the New World* (Toronto: McClelland and Stewart, 1978).

3 G.W. Domhoff, *The Powers that Be: Processes of Ruling-Class Domination in America* (New York: Random House, 1978), pp. 61-62.

4 K.Z. Paltiel, *Political Party Financing in Canada* (Toronto: McGraw-Hill, 1970), especially chapter 2, "Business and Bagmen: the Liberal and Conservative Pattern".

Bibliography

General and Comparative Works

Books

Baltzell, E.D. *The Protestant Establishment*. New York: Random House, 1964.

Baran, Paul A., and Sweezy, Paul M. *Monopoly Capital: An Essay on the American Economic and Social Order*. New York: Monthly Review Press, 1966.

Baum, D.J., and Stiles, N.B. *The Silent Partners: Institutional Investors and Corporate Control*. Syracuse, New York: Syracuse University Press, 1965.

Berle, Adolf A., Jr. *Power Without Property*. New York: Harcourt Brace & Co., 1959.

Berle, Adolf A., Jr. and Means, Gardiner C. *The Modern Corporation and Private Property*. 1932. New York: Harcourt Prace & World, 1968.

Bettelheim, Charles. *Class Struggles in the U.S.S.R.* Translated by Brian Pearce. New York: Monthly Review Press, 1976.

Blair, J. *Economic Concentration*. New York: Harcourt Brace Jovanovich, 1972.

Boccara, Paul. *Etudes sur le C.M.E. sa crise et son issue*. Paris: Editions Sociales, 1974.

Bouvier, J. *Un siècle de banque française*. Paris: Hachette, 1973.

Bullock, H. *The Story of Investment Companies*. New York: Columbia University Press, 1959.

Burch, Philip. *The Managerial Revolution Reassessed*. Lexington, Mass.: D.C. Heath & Co., 1972.

Cardoso, Fernando H. *Autoritarismo e democratizaçao*. Rio de Janiero: Paz e Terra, 1975.

Cheprakov, Victor. *Le capitalisme monopoliste d'Etat*. Moscow: Ed. du Progrès, 1969.

Chevalier, Jean-Marie. *La structure financière de l'industrie américaine*. Paris: Cujas, 1970

Dahrendorf, Ralf. *Class and Class Conflict in Industrial Society*. London: Routledge and Paul, 1959.

Dobb, Maurice. *Papers on Capitalism, Development and Planning*. London: Routledge and Kegan Paul, 1967.

Domhoff, G.W. *Who Rules America?* Englewood Cliffs, New Jersey: Prentice Hall, 1967.

Domhoff, G.W. *The Powers that Be: Processes of Ruling-Class Domination in America*. New York: Random House, 1978.

Domhoff, G.W. and Ballard, H.B. *C.W. Mills and the Power Elite*. Boston: Beacon Press, 1968.

Emmanuel, A. *Le Profit et les crises*. Paris: Maspéro, 1974.

François-Marsal, Frédéric. *Le dépérissement des entreprises publiques*. Paris: Calmann-Lévy, 1973.

Galbraith, John Kenneth. *Modern Capitalism*. Boston: Houghton Mifflin, 1952.

Galbraith, John Kenneth. *The New Industrial State*. Boston: Houghton Mifflin, 1967.

Gillman, J. *The Falling Rate of Profit*. London: Dobson, 1956.

Gramsci, Antonio. *Oeuvres choisies*. Paris: Editions Sociales, 1959.

Guthrie, John A. *The Newsprint Paper Industry*. Cambridge, Mass.: Harvard University Press, 1943.

Hilferding, Rudolf. *Le capital financier*. 1910. Paris: Minuit, 1970.

Kolko, Gabriel. *Wealth and Power in America*. New York: Praeger, 1962.

Kotz, David M. *Bank Control of Large Corporations in the United States*. Berkeley, Calif.: University of California Press, 1978.

Larner, Robert J. *Management Control and the Large Corporation*. Cambridge, Mass.: Harvard University Press, 1970.

Lenin, V.I. *Selected Works*. 3 vols. Moscow: Progress Publishers; New York: International Publishers, 1967.

Lundberg, Ferdinand. *The Rich and the Super-rich*. New York: Bantam Books, 1968.

Martins, C.E., ed. *Estado e capitalismo no Brasil*. Sao Paulo: Ed. Hucitec-Cebrap, 1977.

Marx, Karl. *Capital*. 3 vols. Edited by Frederick Engels. Translated by Samuel Moore and Edward Aveling. Moscow: Progress Publishers, 1965-67.

Marx, Karl, and Engels, Frederick. *Selected Works*. 2 vols. Moscow: Foreign Languages Publishing House, 1962.

Menshikov, S. *Millionaires and Managers*. Moscow: Progress Publishers, 1969.

Miliband, Ralph. *The State in Capitalist Society*. London: Wiedenfeld & Nicholson, 1969.

Mills, C. Wright. *The Power Elite*. New York: Oxford University Press, 1956.

Morin, François. *La banque et les groupes industriels à l'heure des nationalisations*. Paris: Calmann-Lévy, 1977.

O'Connor, James. *The Fiscal Crisis of the State*. San Jose: St. Martin's Press, 1970.

Sampson, Anthony. *The New Anatomy of Britain*. London: Hodder & Stoughton, 1971.

Sweezy, Paul M., and Magdoff, Harry. *The Dynamics of U.S. Capitalism*. New York: Monthly Review Press, 1972.

Théret, B., and Wieviorka, M. *Critique de la théorie du C.M.E.* Paris: Maspéro, 1978.

Tivey, Leonard. *Nationalization in British Industry*. London: J. Cape Ltd., 1973.

Valier, J. *Le PCF et le capitalisme monopoliste d'Etat*. Paris: Maspéro, 1976.

Varga, Yevgenii. *The Great Crisis and Its Political Consequences: Economics and Politics, 1928-1934*. New York: International Publishers, 1935.

Varga, Yevgenii. *Politico-Economic Problems of Capitalism*. Translated by Don. Danemanis. Moscow: Progress Publishers, 1968.

Weinstein, J. *The Corporate Ideal in the Liberal State*. Boston: Beacon Press, 1968.

Wilkins, Mira. *The Emergence of Multinational Enterprise*. Cambridge, Mass.: Harvard University Press, 1970.

Wilkins, Mira. *The Maturing of Multinational Enterprise.* Cambridge, Mass.: Harvard University Press, 1974.

Young, A., & Co. *Top Management Compensation.* New York, 1976.

Ziegler, J. *Une Suisse au-dessus de tout soupçon.* Paris: Seuil, 1976.

Articles

Cardoso, Fernando H. "Desenvolvimento capitalista e Estado: bases e alternativas." In *Estado e capitalismo no Brasil,* edited by C.E. Martins. Sao Paulo: Ed Hucitec-Cebrap, 1977.

Works About Canada

Books, theses and pamphlets

Ashley, C.A., and Smails, R.G. *Canadian Crown Corporations: Some Aspects of Their Administration and Control.* Toronto: Macmillan of Canada, 1965.

Bédard, R.J., ed. *L'Essor économique du Québec.* Montreal: Beauchemin, 1969.

Bouchette, Errol. *L'Indépendance économique du Canada français.* 1906. Montreal: Ed. La Presse, 1977.

Brunelle, D. *La Désillusion tranquille.* Montreal: HMH, 1978.

Buckley, K. *Capital Formation in Canada 1896-1930.* Toronto: McClelland and Stewart, 1955.

Burley, K.H. *The Development of Canada's Staples 1867-1939.* Toronto: McClelland and Stewart, 1970.

Clement, Wallace. *The Canadian Corporate Elite: An Analysis of Economic Power.* Toronto: McClelland and Stewart, Carleton Library no. 89, 1975.

Clement, Wallace. *Continental Corporate Power.* Toronto: McClelland and Stewart, 1977.

Confederation of National Trade Unions. *La Coopérative fédérée est capitaliste.* Montreal, 1974.

Conference Board in Canada. *Canadian Directorship Practices: Compensation 1976.* Ottawa, 1976.

Conference Board in Canada. *Stock Option Plans.* Ottawa, 1976.

Donald, W.J.A. *The Canadian Iron and Steel Industry.* Boston: Houghton Mifflin Co., 1915.

Durocher, René, and Linteau, Paul-André, eds. *Le "retard" du Québec et l'infériorité économique des Canadiens français.* Montreal: Boréal Express, 1971.

Epp, A.E. *Cooperation among Capitalists: The Canadian Merger Movement.* PhD thesis, The Johns Hopkins University, Baltimore, 1973.

Gonick, Cy. *Inflation or Depression: The Continuing Crisis of the Canadian Economy.* Toronto: James Lorimer and Co., 1975.

Gordon, Walter. *A Political Memoir.* Toronto: McClelland and Stewart, 1977.

Heap, J. *Everybody's Canada.* Toronto: Burns & MacEachern, 1974.

Kalbach, W.E., and McIvey, W.W. *The Demographic Basis of Canadian Society.* Toronto: McGraw-Hill of Canada, 1971.

Kilbourn, William. *The Elements Combined*. Toronto: Clarke Irwin and Co., 1960.

Jobin, Carol. *Les enjeux économiques de la nationalisation de l'électricité*. Montreal: A. St. Martin, 1978.

Laxer, Robert M., ed. *(Canada) Ltd.: The Political Economy of Dependency*. Toronto: McClelland and Stewart, 1973.

Léonard, J.F. *La chance au coureur*. Montreal: Nouvelle Optique, 1978.

Levitt, Kari. *Silent Surrender: The Multinational Corporation in Canada*. Toronto: Macmillan of Canada, 1970.

Murray, Vera. *Le Parti québécois*. Montreal: HMH, 1976.

Myers, Gustavus. *A History of Canadian Wealth*. 1914. Toronto: James Lewis and Samuel, 1972.

Nelles, H.V. *The Politics of Development: Forests, Mines and Hydro-Electric Power in Ontario, 1849-1941*. Toronto: Macmillan of Canada, 1974.

Neufeld, E.P. *The Financial System of Canada: Its Growth and Development*. Toronto, Macmillan of Canada, 1972.

Newman, Peter C. *Flame of Power: Intimate Profiles of Canada's Greatest Businessmen*. Toronto: McClelland and Stewart, 1959.

Newman, Peter C. *The Canadian Establishment*. Toronto: McClelland and Stewart, 1975.

Newman, Peter C. *Bronfman Dynasty: The Rothschilds of the New World*. Toronto: McClelland and Stewart, 1978.

Niosi, Jorge. *The Economy of Canada: A Study of Ownership and Control*. Montreal: Black Rose Books, 1978.

Ouellet, Fernand. *Histoire économique et sociale du Québec 1760-1850*. Montreal: Fides, 1966.

Paltiel, K.Z. *Political Party Financing in Canada*. Toronto: McGraw-Hill of Canada, 1970.

Panitch, Leo, ed. *The Canadian State*. Toronto: University of Toronto Press, 1977.

Park, Libbie and Frank. *Anatomy of Big Business*. 1962. Toronto: James Lewis and Samuel, 1973.

Plewman, W.R. *Adam Beck and the Ontario Hydro*. Toronto: Ryerson Press, 1947.

Porter, John. *The Vertical Mosaic: An Analysis of Social Class and Power in Canada*. Toronto: University of Toronto Press, 1965.

Resnick, Philip. *The Land of Cain*. Vancouver: New Star Books, 1977.

Rosenbluth, Gideon. *Concentration in Canadian Manufacturing Industry*. Princeton, N.J.: Princeton University Press, 1957.

Roussopoulos, Dimitrios, ed. *The Political Economy of the State*. Montreal: Black Rose Books, 1973.

Sales, A. *La bourgeoisie industrielle au Québec*. Montreal: Presses de l'Université de Montréal, 1979.

Schull, Joseph. *The Century of the Sun*. Toronto: Macmillan of Canada, 1971.

Stapells, H.G. *The Recent Consolidation Movement in Canadian Industry*. MA thesis, University of Toronto, Toronto, 1922.

Teeple, Gary, ed. *Capitalism and the National Question in Canada*. Toronto: University of Toronto Press, 1972.

Wood, L.A. *Farmers' Movements in Canada.* 1924. Toronto: University of Toronto Press, 1975.

Articles

Clement, Wallace. "The Canadian Bourgeoisie: Merely Comprador?" In *Imperialism, Nationalism and Canada*, edited by J. Saul and C. Heron. Toronto: New Hogtown Press, 1977.

Linteau, Paul-André. "Quelques réflexions autour de la bourgeoisie québécoise 1850-1914." *Revue d'Histoire de l'Amérique Française* 30, no. 1 Montreal (June 1976).

Melançon, Jacques. "Rôle et financement d'une banque d'affaires." *L'Actualité Economique*, Montreal, October-December 1956.

Pentland, H.C. "The Development of Capitalistic Labour Market in Canada." *Canadian Journal of Economics and Political Science* 25, no. 4 Toronto (November 1959).

Rosenbluth, Gideon. "Concentration and Monopoly in the Canadian Economy." In *Social Purpose for Canada*, edited by Michael Oliver. Toronto: University of Toronto Press, 1961.

Rosenbluth, Gideon. "The Relation between Foreign Control and Concentration in Canadian Industry." *Canadian Journal of Economics* 3 (February 1970).

Weldon, J. "Concentration in Canadian Industry, 1900-1948." In *Restrictive Trade Practices in Canada*, edited by L.A. Skeoch. Toronto: McClelland and Stewart, 1966.

Government and Private Sources

Government sources and studies

Annual reports of the major federally-and provincially-owned corporations.

Canada. *Foreign Direct Investment in Canada* (Gray Report). Ottawa: Information Canada, 1972.

Canada. *Revised Statutes of Canada.* Ottawa: Information Canada, 1970.

Canada. Committee on Election Expenses. *Report.* Ottawa, 1966.

Canada. Committee on Election Expenses. *Studies in Canadian Party Finance.* Ottawa, 1966.

Canada. Department of Finance. *Public Accounts of Canada, 1975-76.* 3 vols. Ottawa: Supply and Services, 1976.

Canada. Parliament. House of Commons. Standing Committee on Public Accounts. *Proceedings and Testimony.*

Canada. Parliament. Senate. Special Committee on Mass Media. *Report.* 3 vols. Ottawa: Information Canada, 1970.

Canada. Privy Council Office. *Foreign Ownership and the Structure of Canadian Industry.* Ottawa, 1968.

Canada. Privy Council Office. *Steel Profits Inquiry.* Ottawa: Information Canada, 1974.

Canada. Royal Commission on Banking and Finance (Porter Commission). *Report.* Ottawa: Queen's Printer, 1964.

Canada. Royal Commission on Canada's Economic Prospects (Gordon Commission). *Report*. Ottawa, 1956.

Canada. Royal Commission on Canada's Economic Prospects. *Studies*. Ottawa, 1956.

Canada. Royal Commission on Corporate Concentration. *Report*. Ottawa: Supply and Services, 1978.

Canada. Royal Commission on Corporate Concentration. *Studies*. Ottawa: Supply and Services, 1978.

Canada. Statistics Canada. *Canada Year Book 1976-77*. Ottawa: Supply and Services, 1977.

Canada. Statistics Canada. *Federal Government Enterprise Finance*. Annual. Ottawa: Supply and Services, 1976.

Canada. Statistics Canada. *Provincial Government Enterprise Finance*. Annual. Ottawa: Supply and Services, 1976.

Canada. Statistics Canada. *Trusteed Pension Plans. Financial Statistics*. Annual. Ottawa: Supply and Services, 1976.

Quebec. Department of Consumers, Cooperatives and Financial Institutions. Inspector of Trust Companies. *Report* (annual), 1976.

Quebec. Department of Consumers, Cooperatives and Financial Institutions. Insurance Branch. *Annual Report*. 1976.

Quebec. National Assembly. *Commission parlementaire permanente de l'industrie et du commerce. Débats*. 1978.

Quebec. National Assembly. *Commission permanente de l'industrie et du commerce, du tourisme, de la chasse et de la pêche. Débats*. 1972.

Quebec. National Assembly. *Commission permanente des finances, des comptes publics et du revenu. Débats*. 1974.

Quebec. Parliament. Legislative Assembly. *Comité des régies gouvernementales. Débats*. 1968.

Quebec Securities Commission. *Weekly Bulletin*. Montreal, 1974-78.

United States. Securities and Exchange Commission. *Proxy Statements 1975*.

Private sources

Biographies canadiennes-françaises, 1920-1978. Montreal: Editions Biographiques Canadiennes-Françaises, irregular.

Centre de Recherche et d'Information Socio-Politiques (CRISP). *Répertoire permanent des groupes financiers et industriels*. Brussels, 1975.

Financial Post Directory of Directors. 1931-78. Toronto: Maclean-Hunter Ltd., annual.

Financial Post Survey of Corporate Securities, 1928-46. Toronto: Maclean-Hunter Ltd., annual.

Financial Post Survey of Funds, 1962-78. Toronto: Maclean-Hunter Ltd., annual.

Financial Post Survey of Industrials, 1947-78. Toronto: Maclean-Hunter Ltd., annual.

Financial Post Survey of Mines, 1926-78. Toronto: Maclean-Hunter Ltd., annual.

Financial Post Survey of Oils, 1936-78. Toronto: Maclean-Hunter Ltd., annual.

Moody's Bank and Finance Manual. New York: Moody's Investors' Service, 1976.

Moody's Industrial Manual. New York: Moody's Investors' Service, 1976.

Moody's Public Utility Manual. New York: Moody's Investors' Service, 1976.
Moody's Transportation Manual. New York: Moody's Investors' Service, 1976.
Municipal and Government Manual. New York: Moody's Investors' Service, 1976.
New York Stock Exchange. *Corporate Proxy Statements*, 1976.
Who's Who in Canada, 1912-78. Toronto: International Press Ltd., irregular.

Magazines and newspapers

Commerce, Montreal, 1950-78 (monthly).
Le Devoir, Montreal (daily).
The Economist, London, 1970-78 (weekly).
Financial Post, Toronto (weekly).
Forbes, New York, 1970-78 (fortnightly).
Fortune, New York, 1970-78 (monthly).
Investors Chronicle, London, 1970-78 (weekly).
La Presse, Montreal (daily).
Wall Street Journal, New York (daily).

Index